Dog Lover's
DAILY COMPANION

---

365 Days
of Tips, Tricks, and Techniques for Living a Rich Life with Your Dog

Wendy Nan Rees, Pet Lifestyle Advisor, and Kristen Hampshire

Photography by Kendra Luck

CRESTLINE

This edition published in 2012 by CRESTLINE
A division of BOOK SALES, INC.
276 Fifth Avenue Suite 206
New York, New York 10001
USA

This edition published by arrangement with Quarry Books, a member of the Quayside Publishing Group.

First published in the United States of America by
Quarry Books, a member of
Quayside Publishing Group
100 Cummings Center
Suite 406-L
Beverly, Massachusetts 01915-6101
Telephone: (978) 282-9590
Fax: (978) 283-2742
www.quarrybooks.com

Library of Congress Cataloging-in-Publication Data
Rees, Wendy Nan.
dog lover's daily companion: 365 days of tips, tricks, and techniques for living a rich life with your dog / Wendy Nan Rees, Kristen Hampshire ; photography by Kendra Luck.
      p. cm.
Includes index.
ISBN-13: 978-0-7858-2938-6
  1. Dogs--Miscellanea. 2. Dog owners. 3. Human-animal relationships. I. Hampshire, Kristen. II. Title.
 SF426.R45 2009
 636.7--dc22

                                          2008054257
                                          CIP

10 9 8 7 6 5 4 3 2

Design: everlution design

A special thanks to Anna Gil, owner of Dogpile Dogs, and the crew at Planet Pooch, as well as Diane Livoti and Alison Smith for their unlimited support and for giving access to photographer Kendra Luck at Metro Dog. Thanks, also, to all the great dogs that come there, as well as all her canine friends whose furry faces grace these pages.

Printed in China

contents

THE DOG OWNER'S YEAR

MONDAY / **DOGS 101**

TUESDAY / **TABLE MANNERS AND TRAINING**

WEDNESDAY / **PLAYTIME AND EXERCISE**

THURSDAY / **GROOMING AND HEALTH CARE**

FRIDAY / **HOUSEKEEPING AND CLEANING**

SATURDAY + SUNDAY / **BONDING AND RELATIONSHIP BUILDING**

Foreword
by Kathy Santo

Recently, Wendy Nan Rees contacted me via email, asking me if I would be a guest on her radio show and "talk dogs." Talking and training dogs is my passion—and has been for twenty five years—so I eagerly agreed. On the day of the interview, I had prepared for the normal routine—question, answer, question, answer, go to break, and we're done. But this time was different. Within the first two minutes, I felt as though I was talking to my long-lost best friend. We were finishing each other's sentences and laughing at each other's jokes. By the end of the interview we agreed that we must be long-lost friends, living on opposite coasts!

When she asked me to write the foreword for *Dog Lover's Daily Companion*, I was honored. Before I read the book, I tried to conjure up what type of book would it be. Would it include training advice? Tips for traveling with your pooch? Maybe it would be a book about all the things you can make at home for your dog, from treats to toys? Imagine my delight to see that it is about all that and more!

Simply by opening this book, you start on a year-long journey through all things dog-related! Are you training a new puppy? Common questions that I hear from my dog training students every day are included here in easy-to-understand language. Wondering how to stimulate your dog's appetite? Manuka honey, (Day 4), could be the answer. Have you considered that your dog's zodiac sign might give you insight into his personality? What are the best "workouts" for your breed? All of this and more is explained in detail and in a lively, encouraging voice.

If sage advice on important topics wasn't enough, several days offer craft and handmade gift ideas. I confess, I never imagined I could find time to fit dog-themed crafting into my lifestyle of dog training, raising two (wonderful) children, writing, and so on. My ten-year-old daughter talked me into making doggie place mats (Day 9) and, to my surprise, it was fun and rewarding! Now when I look at my dogs eating their dinner on the mats that we made, I feel proud of our handiwork. (So proud, actually, that we are going to "kidnap" my father in a few weeks and invite him to lend his construction skills to helping us build a doghouse (Days 118 and 119). Many of the fun projects in the book fall somewhere between place mats and doghouse building. You're sure to find one that matches the craft skills (or lack thereof) of everyone!

So read *Dog Lover's Daily Companion*, take notes on the pages, turn down the corners, and read it again next year! You will use this book time and time again. From your beloved dog's puppyhood to adulthood, this will become your roadmap to the wonderful journey of not just dog ownership, but dog friendship.

Kathy Santo is the author of Kathy Santo's Dog Sense *(Knopf, 2005). www.kathysanto.com*

Introduction

Whether your dog is twelve weeks old or twelve years old, you already know the sheer joy that comes with owning a dog. And whether you are a first-time dog owner or you have had one in your life for as long as you can remember, you have experienced the privilege of sharing one's life with a dog. Dogs offer us unconditional love, and if they are treated with respect, trained well, and truly loved in return, they will become our best friend.

This book will help you build that special bond that exists between dogs and their owners, improving all areas of your dog's life, and—most important—your lives together. You've probably long gotten used to your dog's constant chewing, navigated housetraining, and contended with all the barking. Here we offer plenty of ideas for more effectively dealing with those issues, and more. *Dog Lover's Daily Companion* is filled with inspiring ideas, money-saving advice, do-it-yourself projects, and special quick tips—all complete with beautiful photos—that will help you create a warm, loving environment for your dog.

You will learn everything from the practical (getting your home ready for a new puppy and dog-proofing 101) to the whimsical (making costumes for your pet) and the critical (compiling a first-aid kit). You already know that dogs can be our friends, family members, exercise partners, and even our therapists. We hope this book will inspire you to better care for your dog, get creative with home and craft projects, and, most of all, bond with your canine companion.

How to Use This Book

This book is organized as a day minder, with entries creating a complete year's worth of information. Each of the year's fifty-two weeks has six entries.

You can start reading this book from the beginning, following the days of the week through the calendar year, reading one entry each day. You can also read from the middle of the book, the end, or skip around from week to week as inspiration strikes. The most important thing to remember is that you can use this book however you want. Part of owning a dog is that every day is a surprise . . . and this book reflects that spirit—turn to any page and you will find another useful tip. Another (equally enjoyable) part of dog owning is that you and your pet will discover those "old favorites," too—whether it is your favorite routine, your daily walk, or an old stuffed toy. Likewise, you can come back time and time again to your favorite page.

For the entries that describe longer projects, I have included materials lists, timelines, and checklists of everything you will need to have on hand. General checklists for weekly, monthly, twice annually, and once yearly activities are included for quick reference at the end of the book.

What's next? Set aside some time and find a quiet place that is yours alone. (Invite your four-legged friend, if you'd like.) Enjoy this book at your own pace and remember to have fun. You already know how special dogs are. Now, with this book, you will have all the tips, tricks, and techniques you will need for living a rich life with your dog.

The Dog Owner's Year

 MONDAYS are for the **basics** of dog ownership—from bringing home a shelter pup to storing all your pet's toys.

 TUESDAYS are for **table manners and training**—from basic housetraining to finding the right dog bed.

 WEDNESDAYS are for **exercise and playtime**, providing ideas for creating your own toys, dog park etiquette, backyard adventures, and more.

 THURSDAYS are devoted to **health, grooming, and first aid**, exploring everything from building your own first-aid kit to holistic treatments.

 FRIDAYS cover home **organizing, cleaning, and housekeeping** and touch on everything from stain removal to stocking a doggie-craft utility closet.

 WEEKENDS are reserved for **bonding and relationship building**, maximizing playtime, making toys, traveling, and planning special occasions.

A Dog's First Year

YOU'VE PROBABLY HEARD about dog years and the rule about multiplying your pup's age by seven to determine the dog's "human age." Although the equation is not completely scientific, we can count on this estimate to explain why puppies go through their terrible twos, childhood, and adolescence before they turn one year old. By the time our senior dogs are slowing down at age ten, keep in mind that, when multiplied by seven, that decade is equal to seventy human years.

Understanding your dog's fast-paced life is especially important during that first year, when behavioral changes mark rites of passage. Here are some guidelines to help you prepare for what to expect from your puppy. Depending on the breed, some puppies will reach adulthood within a year, whereas others will continue growing (physically) far beyond their first birthday. Smaller breeds tend to mature faster than do larger dogs. Consult with your vet for your breed's expectations, but here's a basic first-year timeline to get you started:

1 to 8 weeks—*baby:* Early development stage; the puppy learns dog behaviors and eventually weans from her mom.

8 to 12 weeks—*toddler:* Human socialization period; the puppy is easily frightened and learns from bad experiences.

12 weeks to 6 months—*early adolescence:* The puppy will test the rules; the equivalent of human puberty.

6 months to 1 year—*adolescence/young adulthood:* The puppy will continue to experiment and test training commands; by now, the puppy is adjusted in the home and part of the family.

Basic Training Starts Early

THE DAY YOU COME home with your new puppy, you'll want to play with her and hold her. She'll be exhausted from the trip, and at first will want a nice snooze. When puppies are so young—usually eight to ten weeks old—we tend to treat them like newborns. The difference is, puppies at this stage are primed to learn, and if you start some very basic training right away, you will both be happy in the long term. The first orders of business are housebreaking (potty training) and getting your puppy acclimated to a collar and leash (see Day 65).

Also, you'll choose a name (see Day 22) and begin calling your puppy when he is eager to come to you. Place him on the ground, walk away, and call him by his name. When he comes, give him a treat. If you are going to be using the clicker training method (see Day 359), start using the clicker as soon as possible with the treat. The dog is able to learn simple commands such as "stay" and "sit down." When you teach a puppy from seven to twelve weeks of age, she never forgets these simple commands. Later on, you can build on this early training experience.

This first stage of training provides valuable bonding time with your puppy. She will learn who is her boss and best friend. She will explore her new environment with your help, and discover boundaries that will keep her safe, thanks to all of your careful puppy-proofing. The "light training" you do at home those first weeks and months will come in handy when you enroll your puppy in a class.

Whether you're a first-time or veteran dog owner, puppy classes are a must. This is where you can socialize your puppy and teach her to play nicely with other dogs so you both can enjoy situations where you may meet other dogs, such as dog parks, and go hiking, walking, or swimming. It is a good idea to go alone first to check out the puppy class to get a feel for the size of the group and the style of the trainer, so you can make a decision if it is the right class for you and your dog. You want to find a trainer who keeps control and knows his or her subject but also encourages laughter and fun. Finding the right class will ensure that both you and your puppy will learn and have fun.

9

Stocking the Toy Box

TOYS GO A LONG way toward fighting boredom, especially for a dog that must be left alone for long periods of time. They can also help prevent your dog from developing unacceptable habits and behavior problems. Toys can serve as a distraction for your dog when you don't have time to play more actively with her. The market is flooded with variety. How do you choose the best toys for your dog?

Toys should be age, size, and strength appropriate. A chew toy should not be so big that your dog can't get her mouth around it, nor so small that she could possibly swallow and choke on the item. Big, strong dogs should have larger, tougher toys.

Toys should be safe for active play. Are there sharp edges, ingestible cords or "whiskers," or pieces that could easily come off? Is the toy made from safe and nontoxic materials? Rope toys are available in several shapes, but the most popular is a bone shape with knotted ends. You want to choose one made of cotton (preferably undyed), as cotton will be digestible should little pieces be chewed off. Nylon or polyester, on the other hand, will not break down in your dog's digestive system and can therefore be dangerous as toy materials.

Toys should be sturdy enough to stand up to your dog's attention. Is it something that will be easy for your pet to tear apart? A damaged toy can quickly become a hazard. Does the toy have internal springs, bead pellets, or other internal parts that the dog could remove and possibly cut her mouth on or swallow? If the toy has a squeaker, is it securely attached so it won't come out?

Some toys that move or make noises contain batteries that can burn your dog's mouth or make your pet sick if ingested. Tennis balls can provide hours of fun, but your dog should not be left unsupervised with one, since they can be chewed up so easily. Inspect your dog's toys weekly for signs of wear. Please never punish your dog for destroying his toys: Remember, the point is for him to concentrate on chewing approved objects and not your shoes.

The sheer joy (tail wagging, playful dancing) your dog expresses when you introduce a new toy is infectious. As you fill a toy bin with new things for your dog to play with, your pet will treat every one as a favorite.

Manuka Honey for Health

KNOWN FOR ITS healing properties, Manuka honey has natural antiseptic and antibiotic properties. All honey contains some hydrogen peroxide, but the level varies depending on the type of honey. Manuka honey, in particular, contains an extra antibacterial property found only in honey sourced from Leptospermum plants. You can purchase it at natural foods stores in aisles where you find supplements and vitamins. Manuka honey is effective for internal and external ailments—some pet owners swear by its ability to clear up skin problems, and others commend the honey's capability to trigger a healthy appetite or settle gastrointestinal unrest. Looking at the honey's label, study the unique Manuka factor (UMF) rating, such as UMF 10+ or UMF 20+. A higher number indicates a greater concentration of healing antibacterial properties.

Applied topically, Manuka honey naturally heals burns, infections, and psoriasis. The honey destroys wound bacteria and feeds the area with sugars, which triggers new cell growth. Using sterilized honey—it is available in a squeeze tube—gently rub a layer over the infected area. Place a bandage or gauze dressing over the wound so your dog does not lick off the honey or leave sticky spots on bedding or furniture.

Squirt Manuka honey on a dog biscuit or spread some on a corner of toast and feed the honey treat to your dog to increase appetite and relieve acid reflux, heartburn, upset stomach, stomach ulcers, or irritable bowel syndrome. (Dogs can suffer from all the same gastrointestinal ailments that we do. In fact, their stomachs are far more sensitive.) You may feed your dog three teaspoon-size (6 ml) servings of honey a day until conditions improve. Note: It's always a good idea to consult with your vet before pursuing treatment of any kind, including all-natural holistic remedies.

Healing Supplements

Your dog can benefit from the natural healing properties of these supplements. Some are available in pill form, which you can administer to your dog by folding the correct dosage into a hunk of cheese or a "pill pocket" treat. You also can chop up pills and mix them with food.

Important Note: Talk to your vet about dosing and whether these agents are appropriate for your pet.

Supplement > Effect

Aloe > itch relief, healing agent

Echinacea > immune system builder

Ginger > settles the stomach

Ginkgo biloba > improves cognitive function

Glucosamine and chondroitin > relieves arthritis and joint pain

Milk thistle > for liver problems

St. John's wort > fights viral infection

Slippery elm > for digestive problems and skin irritation/problems

Vitamin C > antioxidant

11

Hazardous Household Substances

OUR HOMES ARE like candy stores for pooches, who have an appetite for mischief. Puppies are curious; dogs are knee-high detectives, always noticing odds and ends we leave for the taking. Sometimes, those items are products we use every day around the house. There's no need to purge your medicine cabinet and laundry room of such products as acetaminophen or fabric softener. But you should keep these items well out of reach and firmly capped.

If your dog ingests any of these potentially toxic substances, call your veterinarian or poison control center.

Acetaminophen, such as Tylenol and Excedrin

Antidiarrheal products, such as Lomotil and Imodium

Aspirin, all kinds, including low-dose

Batteries, all kinds, typically found in remote controls, watches, hearing aids, toys

Bleach

Breath strips

Chocolate

Citrus-based cleansers

Cough syrups and lozenges

Diet pills and supplements

Fabric softener sheets

Flea and tick products containing organo-phosphates

Glues, especially strong-hold or expanding glue products

Herbal supplements not specifically recommended for dogs or ingested in large quantities

Homemade or commercial molding dough, such as Play-Doh, or clay

Household cleansers, such as ammonia, dishwashing and laundry detergent, scouring powder, drain cleaner, and furniture or metal polish

Ibuprofen/NSAIDS, such as Aleve, Advil, Nuprin, Motrin, or Vicks NyQuil

Lead items, such as old paint, drapery weights, wine-bottle cork foils, and fishing weights

Marijuana, cocaine, and other recreational drugs

Matches

Mothballs

Mouthwash

Pennies (U.S.) minted after 1982 (due to high zinc content)

Phenol-based cleaners, such as Lysol or Pine-Sol

Potpourri, especially liquid potpourri

Prenatal and other human vitamins, especially high-iron formulations

Prescription medications, such as anti-depressants, birth control pills, painkillers, and other opiates

Rat and mouse bait-traps and rodent-control products

Rubbing alcohol

Tobacco and nicotine products such as snuff, nicotine gum, cigarette butts, cigars, trans-dermal patches

Vitamin and mineral supplements not specifically recommended for dogs or ingested in large quantities

What's Your Dog's Zodiac Sign?

YOU DON'T NEED a horoscope to tell you that you and your pooch are compatible partners. For fun, decide whether your dog displays behaviors that are characteristic with her sign. If you don't know your dog's birth date, you can guess by her age when you brought her home.

Aquarius *(January 20 to February 18)*: Revolutionary, self-sufficient, zesty, and headstrong. No one will tell an Aquarius dog how to live. These dogs may have an attitude, but they are deeply sensitive and caring underneath. Life will never be drab.

Pisces *(February 19 to March 20)*: Compassionate, sensitive, intuitive, deeply emotional, a daydreamer. Pisces dogs always lend a helping hand, and they sense their owner's feelings and respond by nurturing.

Aries *(March 21 to April 19)*: Lively, daring, adventure seeking, and independent. These dogs know what they want and they are confident they will get it. They can be impulsive and fearless. They may need help learning how to relax, but their energy is contagious.

Taurus *(April 20 to May 20)*: Practical, cautious, purposeful, persistent, patient, and exceptionally sensitive. These dogs focus on what they want, and they don't mind getting dirty. They have sharp intuition and an active mind.

Gemini *(May 21 to June 21)*: Active, athletic, stimulated, fast paced, and thirsty for new experiences. Your Gemini dog loves meeting people and may need help slowing down. These versatile dogs love to learn and travel.

Cancer *(June 22 to July 22)*: Emotional, generous, intuitive, adaptable, and nurturing. These dogs are receptive to people and their surroundings. They have a maternal nature, an expressive face, and love to play creative games. They are unconditionally loyal and dreamy.

Leo *(July 23 to August 23)*: Warm, bright, motivated, eager to make an impression. Leos are dynamic balls of energy, generous in nature, and very loyal. Your Leo dog loves to travel, has a pioneering spirit, and isn't afraid to blaze the trail. He'll never leave his owner's side.

Virgo *(August 24 to September 22)*: Analytical, investigative, cautious, studious, intelligent, and sometimes demanding. Virgo dogs are quick, logical thinkers. They will excel in training.

Libra *(September 23 to October 22)*: Social, outgoing, caring, youthful, even wacky. These dogs will always be young at heart. You'll find them in the center ring—Libras are the life of the party. They create harmony in their environments.

Scorpio *(October 23 to November 21)*: Strong but silent, determined, loyal, complex, and emotional. Scorpio dogs give 100 percent to those they love. They can be manipulative, but they will never let down their owners. They will work and play tirelessly.

Sagittarius *(November 22 to December 21)*: Confident, jolly, enthusiastic, lighthearted, optimistic. These dogs love adventure and freedom. Fence in your yard for a Sagittarius, who doesn't want to be tied up or restrained. You'll need to help them recognize their limits. They are easily bored.

Capricorn *(December 22 to January 19)*: Practical, down-to-earth, shy, cautious, suspicious of strangers, but committed to completing any task. These dogs are affectionate and loyal—not as adventurous as others, but very trustworthy. They are known for their courage, and keen focus.

Are You Getting a Dog for the Right Reasons?

RESISTING LOVE AT first sight is not easy. Those inquisitive puppy eyes, the touch-me soft fur—her playful nature and happy dance when you greet her—of course you must take home this puppy! Certainly, adopting a dog from an animal shelter is a responsible thing to do. Unfortunately, the decision to bring either a puppy or a mature dog into the family requires more practical considerations. Ignore your tugging heartstrings, at first, until you thoughtfully consider whether now is the right time and whether your lifestyle can accommodate a new "child." Ask yourself the following questions:

Why do you want to own a dog? Adopting a pet on a whim or because a child demands a pet are the wrong reasons. Remember, this dog will be part of your family's life for up to twenty years, depending on the breed.

Do you have time? You cannot ignore a dog when you are tired or get too busy. Dogs require food, water, exercise, care, and companionship every day of every year, for as long as they live. Most shelter dogs are there because their owners didn't realize what an incredible amount of time and energy it takes to care for them.

Can you afford to properly care for a dog? From licenses to training classes, spaying and neutering, veterinarian care, grooming, toys, food, and supplies, the costs may be substantial, especially when added up over the dog's lifetime. Then there could be fees associated with problems your dog may confront: flea infestations, worms, and even cancers. (You can buy pet health insurance. Learn more in Day 207.) In addition to direct costs, there will be indirect expenses. You can count on losing at least one piece of furniture, rug, or household accessory as a puppy teethes and innocently plays with, say, the tassels on your heirloom oriental rug.

Will your lifestyle accommodate a dog? Are you allowed to have a dog where you live? Many rental communities do not allow dogs, and the majority of the remainder have restrictions. Be sure you know the rules before you bring a dog home or if you expect to be moving in the near future. This goes double if you travel and want to take your pet along to inns, motels/hotels, or time-shares.

Is now the time? If you have a child who is not yet six years old, you may want to hold off for a few years. Children should be responsible enough to help with pet care, such as filling a water bowl, and to understand a dog has more feelings and needs than a favorite stuffed animal. Likewise, if you are in school, the military, or travel frequently for your job, and would need to leave your pet behind at home, wait to adopt a dog until you settle down.

Some animals are independent and require their human family members only to "check in" on them periodically—some cats are like this. Dogs are not; they require attention and love every day of their lives.

Will you be a responsible dog owner? Remember that getting your dog spayed or neutered, obeying your community's leash and licensing laws, and maintaining and renewing your dog's identification tags are all requirements of being a dog owner.

Are you ready to care for the dog for the rest of his life? Remember that when you adopt a pet, you are making a commitment to care for the animal for her lifetime, which includes giving your dog love, exercise, companionship, a healthy diet, and regular vet care.

Do you already have other pets? Will they accept a canine newcomer, and do you have the time and patience to oversee the transition period?

If more potential dog owners would ask themselves these questions before they adopt or buy a dog, there would be fewer dogs in shelters today.

Create Personalized Paw-Print Place Mats

Dogs don't mind their table manners when they are thirsty. They slurp, drip, slobber, and sometimes spill water from their dishes. To offset this mess, prepare their mealtime area by laying a place mat underneath food and water dishes. You can purchase place mats at discount and department stores, but they may not be large enough to accommodate a set of bowls. Also, these mats tend to slip and slide when your dog noses around in his bowls, pushing the mat along with his dishes across slick tile or wooden floor surfaces.

Why not personalize your pup's place mats and improve their slide resistance by making your own? Your dog can help with this project— you'll borrow his paw for a "stamp."

MATERIALS

Fabric or paper (several feet [less than a meter] long) to become the mat's top surface

Masking tape

Nontoxic water-based paint, colors of your choice

Disposable plastic or paper bowls (for holding paint)

Sponges (scrap) for stamping designs (optional)

Paintbrushes, various sizes (optional)

Ruler

Scissors

Embellishments, such as ribbon, glitter, or other crafting mediums

Burlap-textured shelf liner (to affix beneath the mat for skid resistance)

1. *Gather your materials.* Set up a place to work outside. Cut the fabric or paper several feet long to give enough room for your dog to walk on its surface. Tape the corners of fabric or paper to the ground. This is your canvas. Pour the paint, one color per bowl, into the plastic or paper bowls.

2. *Round up your dog and calm her down with a treat or two.* Dip one or two paws at a time in the paint and allow her to jump and dance on the fabric. If you have more than one dog, work with them individually; consider leaving the other dogs indoors so they don't get their noses in the paint bowls. (If authentic paw prints are too labor intensive, cut kitchen sponges into paw shapes, dip into the paints, and stamp onto the fabric or paper.) Allow the paint to dry in the sun.

3. *Set your dog's dishes side by side.* Using the ruler, note the total length and width, allowing several extra inches on every side for eating/drinking spillovers. Cut rectangles of these dimensions from your fabric or paper canvas, once its paint has dried.

4. *Embellish the place mats.* Use ribbon, glitter, or any type of crafting medium before lamination, to create different designs. There are limitless options.

5. *Laminate the design.* Most print shops and office supply stores offer lamination services. Or, if you have a wide enough food saver, feed the unlaminated place mats into the saver and operate according to manufacturer's instructions. (Do not use embellished place mats without first laminating them.) To prevent sliding, attach the burlap-textured shelf liner to the reverse side by cutting a rectangle the same size as the place mat and carefully adhering it, applying the sticky side of shelf paper to the back of the place mat.

Let's Play "Which Hand?"

THIS GAME IS simple for puppies to play and requires virtually no training. Do you remember the childhood game, "Which hand is it in?" Usually it was played with something your friend wanted badly, such as a piece of candy. For your dog, the ultimate reward is also a tasty treat.

Here's how to play:

1. *Attention please!* Show your dog the treat and your pooch will know something exciting is in store.

2. *Kneel and conceal.* Facing your dog at his eye level, tuck the treat into one of your palms and place both hands side by side in front of him.

Ask, "Which hand?" Then put your hands behind your back and trade the treat between hands.

3. *Show and reward.* Bringing your hands back in front of you, side by side, ask the question again: "Which hand?" Your dog may lick one or both hands. When the action is correct, reward him with the treat. Repeat this game and he will catch on to the facts that (1) only one hand contains a treat and (2) his guessing right is necessary to get a snack.

Administering Liquid Medicine

PILLS ARE EASY to wrap in cheese or another meaty treat your dog adores. Your pet will barely notice what's buried underneath the "good stuff." Giving a dog liquid medication requires more practice and a bit of strategy. Let's walk through the process:

1. *Prepare the syringe.* Your vet will supply a syringe to "upload" the liquid medicine for dropping it into your pet's mouth, or you can purchase one at a pharmacy. Open the bottle of liquid medication and fill the syringe to the proper dosage.

2. *Stabilize the dog.* You might ask someone to help hold your dog the first time you administer liquid medication. Tip back your dog's head by placing one hand on the top of the dog's head, and the other hand (with the syringe) underneath her jaw. Before administering liquid medication, you must stabilize your dog's head.

3. *Insert the syringe.* With the dog's head tilted back, put the syringe in her mouth toward one back corner, tilting it slightly toward the back of her mouth. This position will ensure that more liquid goes down the hatch, even if your dog squirms during the process. If you put the syringe in straight, and she makes a quick head move to the right or left, your liquid will spill onto the floor.

4. *Reward your dog.* Once the medicine has been swallowed, praise your dog and give her a tasty treat to reinforce her cooperation for a job well done. Clean out the syringe and place it in a designated plastic box (a pencil box works well), labeled "liquid medication syringes."

Munching on Grass

YOUR DOG PERIODICALLY treats the yard as an all-you-can-eat salad bar, munching on the green grass like a cow. No, your dog is not having an identity crisis. Sometimes, dogs eat grass when they are sick to their stomach. If your pooch feels nauseated, her first instinct is to clear her belly of the "bad stuff." That could be too many treats, or even pet food that just didn't sit well. Grass acts like ipecac, helping your dog to vomit. So if you notice your dog eating grass, take away food and water and watch your pet's behavior carefully. If you see her slink around with her tail between her legs, you should usher her outside. This is a clear sign that she is about to get sick. As you notice her activity returning to normal, allow small amounts of water throughout the day. Return to pet food once you are sure her stomach has stabilized.

Aside from indicating sickness, grass munching may indicate that your dog is not getting adequate fiber from her diet. However, if you are feeding your pet premium dog food, you can rest assured that nutrient deficiency is not the problem. Your dog probably just needs to throw up, and grass is a sure way to trigger the response.

If the need to eat grass or vomiting persists for more than a day, however, do check with your vet, as there may be some medical reason why your pet is feeling queasy.

Note: Not all dogs eat grass to vomit. Some breeds do this to add bulk to their diet.

The Budget-Savvy Dog Owner

DOG OWNERSHIP CAN get expensive if you splurge on the latest toys and do not invest in your dog's health. Consider these spendthrift measures to cut the cost of dog ownership without compromising your dog's wellness or happiness.

• Start your dog early on an exercise program, and try not to overfeed your pooch. Health, exercise, and diet go hand in hand, and a healthy dog will be less expensive to take care of.

• If you're not attached to your vet, shop around. Prices can vary widely from one office to another. Ask your friends and neighbors for recommendations. But don't choose a vet on price alone; the right vet will save you money in the long run. (See how to find a vet, Day 46).

• Having your pet spayed or neutered is not only ethically the right thing to do but can save money. Dogs who have been fixed are at less risk for many cancers, and don't produce puppies that come with expenses of their own. Many humane organizations offer low-cost spaying and neutering—and low-cost vaccinations.

• Never be afraid to ask for discounts: Some vets offer multiple-pet discounts as well as discounts for senior pet owners.

• Ask your vet for a prescription for any medications, as opposed to buying the medication directly from the office. Most people don't realize that 75 percent of the drugs that vets use are approved for people and can be purchased for much less in generic form at your local pharmacy, perhaps even with pet-palatable flavorings. Also, ask your vet if a less costly over-the-counter or alternative remedy might be suitable for the situation. NEVER give any medication to your pet without checking with your vet first.

• If your pet is ill and your vet is unable to arrive at a diagnosis or an effective treatment, get a second opinion. This may cost more up front, but can save hundreds or thousands of dollars in the long run if the second vet can identify the problem sooner and more effectively.

• Pet stores, dog parks, and even humane societies can help you find low-cost training classes. Be sure you always check the trainer's credentials, and ask friends and family for recommendations. Every puppy should at least go to the basic puppy training classes. If you can't afford a trainer, get a book on training your dog and do it yourself.

19

Containing Your Puppy Indoors:
Crates, Gates, and Playpens

GATES, CRATES, AND PLAYPENS can be sanity savers while you're training your puppy or protecting off-limits rooms from becoming doggy dens. Any dog, be it a puppy or adult, wants to explore. Because you can't keep an eye on your dog every minute, you should create boundaries by putting up barriers that keep your pet in a dog-approved space. Puppies require even more restrictions. You may decide to limit your puppy's roaming to just the kitchen (or any other room with an easy-clean floor). Decide in advance where your puppy or dog is allowed in the house. If he gets a taste of that off-limits room just once, you can bet he'll work hard to reenter it.

A crate is a safe retreat for your dog and should be sized to fit your dog to allow for room to stand up and turn around inside it. You can downsize a larger crate by blocking off the back. Have a piece of sturdy cardboard or wood cut to fit at a hardware store and sand the edges. As your puppy grows, you can move the plastic farther and farther back in the crate until your pet doesn't need the divider anymore. See Day 30 for more about crates.

Gates are an easy way to confine your dog to certain rooms if you don't want to have a house full of closed doors. Gates allow you to keep an eye on your dog when you're in another room. They come in different styles, both temporary and permanent. They are readily available at larger department and discount stores and are easy to install.

Playpens can be a great solution if you don't want to deal with gates. Just be sure the pen is large enough for your puppy to play freely. Many playpens can be used outside, too, and they're nice to have if you travel. Playpens shouldn't be used as full-time babysitters, though. Your puppy needs to have some freedom so she can learn what she needs to learn, to someday have full run of the house.

The Language of Barking

DOGS HAVE SEVERAL kinds of barks. If you get attuned to the different barks you may hear, you will be able to understand your dog better and be better able to deal with the problem. As a friend has told me many times, "A barking dog has a lot to say. We need to learn to understand."

- The warning bark is deep and loud: "Hey, Mom—look out!"

- The middle-pitched, not too loud, and not too strong bark is saying, "Hey, please come get me. I want to go out."

- The short bark that is almost a whine means, "Hey, I have to relieve myself right now!"

- The happy bark is excited: "Come play with me—let's go to the park!"

- The anger bark: "Hey, look at that squirrel! I must go get it!"

- The loud bark that comes in short waves says, "Hey, it's dinnertime now!"

- The play bark that means your participation is needed: "Hey, I can't reach that ball—I need help please."

- The growl is a kind of warning bark: "Leave me alone!"

- The whining and crying bark is to get your attention: "Hey, look at me! Look at me! Look at me!"

- The yelp means, "Run fast! I'm hurt, or stuck!"

Don't reward your puppy's whining, or attention-seeking barking, or your pet may never grow out of it. You don't want to teach that affection or a treat will reward whining.

Are they Playing or *Fighting*?

PLAYTIME AMONG DOGS can look like a competitive match. Whether you take your pet to a dog park or arrange play dates with neighbors' and friends' dogs in a safe, fenced-in area, you should learn what healthy play looks like. Normal dog play can look rough and tough—you may hear some yipping (but not yelping) and a bit of growling (sing-song growls, not low nasty snarls). That's the sound of happy dogs interacting and taking turns talking back to one another. Monitor sounds, and if you notice urgency, pain, or aggression in dogs' voices, run interference. Leash both dogs and stop the play session.

Pay attention to dogs' body posture. They will take turns being the "alpha" on top; they will alternate chasing. A submissive dog will introduce himself by lying on his side or crouching so the other dog can sniff and "meet" him. The shy dog should come out of his shell if play is healthy, acting as an equal participant in the jumping and chasing.

It is healthy for dogs to play in a sort of dancing pose, standing on hind legs in an embrace, where one dog is the lead. As long as they take turns being the lead, or alpha, the couple can dance all they want!

Monitor dog play, especially when your dog is meeting a new friend. Here are some danger signs to watch:

- *Ganging behavior*: Watch that dogs play fair and don't pick on one participant.

- *Unequal matches:* Size isn't everything; some big dogs are intimidated by small, feisty characters.

- *Overdomination:* One dog is clearly in charge and aggressive, not allowing the other to chase back or take a turn being on top during some playful wrestling.

How to Give Pills to Your Dog

WHEN YOUR DOG is sick and needs medication, it can be as distressing for you as it is for your pet. Once your vet has prescribed pills for your dog, now what?

Giving medicine should not involve shoving the medication down an animal's throat. A puppy can be trained to take medication by using positive reinforcement and making the dog feel he will be rewarded. Remember, using a patient, calm tone of voice helps convey that message. You are trying to help your dog, not scare him.

With an older dog or one that resists taking medication, sometimes you must get creative. Offering a pill hidden inside a treat is the easiest approach. You can purchase commercial pouch-shaped treats with tempting flavors at your vet's office or any pet store—just pop the pill into the pocket and it will be swallowed along with the treat. It's just as easy to make your own with something your dog absolutely loves (such as folded liverwurst patties). It may be peanut butter, hot dogs, cheese spread—anything you know your dog is going to eat. But watch out! Dogs are pranksters and may eat the entire treat, then spit out the pill when you have left the room. If necessary, crush the pill and blend it into something soft, such as peanut butter or a small amount of your pet's favorite canned dog food.

Your last resort is to give the pill manually. Talking calmly at all times, gently open the dog's mouth and place the pill as far back into your dog's throat as you can. Close the mouth and gently hold it closed while you stroke his throat until he swallows. As soon as your pet swallows the pill, provide a ton of affection and a yummy treat so he'll remember the positive reinforcement and not the unpleasantness of having to take medicine. This is an art, so please do not get discouraged if it does not work the first few times.

> Never give your dog acetaminophen, ibuprofen, aspirin, or any other "people" medication without your vet's consent.

Calming Your Anxious Dog

DOGS HAVE DIFFERENT personalities, and some are prone to anxiety and nervous behavior. The reason for your dog's skittish reaction may be obvious: a stranger enters your home; he hears loud thunder; he is exposed to a new environment, such as a friend's home. Some common signs of anxiety include crying, loss of appetite, digging, eliminating in an "off-limits" place (not outside), never leaving your side.

Your dog can overcome anxious behavior by learning that the trigger (a stranger, sound, or situation) is "safe." Here are some tips for calming a dog that displays the above side effects of nervousness.

Loss of appetite. Sit with your new dog and feed him by hand to show that no one will take away the food. Talk to him gently, coaxing him to take a bite. Let the dog put his nose into your hand to take food. Never force feed.

Crying. If your dog cries when you leave the room, take him to a safe place: his crate. Or, set up a play pen so he can move around more freely. If you give your puppy full run of the house too soon, he may feel uncertain when he cannot see you and react by eliminating or crying.

Eliminating. Your dog will not want to go potty in his crate. Dogs are careful to keep neat beds, and they will work very hard not to soil their safe zone. (If they do, it is almost always an accident and the dog may mope or feel sad.) By crate training your dog, you can rest assured that your dog will not eliminate when guests visit or when you leave the house and he gets scared from a strange sound or simply because he is alone.

Never leaving your side. You can't spend 24/7 next to your dog, though you both may prefer it that way. You will leave, and your dog will learn to stay home alone for some time. By bedding the crate with towels that contain your scent, he will be comforted and know you will return home.

Mom, I'm Scared!

If on a walk, your puppy is frightened by a loud truck rolling by, a cyclist, garbage cans stacked at the end of the driveway for trash day—the possibilities are endless—take these steps to calm your pet:

- *Resist the urge to console.* Do not pick up your puppy and coddle him. He will think you are praising him and think that there is, indeed, something to be scared about.

- *Lighten up.* Using a joyful tone, pal around and play a little game. Let your puppy know this scary moment is nothing to fear—you're both having fun.

- *Get near the "scare."* If a parked truck is scaring your puppy, ease him close to the truck and use a consoling, comforting voice as you say, "That's okay," or another reassuring comment.

Giving Back: Your Dog Can Be a Blood Donor

THERE ARE MANY ways for people to give back to other people. Did you know that your dog can also make a contribution to the dog world? By allowing your dog to donate blood, you just may be saving the life of another dog that is ill or has been in an accident.

The dog world could use a few more "good men" to help those in need. Currently only large and medium dogs are allowed to donate, because blood packs small enough for a toy or little dog do not yet exist (the medical industry is working on it).

Your veterinarian can draw the blood from your dog, and the process is really very simple. Your dog is laid on her side in a quiet room with a front leg extended, which is usually where the best veins are located. While you talk to your pet and keep her calm, the needle is inserted into the vein and the process begins. The actual drawing process takes roughly five to ten minutes. Approximately 450 ml of blood is drawn and mixed with an anticoagulant to prevent clotting. You will need to block out about 45 minutes for the entire process; most of that time is to make sure that your dog is healthy and feeling okay after the procedure.

Your dog does not have to be a purebred and can donate blood up to four times a year. One donation of blood can save the lives of up to four other dogs. After your dog has donated a few times, she will get used to the process and become more relaxed. After all, who wouldn't love getting a rest in a dark room while being given a calming massage, not to mention the treats that are in store after the process is over.

One of the other benefits of being a dog blood donor is that you will receive a comprehensive blood panel, free of charge, which lets you know your dog is hale and hearty. Dogs are not paid for blood donation, but many veterinarians offer a goodie bag with toys and treats. How many dogs do you know that are going to turn down free treats and toys?

If you are interested in having your dog donate blood, here are a few things to consider:

- Does your dog enjoy her vet visits?

- Does she greet the vet with a wagging tail?

- Is she relaxed at the vet's office?

- Is your dog the correct size and weight? Your vet can help you determine this.

- How do you personally feel about giving blood? Is it okay with you?

- The calmer you are, the better your dog will be about it.

There is a saying that "every person who walks through your life changes it"—it is the same with dogs. What better way to show your special companion how much you love her than by enabling her to help another dog?

What's in a Name?

SOON AFTER YOU bring home your new puppy or dog, you'll begin the name game. What should you call your new friend? If you adopt a dog that has been previously named, you *can* teach him a new name, but it will take some training. In any case, consistency is key with training, so decide early what to name your dog and stick to it. Here, we'll assume you are naming a new dog.

Name possibilities are endless, some of which you may not want to call out loud. (Do yo u want to yell, "Come home, Stinker!" every day?) While you may have the perfect pooch name picked out before you bring your puppy home, keep an open mind until you get to know your new friend. It's okay to wait a few days to name your pup. You may learn that her spunky nature disagrees with the name Grace. Or perhaps your pet's sly behavior suits the name Brutus but not Fido.

Brainstorm a list of possible names, and keep these pointers in mind as you select a winner:

- *Noah sounds like "no."* Names that rhyme with no could be confused for the command no. A dog named Noah that hears "No!" will be excited you called his name and will not get the message to stop a bad behavior.

- *Keep it short.* Two-syllable names are best. Practice saying the name and see how easily it rolls off your tongue. If you choose a name that is too long, you'll probably resort to a nickname anyway.

- *Test the name.* How does your dog respond? Of course, he will not realize it is his name at first, but if you get an adverse reaction, you may wish to reconsider the moniker.

You can also search online for name ideas. You'll find typical names for your dog's breed, most popular names, Hollywood names, historical names, political names. Here is a list of prompts to get your creative juices flowing:

- What physical characteristics make your dog special? (Why do you think there are so many dogs named Spot?)

- What was your favorite childhood movie or book character?

- Name your favorite flowers or plants: Daisy, Rose, Basil . . . the list goes on.

- Can you think of foods that would make interesting dog names?

- Consider your favorite hobbies and the jargon associated with them. Music, dance, crafts, and sports terms can double as inventive dog names.

- Avoid naming your dog after someone you know personally, unless the individual has a great sense of humor and is fond of dogs.

- Peruse baby name books, where you'll find hundreds of possibilities.

Contending with Chewing

CHEWING IS A PUPPY'S way of exploring the world by mouth. Taste and smell are strong dog senses (see Day 232), and as your puppy gets acclimated to her new home, she will naturally use her mouth to fulfill her curiosity. Babies do a similar thing when they get their hands on an object they find interesting. Beyond environmental discovery, chewing is a part of a puppy's teething process. When adult teeth cut through a puppy's gums, the feeling can be painful, and she will try to alleviate this discomfort by chewing. Try giving the pup frozen teeth soothers (learn to make them in Day 108). Finally, chewing can be a sign of boredom if a dog is not getting enough exercise or there is a lack of appropriate chew toys and bones for your new pet to sink his teeth into.

No matter the case, you should take three steps to prevent chewing and satisfy your dog's need to exercise her mouth.

- First, apply a stop-chew solution to furniture legs, throw-rug corners, any tempting area or object your dog has taken a liking to and has a habit of chewing.

- Second, provide your dog with safe chew toys (see Day 3) so he does not look around the house for alternatives, such as your shoes.

- Third, be sure your grown dog is getting enough exercise and playtime so he does not resort to chewing your valuables. Your pet will be happier, and so will you.

When you see your dog chewing something he shouldn't, take it out of his mouth and replace it with an appropriate chew toy, then praise him. Your dog wants to please you, so the more positive training you provide, the faster he will learn.

Recipe for a Stop-Chew Solution

To make your own stop-chew solution, mix equal parts of cinnamon, clove, and nutmeg essential oils (from a natural foods store) in a clean glass container with a lid. You can use this blend full strength by applying a small amount with a rubber glove directly to the surface the dog is chewing. To make a spray, place the oil blend in a glass spray bottle and add a small amount of very hot water. Shake well and spray on surfaces you want the dog to avoid. Note: Never use this stop-chew solution on painted surfaces, and test other surfaces in an inconspicuous area before applying to be sure it will not cause damage. Store any unused solution in a cool, dark place—the refrigerator is great.

STOPPING AN ADULT CHEWER

If a grown dog is chewing and it's a new be-havior, you need to look at the dog's day. Ask yourself these questions:

- Is my dog getting enough exercise during the day?

- Is my dog mentally stimulated during the day while I am at work?

- Is my dog chewing only when I am away from home?

A yes answer to any of these questions indicates that your dog may be chewing because he is bored. Before leaving the house, take your dog for a long walk and do your training to stimulate his mind and body. Provide your pet with chew toys to keep him busy while you are gone. Chew toys that can be stuffed with an edible filling (such as those made by Kong or the Tire Biter line of toys) can be especially helpful. You can fill them with commercially prepared fillings, or make your own with peanut butter, spray cheese, or any similar filling your dog loves. You can even mix in chopped hot dogs or cold cuts. Try freezing the filled toys to add to the chew time. Discard any food-augmented chew toys that have been out at room temperature for more than four hours.

Yes, Puppies Do Flirt!

THAT PLAYFUL BOW male dogs use to invite a female to play may be a loaded request. Sure, playtime is the idea, but the male will go out of his way to play nice, handicapping himself into disadvantaged positions so the female can "win" at puppy games. The male dog just wants to keep the play going. He is usually willing to lose a game if he can win some love in the long term.

It has been observed that in puppy litters, young male pups are more likely to bow to females to invite them to play. The female–female sessions, however, tend to be more aggressive and tense.

Basically, consider how children act on a playground. Girls may argue or fuss with one another, and boys will always try to please them.

So next time that the neighbor dog comes knocking for a play date with your girl, you can rightly question whether the male just wants to be friends.

Maintain Medical Records for Your Pet

KEEPING ALL OF your dog's essential information in one safe place ensures that in an emergency, you'll be able to find the necessary information ASAP. File the following information in a place that is easy to remember and access, such as the front of your filing cabinet or a designated drawer in the kitchen. And always remember to make sure your dog's vaccinations are up-to-date.

- Medical records
- Vet info
- List of emergency phone numbers, including a poison control center
- Training history
- Groomer
- Boarding
- Diet
- Medications
- Allergies
- Food and toy preferences
- Personality (for example, friendly toward people in uniforms)
- Vaccination records (starting at 8 weeks old)
- Registration
- Rabies vaccines (between 4 and 6 months of age, then annually or semiannually per state law)
- Spay/neuter record
- Diseases/conditions (both resolved and ongoing)
- Worm records (bring stool sample on first visit to vet)

How Much Did You Say That Checkup Costs?

The cost of vets can rival our own doctor's fees. The price of veterinary care has increased at twice the rate of overall inflation. Because of advances in vet care, some very expensive "human"-style treatments are now available, including kidney transplants, chemotherapy, knee replacements, and pacemakers. Consider obtaining pet insurance when your dog is a puppy. If you purchase it early in your dog's life, you may pay a lower deductible and maximize the insurance benefits over time. There are many different types of insurance, so be sure to talk with your vet to find the best policy for you and your dog.

Bells: Old-Fashioned GPS for Dogs

IF YOU LIVE in the country, you may wish you could put a GPS tracking device on your dog—and you can, with GPS collar devices on the market that allow you to program coordinates for your property perimeter so the system can alert you if your dog escapes. These devices are great for gadget-loving dog owners who don't mind shelling out to get the latest technology. A simple Internet search produces an array of GPS collar setups for your pooch.

If you want to keep it simple, attaching a bell to your dog's collar will work double-duty as a tracking device and scarecrow. Here's why: You'll hear your dog coming and going, and if the bell sound disappears you can bet she wandered past her boundaries; plus, the ringing will alert animals such as squirrels to keep their distance.

Ideally, the bell will scare off the critters before the dog notices their presence, preventing an all-out chase.

You can purchase jingle bells at most pet stores. Craft store jingle bells do not resist chewing and could become harmful to your dog. Secure the bell on to your dog's collar with a sturdy ribbon, or hook securely onto the ring holding your dog's tags. At first, the noise will agitate your dog—she'll have a similar reaction to when you placed a collar around her neck for the first time. But she will quickly get used to the sound and feel of the bell, and you'll appreciate the low-maintenance tracking device, especially if your dog is trained off-leash and has the run of the yard.

Memories . . . Keeping a Dog Journal

A DOG JOURNAL is a great place to collect memories and photographs of your dog. Amusing stories and silly pictures will remind you why you love your dog when your pet is trying your patience, and can be a comfort when you're feeling low.

Your memory book can contain written passages, photo collages, interesting one-liner recollections, or even memorabilia that you collect while traveling with your dog. If you can draw, bring out the colored pencils and put in some sketches. Paste in mementos of your travels together, such as train tickets or camping passes. Use your imagination to record not just the special times, but the everyday, too.

Journals come in a wide variety of styles and forms. Craft stores have fancy scrapbooks with large, removable pages. Bookstores, art supply stores, and office supply stores have dozens of blank books to choose from in a range of sizes, some with lined paper and others with plain paper. If you want to make entries every day, you might even consider a daybook calendar, which has a dated page or spread devoted to each day. Even a simple spiral notebook will do.

Creatively decorate the pages if you wish. Craft and scrapbooking stores have a huge selection of decorations: decorative papers, stickers, rub-on transfers, stamps, three-dimensional embellishments. Use colored pencils, markers, paints—whatever strikes your fancy. There are no rules. Check out books about art journals, for inspiration.

How Dogs Respond to Babies and Children

A DOG CAN BE a child's best friend, but some breeds inherently don't get along well with children, and not all children get along well with dogs. Most problems occur with younger children. If your child is under age six, you may want to wait before adding a dog to the family until you are sure that all family members understand what "gentle" and "leave the dog alone" mean.

Of course, if you already have a dog and find out that you have a baby on the way, that's a different story. Most dogs tend to do fine with new babies. The concept of a "puppy" is innate, and although a human pup doesn't have a tail, most dog breeds tolerate, and even love, our babies. As you make plans for your new arrival, discuss with your partner how you will handle the dog's exercise and attention needs while you are getting used to being parents.

As your baby becomes a toddler, arrange to keep some distance between the child and the dog, and supervise their interactions. A fenced yard is always helpful, and you can keep them separated in the house by using a baby gate between rooms. Dogs that get some kid-free time every day are more likely to tolerate your two-year-old.

Remember that you, as the adult, are responsible for training both your child and your dog. Until you are completely sure that both of them understand how to safely interact with each other, never leave them alone together.

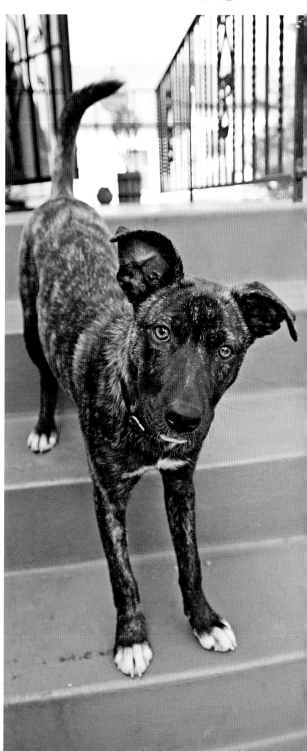

The Crate: Your Dog's Safe Haven

BEFORE DOGS WERE domesticated, they sought out dens in the wild, which were safe places to sleep, hide from predators, and raise their families. Today, the crate replaces the den for domesticated dogs.

Most reputable breeders suggest a crate as a safe place to keep a dog when you are not able to be around to watch what she is doing (or getting into). Dogs are masters at occupying themselves without help from humans! Sometimes what they choose to play with is either dangerous for them or destructive to the house. You are responsible for your dog's safety, and that means if you cannot watch her, she is better off spending time in her crate. Trust comes with age. Eventually, usually after a dog's first birthday, you can leave her at home for short periods of time, setting limits by gating her in the kitchen or a "safe room." As your dog is trained, she will learn boundaries and you will not have to keep such a close eye on her all of the time.

When exactly should you crate your dog? The crate is ideal when she is ill or recovering from surgery and needs to be in a safe, confined place where she can rest quietly. (You'd hate to have to take your dog back to the vet for restitching after she raced all over the house during recovery.) A crate is also great for long naps, and for sleeping at night if the crate is close to your bedside so you can monitor her noises. (She will let you know if she needs to go potty, because dogs do not want to mess their beds.)

Crates are essential when you leave the home. Mind how long you leave your puppy in a crate. She will tolerate a couple of hours alone at a few months' age, and as her capability to wait longer for bathroom trips increases, so can her crate time.

Still, a crate is not a cure-all. Your dog needs exercise and social time in the house with you. Never put your pet in a crate as punishment; rather, use the crate as a discipline. She will quickly learn that the crate is her "corner" where she must go for time-out when she is bad. If your puppy needs crate time to settle down, lure her into the crate with a treat and reward her with praise and hugs when she obeys. She will recognize that the crate is where she wants to be after you show and tell her that it is a safe, comfortable place.

35

How to Make a Dog Photo Album

ADD A SPECIAL touch to a purchased photo album with a custom canine-themed fabric cover. An album makes a nice new dog shower gift, and it is also a thoughtful present for grown children who go away to college or move out of the home.

MATERIALS

A plain photo album

Fabric (the amount will depend on the size of your album; lightweight cotton will work best for this project)

Fabric chalk or washable fabric marker

Fabric glue

Fabric scissors

Pinking shears

Fabric appliqués that coordinate with the base fabric (bone shapes, doghouses, letters to spell out your dog's name—whatever you like)

Heavy paper (for the inside front and back covers; you can use scrapbooking paper with a dog design on it or plain paper of any color)

MAKING THE COVER

1. Lay out your fabric on your work table, right side down. Smooth out any wrinkles.

2. Position the open photo album on the fabric. If the fabric has a pattern, make sure it is lined up with the book the way you want it to be.

3. Using chalk, mark your cutting line on the fabric, about 2 inches (5 cm) from the edge of the album all the way around.

4. Cut out your fabric with the fabric scissors.

5. Apply fabric glue to the outside front and back covers and spine of the album.

6. Wrap the fabric around the closed album, making sure the pattern is lined up the way you want it to be. Smooth out any wrinkles. Allow this to dry thoroughly.

7. Trim the fabric evenly around the edges of the album with the pinking shears, leaving about 1 inch all around.

8. Depending on how your photo album is constructed, you may need to use the fabric scissors to cut slits straight in from the edge of the fabric to the edge of the album at the points where the cover bends.

9. Fold the one corner of fabric in at a 45-degree angle and tack it to the inside of the cover with glue. Repeat with the other four corners.

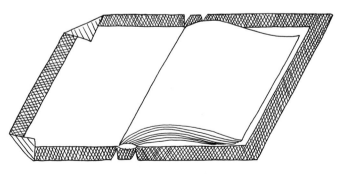

Assembly diagram of photo album cover

10. Fold the sides in and secure with glue.

11. Fold the bottoms and tops in and secure them with glue.

12. At this point, unless you have a photo album with a thin, folded spine, you should have two flaps of fabric sticking out, one each at the top and bottom of the spine. Depending on how your book is constructed, you may need to trim these closer before folding them over and gluing them down.

13. Smooth out any wrinkles and allow all the glue to dry.

MAKING THE ENDPAPERS

1. Measure the inside covers of your book and cut two heavy pieces of paper to ¼ inch (6 mm) shorter and ⅛ inch (3 mm) narrower than that measurement.

2. Glue the papers over the fabric on the inside front and back covers to cover the edges of the fabric. If you position your paper with the edge in the crease, you should have an even ⅛-inch (3 mm) margin around the edges. Allow the glue to dry.

3. Decorate the front of your photo album by gluing on the fabric appliqués with fabric glue. Allow the glue to dry.

4. Add your photographs and enjoy your album!

The Fifteen-Minute Makeover

YOUR DOG IS having a bad hair day. Her long hair is matted, scraggly, and she is feeling all-around yucky, lacking in confidence while strolling down the street for her daily walks. Usually, she struts around your block as if it is her personal red carpet. Her nails scratch on the kitchen floor and, although you blame the favorite chicken broth–soaked rawhides for her offensive breath, the truth is you have been slacking on her oral hygiene.

You can clean up your dog's act in fifteen minutes, and in the process restore her queenlike confidence. Maintenance in between grooming appointments will keep her healthy as well. Clean fur carries fewer allergens and is softer to touch. Some dogs actually welcome the cleaning, knowing their reward will be more lap time. Follow this regimen for a quick makeover that will please you both.

Shampoo and condition: Wash smaller dogs in the kitchen sink if you have a handy spray attachment. Medium and large dogs must be bathed in the family bathtub or laundry tub. Always use lukewarm water so you don't burn the dog or dry out her skin. Test the water's temperature on the inside of your arm before soaking the dog.

Towel off and blow dry: Absorb excess water from your dog's coat with a bath towel or chamois. Long-haired dogs can benefit from a blow-dry with a special dog's hair dryer. This tool speeds the drying process and allows you to simultaneously remove tangles with a comb.

Brush teeth: Using a canine toothbrush and toothpaste, give your dog's pearly whites a good cleaning. You can find varieties flavored with peppermint, beef, and chicken. (See Day 65 for more details on oral hygiene.)

Clean ears and eyes: Squeaky-clean ears and bright eyes are signs of a healthy dog. You can purchase prepackaged, presoaked ear pads and wipes for convenience. See Day 291 for detailed cleaning instructions. Cleaning solution also comes in gels and liquids that you dispense and massage into the ear. Eye wipe pads also make an easy job of cleaning the "sleepers" that collect in the corners of your dog's peepers. You may also use drops. Check with your vet for recommended eye and ear solutions.

Doggy Hair Dryer

Owners of short-haired dogs get off easy— a quick rinse, shampoo, and shake-off later and their dogs are "groomed." Long-haired dogs require more maintenance, and because their fur tangles easily and takes longer to dry, you may opt to use a doggy hair dryer to speed the process. Never use a human hair dryer on your dog. An exception: when the blow dryer is on a cool setting and you are constantly moving it back and forth, dispersing the air along the dog's body. Ideally, purchase a special blow dryer tool for dogs from a catalog or pet store. Dog blow dryers are safe, effective, and especially designed to not burn the dog or dry out her skin.

Make Your Own Dog Bar Soap

THIS ALL-NATURAL soap is a fun craft project and great for your dog's skin. It also makes a perfect gift for a dog owner. The process is so easy that you'll soon be able to personalize this recipe, adding your own special touches.

We use the melt-and-pour method of soapmaking, which is the least time consuming and can be done in the microwave. Consult with the expert at a natural foods store when selecting your essential oils. Some oils can irritate the skin; on the other hand, citronella, tea tree, and/or lemongrass essential oils will help repel fleas and ticks.

MATERIALS

All-natural, unscented, 100% olive oil (castile) soap

Microwaveable container, such as a large glass measuring cup

Essential oil(s) of your choice

Exfoliants (optional), such as citrus peel or steel-cut oatmeal—anything that is all natural, nontoxic, and not sharp

Clean soap molds (generally available from soap suppliers in standard or fun shapes, or use your own plastic containers)

Kitchen thermometer

1. Chop the soap into chunks and place in the microwaveable container.

2. Melt the soap in the microwave oven. Each device behaves differently, so start at half power and heat for 2 to 4 minutes at a time, stirring between stages. You do not want to overheat or burn the soap, so check often until you know how quickly it melts. The soap base should be completely melted and at a temperature between 155° and 165°F (68° to 74°C). Once you have reached this temperature, stir it again slowly to make sure it is uniform, then let it sit for a few moments, allowing any air bubbles to rise to the top.

3. Add a few drops of essential oil for fragrance and stir slowly, avoiding creating more air bubbles.

4. Add exfoliants, if desired. Again, stir slowly to avoid introducing air bubbles. It is recommended that all your additives, including essential oils and exfoliants, not exceed 2 percent of the entire soap solution.

5. Pour the soap into the molds. Best results will be obtained if the soap is poured into molds at 150° to 155°F (66°to 68°C). Pour very slowly to avoid creating air bubbles. Once poured, the soap bars should be handled carefully and left to cool completely, about 24 hours.

6. Remove the bars from the molds and wrap them immediately to retain an attractive appearance. The soap bars should be stored at temperatures between 40° and 86°F (4° and 30°C).

Custom Dog Character Soaps

Clear soaps can be personalized with a photograph of the recipient dog. Cover the photograph with a plastic coating, such as cling wrap, packing tape, or laminating sheets. Fill the soap mold halfway and allow it to set. Place the photograph on the soap, then fill the mold with more melted soap.

You can also make soap on a rope so that when you are washing your dog, you never have to worry about losing the soap or a bottle falling over. Just drill a hole in the finished bar, thread onto a rope, and tie a knot.

Reading Doggy Body Language

You know your dog well enough to tell when he is excited (wag-wag-wag), depressed (moping), and timid (attached to your side). But tuning into your dog's body language can lend more clues to what's going on in his head. Dogs would not score big at the poker table. Their movement and mannerisms bluntly reveal emotion. You'll never have to worry about whether your dog is hiding his feelings from you. Look at his tail!

Here are some typical body and tail movements and what they mean:

TAIL WAG TRANSLATIONS

Tail, up and wagging: happy, positive

Tail up and wagging quickly: anticipation, excitement

Tail straight out (horizontal) and wagging: steady, caution, worry

Tail relaxed, slight wag: contentment, ease, life is good

Tail up, quivering: nervous but friendly

Tail sweeping broadly: pre-attack anticipation, nervousness

Tail tucked between legs: submission, fear, anxiety

BODY MOVEMENT MEANING

Bowing down, front paws to the ground: an invitation to play

Nudging nose: attention-seeking, an invitation to play (more)

Pawing: a nagging invitation to play (please!)

Scratching back paws after eliminating (the kick): marking territory; a visual reminder, aside from the excreted scent, to tell other dogs, "I live here"

Scratching front paws (digging): tension, insecurity

Frozen body: threatened, scared, something is happening

Mounting (humping): dominance

Stalking, slow moving: fearful, "hunting," listening and watching

Flickering tongue: submission, anxiety, fear

Smiling: submissive grin, or aggressiveness if accompanied with a snarl

Licking your face: Subordination, affection

Your Children and Your New Pet:
Tips to Help along the Way

SHARING THE RESPONSIBILITY of pet ownership with your children can be a valuable experience for them and can take some of the load off of you. Before you bring home your new puppy or dog, hold a family meeting and discuss what caring for a dog requires. Help your children understand the issues by relating the care and training to their own experiences. Explain that puppies are like babies, and the whole family will help care for this new family member. It is not excessive to say, "Our new puppy will need to learn potty training just like you did, and we will have to help her."

Discuss reasonable tasks the children can help with and talk about how the family will incorporate pet care into the daily schedule. For instance, decide who will be responsible for taking the dog out first thing in the morning. Talk about how to handle and pet the dog. Children think they are showing love, but many times their tight-squeeze embraces can hurt a puppy. The key here is to set the stage before puppy comes home so everyone is prepared. Do not let your children con you into believing they will take care of all the dog's needs.

Assign your children age-appropriate tasks. Here are a few examples of what you may expect.

TODDLER

A toddler can help parents with pet care simply by being involved—"helping" a parent fill food and water dishes, grooming, going with you to take the dog for a walk or to the veterinarian. The toddler can give the dog a treat for good behavior such as getting into his bed or crate before the family leaves the house. Toddler and pet both enjoy these interactions.

THE 5- TO 7-YEAR-OLD

This age group is capable of doing some feeding, watering, and grooming without parental help. Still, you can't expect that a child this age will remember to do these jobs without friendly reminders from Mom or Dad.

THE 8- TO 12-YEAR-OLD

Tasks requiring a greater level of responsibility, such as walking the dog, can be introduced at these ages, with supervision. It is not advisable to have a child under ten to twelve years of age walk a dog without adult supervision. However, the child can feed, water, and play with the dog alone (depending on the dog's temperament, size, and exercise area).

TEENAGER

Depending on your teen's maturity, you can sometimes allow him/her to take full responsibility for the dog, including feeding, cleaning up after him, driving to the veterinarian, and exercising the pet. Allowing the teen to take the dog to obedience classes can also be a good bonding activity for both.

41

Training Special Service Dogs

SPECIAL SERVICE DOGS serve as eyes for those with visual impairments and they listen and work like a set of fine-tuned ears for people who are deaf or hard of hearing. They may also be used to fetch out-of-reach items or perform other services for people with other disabilities, such as those who need to use a scooter or wheelchair. Dogs are wonderful companions and valuable helpers for individuals with disabilities of all kinds, particularly sight and sound. The most popular breeds of service dogs are Labradors, German Shepherds, and Golden Retrievers.

Even within these highly trainable breeds, not every dog has the disposition to work as a service dog—or to go through the rigorous training required to be certified as such. At twelve weeks of age they go to live with a foster family and start basic training, which includes intense lessons in obedience, socialization, attention, and concentration.

At age two, these dogs are sent to a special training school, where they learn tasks that will help them in the "real world," such as opening and closing doors, retrieving objects, alerting humans to sounds such as doorbells or smoke alarms, and guiding people around obstacles. Only a handful of dogs in each class will pass the training program and exhibit the temperament to be a successful service dog.

The training may actually be the easy part of owning a service dog. How would you feel after bonding with a puppy for two years, and then having to give the dog to someone else? It takes a strong and selfless family to volunteer to raise a puppy from twelve weeks to two years and then have to give the dog away. Raising and guiding a service dog through his training years is a tremendous social service—and incredibly admirable. While this training is extensive and expensive, many of those who need service dogs receive them free of charge through the generosity of donors and sponsorship programs.

Matching Dogs with Disabled Individuals

Individuals who adopt trained service dogs (handlers) have a thirty-day evaluation period to be sure the dog is an appropriate match. Just because a service dog knows how to open doors for her blind owner does not mean the pair will live happily ever after. A dog's energy level, sensitivity (to loud noises, a boisterous owner), affection (some want a highly attached dog, others prefer an independent service pet) are all factors that weigh into the decision to keep the dog. Handlers should assess their own disposition and their expectations of a service dog. And trainers should evaluate the dog's disposition and clearly communicate the ideal environment for the dog. This way, everyone is on the same page and both dog and handler will be happy for years to come.

Some owners train their own dogs for service. They are responsible for finding a good handler "match" for their dogs. Here are some questions to ask a potential handler:

• Do you want a dog that is affectionate and wants to sit by you, sleep near you, never leave your side? Or, do you prefer a dependable but independent service dog?

• Describe your background with dogs. Did you own a dog growing up? First-time dog owners will need "human training" skills to adapt to living with a dog.

• What is your daily activity level? Do you go for regular outings and move around the house often? Are you sedentary, spending most of your days sitting or in bed?

• How important is dog breed and size?

Making Your Own Dog Blanket

Sewing your own dog blanket is easy and can save you a lot of money. Plus, you get the satisfaction of putting your time, effort, and love into making something special for your dog. Don't stress about your sewing skills! If necessary, you can make this a no-sew project by using nontoxic fabric glue. Keep in mind, your seams will not be as secure, and the finished look of a hand- or machine-sewn blanket is much more polished. But if you are not inclined to thread a needle or do not own a sewing machine, the crafter's approach is just fine.

MATERIALS

Fabric, ½ to 1 yard (45.5 to 91.5 cm)
(see steps 1 and 2)

Fabric scissors or pinking shears

Straight pins

Sewing thread in color of choice (optional)

Sewing machine or hand-sewing needle

Ribbon trim (optional)

Nontoxic fabric glue (optional)

1. Choose a cozy fabric you can wash in the washing machine. Try synthetic fleece, which can be found at most fabric stores. Flannel is another good choice.

2. If you are making the blanket to fit a particular area, such as a dog bed or crate, measure the area. If you don't need it to be a special size, a good rule of thumb is to use the whole width of the fabric and anywhere between a half yard and a full yard long, depending on the size of your dog. This will make a nice size for on the couch or in the car. Cotton fabrics will shrink a little when washed, so allow an extra couple inches (5 to 8 cm) on each side so your blanket does not come out of the dryer sized like a doormat.

3. Cut the fabric. Cut woven fabrics such as flannel with pinking shears to avoid frayed edges. Synthetic fleece will not fray (and does not need hemming), so cut it with regular fabric scissors.

4. Wash and dry the cut fabric.

5. To hem the edges, turn each edge under at least ¼ inch (6 mm) and pin in place. Sew the seam on your sewing machine or by hand, removing the pins as you go. Choose thread that coordinates with your fabric. Snip all the extra threads close to the blanket. (If you are not going to sew the hems, just skip this step.)

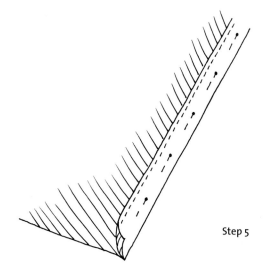

Step 5

44

6. You can attach ribbon trim by sewing it on or using nontoxic fabric glue, if desired. Attach securely, not in bows or streamers, so that your dog cannot chew off and swallow any loose ends.

7. Double-check to be sure all the pins have been removed and threads have been snipped, and wash and dry the blanket again.

8. Arrange the blanket and place a treat on it. Call your dog over to introduce her to her new blanket and offer a treat and praise. In no time, your dog will know this is her blanket.

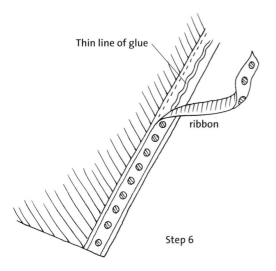

Thin line of glue

ribbon

Step 6

If you are adept at hand-sewing with a needle and thread, embroider the dog's name on a corner of the blanket. (Any blanket can be professionally monogrammed, too.) Also, the blanket can double as "wrapping paper" for a small bag of treats or other gift.

Maintain a Dog Health Journal

A HEALTH JOURNAL is a valuable tool for keeping track of your dog's total health history, not just his vaccination records. If you've ever had to give your own health history to a new doctor, you'll recall how difficult it is to remember the specifics for yourself; remembering it for your dog can be even harder.

Keeping a record of your dog's health history along with notes about his development and activity can help you and your vet track problems. Having a well-maintained health journal will help when transitioning between vets if you move, too.

Creating a health journal doesn't have to be a big project. You'll need a spiral notebook or binder with pockets in which you can save all the notes the vet sends home and space to take your own notes. Keep track of vet visits and outcomes, changes in diet or activity, medications and supplements, illnesses, allergies—anything that relates to your dog's health. Be thorough, and date each entry. If you like, you can use dividers for each year, or even each month within a year.

No matter how you choose to format your journal, it will be an asset for you and your dog in keeping him healthy and happy.

A Pet-Safe Lawn Care Program

A GOLF-COURSE GREEN lawn probably is not safe for your dog. Achieving that emerald luster requires applications of fertilizer, herbicide, fungicide, lime, grub treatment, insecticide, and other growth stimulators. These treatments pose little threat to humans if they walk across the lawn wearing shoes, especially if those shoes are removed before entering the home. Dogs' paws, on the other hand, are bare skin fully exposed to grass, a surface with which they are in contact several times a day. Plus, dogs frequently lick their paws to clean them.

A number of dangerous side effects result from exposure to lawn care products. Immediate signs that your dog has ingested toxins include diarrhea, foaming at the mouth, stomachache, excessive hyperactivity, drooping or glazed-over eyes, and profuse panting. Long-term effects of using products that contain toxins can range from seizures to death.

Some believe that health conditions such as bladder cancer are aggravated by lawn care products. Breeds known for intense self-hygiene are especially susceptible. Female Scottish Terriers, for instance, are known for frequent preening and paw licking.

Now the dilemma: You do not want your dog to lick up harmful toxins, but you also want a presentable yard. Can you have it all? Yes and no. A truly organic lawn care program replaces chemicals with cultural practices, such as aeration, dethatching, and applying topdressing. No commercial lawn product, even if it is advertised as "all natural" or "organic," is ideal for a dog owner's lawn. Yes, they may be less potent options—liquids tend to be more potent than granular formulations, for instance. But they often still involve some kind of chemical—don't assume you are totally toxin free with any commercial substance or lawn service. Read labels thoroughly and ask questions.

SOME PRACTICAL SOLUTIONS

- Only treat the front yard and forbid your dog to enter this area.

- Choose manure-based organic products for topdressing rather than commercial counterparts. Plant native grasses and stop worrying about your curb appeal.

- Seek out purely organic lawn care brands. (The side effect from manure-based products is a distinct cow-farm smell for a few days following application, but the substance is toxin-free.)

- Use undyed mulch made from compost or natural, untreated wood chips.

For more information, contact your local university extension office to gather more information on cultural practices appropriate for your area, so you can prevent rather than treat lawn disease and, therefore, maintain a green lawn without using chemicals. Your dog will thank you for it. (See Resources, page 318.)

Safe Walks in Treated Neighborhoods

Just because you decide to not use chemical lawn care products does not mean your dog is 100 percent protected from exposure. If you live in a neighborhood where curb appeal matters—and this describes most suburban subdivisions—be careful where your dog wanders during walks. Keep your pet on the sidewalk. Scope out "safe" lawn areas for him to eliminate in advance. If the lawn looks especially green and manicured, the lawn or mulch has a detectable chemical odor or the mulch has been dyed, or those tiny colored flags protrude from the ground, steer clear. Toxin build-up happens over time. Take steps to avoid treated areas to protect your dog's long-term health.

Journal Prompts, Part 1

YOU CREATED A beautiful journal to store memories shared with your dog. You want to fill the pages with all of the comedy and error that rearing a puppy and sharing your life with a dog entails. But when faced with a blank journal page, you draw a blank. Don't fret! Writers use prompts to spark creativity—so can you. (See Days 90–91, 146–147, and 209–210 for more journal prompts throughout the year.)

- Do you remember your puppy's first night at home? What were your biggest fears then? What made you laugh?

- Describe your dog's first experience with snow.

- Measure your dog every month during his first year and record his growth in your journal. Looking back, do you recall the day when your puppy was too big to cradle?

Choosing a Low-Shed Dog Breed

ARE YOU THINKING about adopting a dog? If you love dogs, but not the constant shedding that will cover the floor and furniture of your home, don't worry. There are a wide variety of low-shed dog breeds to choose from. Here are some naturally low-shed options:

Bichon Frise: This sweet, affectionate dog barely sheds at all. In fact, many doctors recommend this breed for their patients with allergies. However, you will have to take your dog in for a monthly professional grooming and brush his coat every few days to prevent matting.

Chinese Crested: This dog breed has very little hair save a crest on her head and tufts at her feet, so there is very little to shed. This variety is a shy dog that is happy with a bit of indoor playtime. For this reason, the Chinese Crested doubles as a great apartment dog (see Day 337.) There is also a "powder puff" version of this breed that has fur but minimal shedding.

Poodle: Although Poodles have long been stereo-typed as a frou-frou breed, they were in fact originally hunting breeds. Their dense, lofty coat protects them from the cold when they entered the water after a bird. In fact, the fancy fur cuffs you see at shows was originally intended to protected their joints from the cold when hunting. A Poodle's traditional cut is optional, however, such styling can truly be low maintenance.

Other low-shed breeds are the Affenpinscher, Bedlington Terrier, Brussels Griffon, Dandie Dinmont Terrier, Irish Water Spaniel, Portuguese Water Dog, Shih Tzu, West Highland White Terrier, and Yorkshire Terrier.

If you are worried about allergies, remember that it is usually an animal's dander—and not the fur—that causes sniffles. Even dogs that shed very little may not be allergy-friendly. (See Day 235.)

Leashes Are Not One-Size-Fits-All

LEASHES ARE IMPORTANT training and control tools for your dog. They come in a variety of styles and colors and are available with embellishments ranging from ribbon to real jewels. You can be fashion conscious when it comes to which leash you pick, but remember that safety and control should always be the most important consideration.

Leather is strong and flexible, and after a short time it becomes soft and supple. However, it is more expensive than other options.

Nylon is great because it is virtually impervious to water and comes in many colors. It is perfect for those with especially strong animals. Nylon has no "give," so it's a fine choice for training.

Hands-free or bungee cord leashes are new leash options. They come in long lengths and attach to your bike or your belt for when you want to tour hands free with your pup. But be warned—your dog must be well trained before using one of these, especially since they are attached to your or your bicycle.

Retractable leashes consist of a long cord that unwinds from a lightweight housing and have a thumb brake. You will have to work with them a bit to get the hang of them, but they are light and easy to carry. Consider your pet's temperament: If your dog sees something she likes and takes off, the long leash may unwind quickly and your dog may become tangled or injured; also, the long length of leash may become a hazard, especially if there are other dogs and dog owners in an area where it may quickly unwind.

To prevent your dog from chewing her leash, rub a little bit of clove oil or stop-chew mixture into the leash or collar. (see Day 23 for directions on how to make your own Stop Chew.) One taste of this and your pet will leave it alone.

Search and Rescue Dogs

SEARCH AND RESCUE dogs (SAR dogs, for short) are a special kind of working dog that receives rigorous specialized training to help find people who have gone missing, criminals on the run, and even disaster survivors. They are invaluable in finding survivors of disasters such as earthquakes, avalanches, and mudslides. They are especially helpful on a night search, when human rescuers' sight is limited. Aside from searching for people, SAR dogs are trained to search and sniff out contraband or identify cancer in medical settings. A dog's sensitive smell and hearing can help a well-trained pooch save and protect lives.

A search and rescue dog develops a deep bond with his owner, and in most cases they stay together for life. This bond enables the dog and his partner to work together seamlessly.

Many large breeds are suitable for search and rescue work, including Boxers, Doberman Pinschers, Labrador Retrievers, and Golden Retrievers. Training for this job should be started as early as possible; many trainers begin training puppies as early as six to eight weeks old. The physical terrain that search and rescue dogs have to traverse is often uneven and difficult, so these dogs receive extensive agility training to help them navigate future obstacles. They also receive advanced training in obedience, retrieving, tracking, and searching. SAR dogs generally work for a toy reward, not food; as a result, they perform their job out of love and a sense of fun and adventure.

Many rewards are associated with this job, but it takes a lot of work and dedication from you and your dog. If you are interested in this fulfilling career for your puppy, check with your veterinarian or local police department for possible training resources.

Jobs for a Search and Rescue Dog

SAR dogs are trained to specialize in certain search and rescue techniques, much like people choose a major course of study in college.

Air scent dogs track by smelling shed human skin cells that float in the air.

Trailing (tracking) dogs search by smelling the ground for a missing person's scent.

Water search dogs work along shorelines and on boats with search teams.

Human remains detection (cadaver) dogs find dead bodies by detecting scents rising from the soil, similar to how dogs find buried bones.

How to Choose a Vet (or Find a New One)

A VETERINARIAN IS an adviser, a medical expert, and someone you can rely on for emergencies. You should feel comfortable expressing concerns to this person and asking questions—even the most basic ones, such as, "How much should I feed my dog?" You will turn to your vet when your dog experiences health issues, and your vet can serve as a valuable counselor as you raise your dog. You will share some of the most exciting and devastating moments with your vet. Do not make this decision without "interviewing" your vet and choosing a medical expert with whom you are compatible. (It helps if your dog warms up to the vet, too.)

Seek recommendations from friends and family members who have pets of their own. Check out any and all options that are viable so you find the one you like best. Call the vet's office, explain that you are looking for a new vet, and ask if they would be willing to let you come in to meet with them. Make a list of your questions and concerns so you can discuss them with the veterinarian. (Also, don't discount the distance between you and the vet's office—if you have an emergency, you don't want to be two hours away.)

Visit the vet's office without the dog. Observe the office without the distraction of your dog. Try to arrive at the appointment early and talk to the people in the waiting room. Do they like the vet? What is the vet's bedside manner? Ask for a tour of the office. Are the facilities clean and tidy? Is the staff friendly and professional? Does it look as if there is a backlog of people all waiting with appointments?

Discuss your questions and concerns with the veterinarian. Inquire about their fees and office hours. What are their routines and policies if your dog has to board? What is their exercise program like? Are you allowed to bring your dog's food and treats, or is the dog fed something else when at the vet's?

How Do I Find a New Vet?

You've brought your new puppy or dog to the vet at least once, possibly several times. However, something happened at the vet that upset you—a personality conflict, irresponsible medical advice, or the like—and it's time to find a new medical expert. How do you go about it? Put any guilt aside and begin the interview process for a vet you trust. Here's how to find that person:

• Ask your dog-owner friends and the breeder/ kennel where you adopt your puppy for referrals.

• Call each veterinarian on your list to schedule a consultation before you bring home your new puppy or dog. Your vet can provide valuable tips for selecting a puppy and supply you with questions to ask the breeder or other source.

• Find out whether there is a fee for your visit.

• How close is the vet's office to your home? While the closest option might not be the best fit, consider the distance you will drive for routine appointments and in case of emergency.

• What are the clinic's hours of operation? Find out how the office handles emergency calls after hours, too.

• Aside from meeting with the vet, ask to be introduced to the staff so you can learn who is behind the scenes and how the clinic operates.

• Sit in the waiting room for a while to soak up the atmosphere and find out how the staff interacts with patients.

After your visit, consider your experience and fill out this worksheet, which will help you decide whether the vet you interviewed was the right match for you and your dog.

Veterinarian's Name:

Date of Consultation:

☐ Did you feel comfortable talking with the doctor and staff?

☐ Are the doctor's philosophies and communcation style in line with your own?

☐ Would you feel comfortable asking him or her any question, however silly it might seem?

☐ Is the staff friendly, efficient, and helpful?

☐ Is the office easy to reach and is the staff accessible in case of emergencies?

☐ Is the office inviting to adults and your pets, or is it sterile or messy?

☐ Does the vet seem to know about the latest medical advances?

☐ Finally, look around: What reading materals are displayed for your reading pleasure? Are there materials for you to take with you? Are they interesting and educational?

☐ Do they offer grooming, boarding, or taxi services?

How to Clean Your Collars and Leashes

CLEANING YOUR DOG'S leashes and collars is a very easy task and one you should do whenever they get noticeably dirty, or at least every couple of months. Different materials require different cleaning methods.

NYLON/CLOTH

First, inspect the collar and leash for any deep stains. Pretreat them with a store-bought stain remover or a paste of about 2 tablespoons (28 g) of borax dissolved in ½ tablespoon (7 ml) of warm water. Rub the paste on the stains, then place the collar and leash in your washing machine with a couple of large towels. The towels help with the agitation process. Add laundry soap, but don't use bleach or fabric softener—these will just fade the fabric and collect dust and dirt after drying. Run the normal wash cycle. Dry them in the dryer with the towels for 10 minutes, or let them air-dry.

LEATHER

Leather leashes cannot be laundered in the washing machine, but keeping them clean is not a big chore. Saddle soap and products for cleaning leather are widely available. For commercial leather-cleaning products, just follow the manufacturer's directions, since each formula works a little differently.

Saddle soap is a clear glycerin soap that is used with a natural sponge and a small amount of water. Wet the sponge, wring it out well and rub it on the saddle soap bar to collect a small bit of soap. Fold the sponge over the leash or collar and rub until clean. Rinse the sponge with warm water, wring out well, then rewipe the leash or collar to rinse. Allow it to air-dry. Use as little water as possible, to avoid ruining the leather. Once the leash is clean and dry, you may want to use a leather conditioner to help protect the leather.

Camping with Your Dog

YOU, YOUR DOG, an open fire, and an open sky—camping is a getaway you can both enjoy. With appropriate planning, you and your dog can enjoy friendly campground accommodations and lots of quality time in the natural world, playing in the great outdoors. Before you depart on your trip, call the campground to find out their pet policies. If possible, request a site that is away from other campers, just in case your dog wants to howl at the moon. On a serious note, not all campers are dog lovers, so it's important to respect others who pitch a tent at the grounds (or park their campers). Choose a site that offers plenty of shade if the weather is hot or plenty of sun if the weather is cold. Try to keep the barking to a minimum and the dog's high jinks under control. You don't want to invite any complaints from other vacationers.

Always follow leash laws. Know your dog: If there is any risk that your pet will bite another dog or a human, bring a muzzle. And just as you would anywhere else, always clean up after your dog, following the campsite's policy for the disposal of such wastes.

Pack a stake and long leash so your dog can participate in your campsite fun. Never let your pet wander or leave it unattended—You never know what animal (wild or domesticated) can be nearby. Consider bringing a portable enclosed pen: With one, your dog can enjoy the outdoors with your family and help to keep everyone else safe at the same time. Always keep plenty of water within reach and keep anything that can possibly get entangled in his leash out of your pet's way.

Puppy Personalities and What They Mean to You

THE TIME YOU SPEND observing and interacting with puppies in a litter will help you choose the best pick for your lifestyle, if you want a very young animal. Many dog experts say that it is impossible to determine a dog's adult personality at less than eight weeks of age, which is when you would visit a breeder to choose a puppy. If you decide to go to a shelter, "puppy" can mean a dog is merely less than one year old, and by then, her personality has been partially molded by the environment and you will get some real clues during the time you spend "interviewing" the pup. Here is how to identify personality characteristics in a younger dog, should you choose to obtain your pet from a breeder.

AT THE BREEDER

You have arrived at the kennel and the breeder introduces you to a playful litter of five pups. You crouch down, and a couple of the puppies scurry over to you, vying for your attention. You pick one of them up and she cozies up in your arms, not struggling in the least to get down. (These are both good signs of an outgoing, nondominant personality.) You watch the rest of the playing puppies and notice one generally assumes a supine position or rolls over on his side when the other puppies are roughhousing. This dog is submissive, perhaps a little timid but not at all aggressive. You see one puppy that is smaller than the rest, and her antics seem to make her the class clown of the bunch. She's rolling around, taking turns palling with the others, and sniffing you out, too.

IS THE PUPPY A GOOD MATCH?

Just as people interact differently in "group play," so do puppies. Although you can't determine whether a puppy will make the ideal family dog at such a tender age, consider these points to determine a good match:

- Does the puppy enjoy being with people? How does the puppy respond to your presence?

- When you move—stand up, crouch down, walk among the puppies—is the puppy afraid or playful?

- How does the puppy respond to being held?

- Does the puppy play with her littermates, or shy away from the group?

Remember, you are visiting the litter on a single day, at a certain time. Talk to the breeder about the behavior you see and ask questions about the puppies' social tendencies. And keep in mind that the environment in which you raise the puppy will have the greatest impact on her personality and temperament. Your responsibility as a puppy owner is to create a safe, loving home and to train her so you can both live happily ever after.

Choosing a Puppy

Observing a puppy litter is a lot like watching children at a playground. Each puppy develops a distinctive social role when interacting with the bunch. Here are some common personality references that may help you make a decision:

• *The pick of the litter:* This is the dog the breeder usually saves for showing. Not all breeders save a pup from the litter, though, so never assume that the "pick" has already been plucked out of the litter.

• *Second pick of litter:* Often this may not be the top show dog but he is still a beauty of the litter. Both the pick and second pick are playful, outgoing, and will run to meet you.

• *The middle group:* These can be one to four puppies in the litter; they are usually the followers in the pack. Being a "follower" is not a bad thing. These puppies will be the star at your home, and by providing a healthy and loving environment for your pup, she will grow to be a perfect "pick."

• *The shy and passive puppy:* This can make a great dog for the right person, but might not be the best dog for a family if she shies away from noise and commotion. But remember, when you take the puppy from her litter and introduce her to your home, she will learn she is in a secure place. Some puppies who are shy at six to eight weeks grow into quite playful puppies and dogs once they learn more about the world around them.

• *The runt:* This is the smallest puppy, and she can make a wonderful pet. She usually ends up a smaller dog of the breed, but not always, as runts can eventually grow to the height and weight of the rest of the litter. If she does remain petite, you may find you enjoy having a smaller dog of the breed. Runts are often perfectly healthy; they are just undersized, compared with their littermates.

Setting the Table for Your Dog

YOUR NEW DOG will need dishes of his own, and the selection you'll find for such a basic need may be your first introduction to the vast world of pet goods. You can spend as much as you want on such basics as bowls for kibble. But what does your new pooch really need?

Dog bowls are often made of stainless steel, ceramic, or plastic. In pet boutiques, fancy dishes can cost as much as a place setting of china. On the other end of the price range, discount stores and pet supermarkets carry a host of bowls for dogs. Pace yourself on some of these initial purchases, especially for puppies. As they grow, they will require larger feeding dishes, different collars and leashes, bigger toys . . . the list goes on. Spend prudently on startup essentials. A sturdy stainless-steel bowl may be your best investment.

Stainless-steel bowls will never chip. A damaged china or glass bowl could lead to your dog's ingesting sharp shards that could scratch, cut, and damage his mouth and digestive system. Just as people are cautious about certain plastic drinking bottles because of their potential to leach toxins, you should also consider your dog's health when choosing eating and drinking vessels made from plastic. Your dog will not get sick one day out of the blue because of a plastic dog dish. But over time, she will be better off drinking from stainless steel, which has no reported leaching risk factors. Plastic bowls are acceptable for dry food only. If you do use china, use modern, not vintage pieces, to be sure their composition is lead free.

Buy bowls that are sized for how large your dog will be when fully grown. This way, you will save yourself the expense of buying new bowls as your dog grows. Bowls should be sturdy and sufficiently heavy so as not to topple over when your dog is enjoying her meal.

Always place food and water dishes in the same place. Choose a spot that is not in a high foot-traffic area but is visible and easy for your dog to access. You don't want to hide food and water dishes, but you also do not want to trip over them. Protect the floor with a vinyl place mat so food and water that slops out of dishes can be easily cleaned up. (Learn how to make a personalized paw-print place mat on Day 9.) To provide ergonomic eating conditions for a larger or elderly dog to reach down into bowls at floor level, consider raising the bowls to your pet's nose height. (Learn to make a dog feeder in Day 184.)

Your Four-Footed Running Buddy

WHETHER YOU'RE A seasoned runner or a beginner starting a training program, dogs are motivated, reliable running partners. You will both benefit from the thorough workout. If your goal is to run with your dog, consider adopting a working/hunting breed that is built for endurance and has the energy and stamina required to run distances. Some dogs are natural runners, including Retrievers, Labs, Australian Shepherds, Border Collies, Doberman Pinschers, German Shepherds, and German Short-haired Pointers. Keep in mind, dogs that may be the best running partners are not necessarily the best family dogs. Be sure to consider your priorities.

Train your dog to run with you when he is a puppy and he will learn to expect an endurance workout. Advice for humans and dogs: start slow. Increase mileage gradually, stay well hydrated, stop immediately if there is discomfort or pain, and tune in to the dog's signs of fatigue. Before beginning a dog-running program, visit your vet and discuss your training plans. Your dog needs a clean bill of health and the vet's blessing before you both pound pavement.

Keep in mind the following training tips:

Start slow and easy. Always warm up by walking, then accelerate into a short jog and ease into your running pace. Cool down with a walk before returning home.

Tune in to pain signals. Your dog wants to please you and he'll run through pain to keep up with your pace. Stop if you see your dog tiring or struggling in any way.

Hydrate often. Fill a water bottle for your dog and stop if he is panting heavily or excessively salivating. Potential side effects of heat sickness also include vomiting, red gums, increased heart rate, diarrhea, and weakness. In hot weather, run early in the morning or after the sun goes down in the evening.

Examine paw pads. You get to wear fancy, shock-absorbent footwear. However, your dog runs on his bare pads, which are soft if he is just starting to run with you. Gradually build up endurance by walking, jogging, running, and cooling down. His pads will gradually toughen and you can increase your running time. Examine the pads for soreness and wear. Consider using a pad guard product to protect your dog's paws.

Spaying Your Female Dog

SPAYING A FEMALE dog, also known as "fixing" or "sterilizing," is more complicated than neutering a male dog because it requires entry into the abdomen and removal of the reproductive organs, including the ovaries, Fallopian tubes, and uterus. This is done under general anesthesia. She recovers in 2 to 3 days and needs to be kept still and quiet (to avoid trauma to the wound or internal bleeding) for 7 days. After that, the stitches or staples are removed.

The benefits of spaying your female dog include the following:

1. Spaying eliminates the possibility of your dog's developing cancer of the reproductive system and lowers her risk of breast cancer.

2. Removing the ovaries causes a reduction in hormone levels, which may have a calming effect on her attitude and behavior and willingness during training.

3. If you have more than one female dog in your home, spaying one or both will help lessen dominant and aggressive behavior.

Both male and female dogs are susceptible to gaining weight after being fixed. To avoid weight gain, it is critical that you feed your dog a healthy, low-fat diet after she is fixed and provide her with many opportunities for exercise. Exercise should occur on a daily basis, not only for its beneficial effects on your dog's body, but also for her mind. Studies in humans have shown that people who exercise regularly had a lower incidence of cardiovascular disease and also were less likely to experience anxiety and depression than those who did not exercise regularly. The same goes for our four-legged friends. Providing your dog with the appropriate diet and regular exercise is your responsibility. In return, you will have a healthy, happy companion who will be less prone to illness and will live longer.

Help! My Dog Swallowed a...

SOME DOGS HAVE a reputation for swallowing objects around the house—large, unusually shaped, edible, or not at all. Aside from ingesting the usual rawhide bone, dogs can choke down the most unusual items: remote controls, tennis balls, prescription eyeglasses, socks, an entire loaf of bread, coins, the list goes on.

The problem is, sometimes your dog secretly wolfs down objects and doesn't display side effects until several days later. Signs of intestinal obstruction may not be visible for days or even weeks. Symptoms vary depending on the location and severity of the obstruction.

If your dog tends to swallow objects and you are missing something that you strongly suspect may have become your pet's latest meal, don't wait—take your pet to the vet and ask for an X-ray.

> Immediately call your veterinarian if you notice any of these signs: vomiting, diarrhea, loss of appetite, lethargy, depression, weakness, dehydration, abdominal pain and/or distention, fever or below-normal body temperature, dehydration, or shock.

Craft a Perfect Pooch Bed/Storage Basket

THIS HOMEMADE DOG bed is a gift that can be assembled quickly. Size the tub to fit the puppy, then the bed can store toys or grooming tools once the pup outgrows it.

MATERIALS

Plastic or metal washtub

Nontoxic paints and brushes or stamps, for embellishment (optional)

Cushion or decorative pillow sized to fit in the tub

Fleece blanket, or 1 yard (91.5 cm) of fleece material from a fabric store

Several puppy-safe toys

1. With nontoxic paints, brush the dog's name or stamp the desired designs on the side of the tub (optional). Allow the paint to dry.

2. Set the cushion inside the washtub, or cover the bottom of the tub with a fleece blanket.

3. Place a couple of puppy-safe toys in the bed.

Think beyond the tub. You can create several variations of this project, depending on the bed base you choose and the fabric selected for its interior. Plastic basket weave–style storage boxes come in a range of colors. Stay away from wicker baskets unless the bed is for an adult dog (toy-size or small breed) that is past his chew-on-everything stage.

Sew additional festive bed inserts. Consider making several bed inserts, using holiday-themed fabric. Purchase 2 yards (185 cm) of fabric, double it over, wrong sides facing, and sew the three open sides, allowing a 6-inch (15.2 cm) gap. Pull the right side out through the gap. Stuff with polyfill and hand-sew the gap together.

Choosing a Purebred

AFTER STUDYING DOG books and learning about various breeds, you may decide that you want to bring home a purebred puppy. Certainly, there are breeds that go in and out of style—you'll see lots of Dalmatians one year and many Beagles the next. For better or worse, popular culture trends drive demand for certain breeds. Be sure you choose a breed based on her temperament and compatibility with your lifestyle, not based on this year's dog show winner or because you want a pooch just like the one your favorite celebrity totes.

After deciding what purebred dog you want, investigate breeders by looking in newspapers or online, or contacting breed kennel clubs to learn about reputable breeders.

A responsible breeder will:

- Find out whether you want your dog as a pet or for companionship, working, or competing. Working and competing can entail showing the dog in confirmation shows. Some breeders will require that the new owner co-own the dog with them so that she can be shown in confirmation, if the breeder feels that the dog's allover confirmation is good enough.

- Provide at least a three-generation pedigree with championship titles, if applicable.

- Provide certifications proving that the puppy's parents' hips, elbows, and eyes are free of defects. Remember, however, that although the owner may have certificates that the dog's parents may be free of defects, this does not guarantee that the puppy you choose will not have these problems later on in her life.

- Ask many questions, even getting nosy. Responsible breeders want to be sure their dogs are sold to customers who will give them the best possible lives. You, as a prospective client, must also ask questions, especially if you are a first-time dog owner or if the breed you are considering is new to you. Check out the breeder's own requirements for the breed to make sure that if you need to make modifications to your house or property to accommodate the puppy, such as installing a fence, you will be able and willing to do them.

Some breeders require that if sometime in the future you can no longer keep the dog, you will return her to the breeder, who can then ensure that she has a good home. Be sure you understand all the provisions of the purchase contract, including those related to any unforeseen health issues that you may encounter in the future with your new puppy.

All-Natural vs. Organic Pet Foods

WHAT DO "ORGANIC" and "all-natural" really mean? These descriptions are slapped on nearly every consumer product, edible or not, on shelves at pet supply outlets, and even turn up in clothing shops. What do these titles really signify for consumers? Is "organic" better than "all-natural," and how do we define these designations? What about pet foods labeled "human grade"?

The farm-to-table movement has hit the pet industry in a big way, so we're getting back to the food group basics and sourcing much of our food from the earth via growers. In pet food aisles, the demand for fresh ingredients has caused an eruption of "all-natural" labels. The Association of American Feed Control Officials (AAFCO) has an official definition for "natural":

Natural: A feed or ingredient derived solely from plant, animal, or mined sources, either in its unprocessed state or having been subject to physical processing, heat processing, rendering, purification, extraction, hydrolysis, enzymolosis, or fermentation, but not having been produced by or subject to a chemically synthetic process and not containing any additives or processing aids that are chemically synthetic, except in amounts as may occur unavoidably in good manufacturing processes. (www.aafco.org)

Quite a few loopholes are allowed in "natural" processing. Although pet food manufacturers are instructed to not mislead and to list every ingredient in the product, many companies buy vitamins, minerals, and other additives from large distributors some of whose requirements may not be as stringent. There is no AAFCO definition for "human-grade food." "Organic" is carefully defined by the USDA's National Organic Program, but pet foods must be grown without pesticides, artificial fertilizers, genetic modification, irradiation, or sewage sludge to earn "organic" designation.

So what does this mean for you?

- Carefully scrutinize ingredients in "organic" pet foods. If the company name is "Organic Pet Food Delight," the food isn't necessarily organic. The USDA does not regulate company names, leaving an open door for misleading marketing (see organic categories chart below).

- Seek out pet foods that list protein as a top ingredient—not a filler or by-product.

- Do not be misled by "human grade" labels on pet foods. There is no strict definition of what this means—room for misleading marketing.

- Ask your vet for pet food recommendations.

The following categories represent standardized terms in the United States. Categories may vary from country to country, and may change over time.

All Organic: Must be 100 percent. Can be labeled as such and display a Certified Organic seal on packaging.

Organic: Must be 95 to 99 percent organic; can display Certified Organic seal on packaging.

Made with Organic Ingredients: Must be 70 to 94 percent organic; can say "made with organic ingredients" on package, but cannot display the organic seal.

Less than 70 percent Organic: Can list organic ingredients on the information panel, but cannot use the word "organic" on packaging.

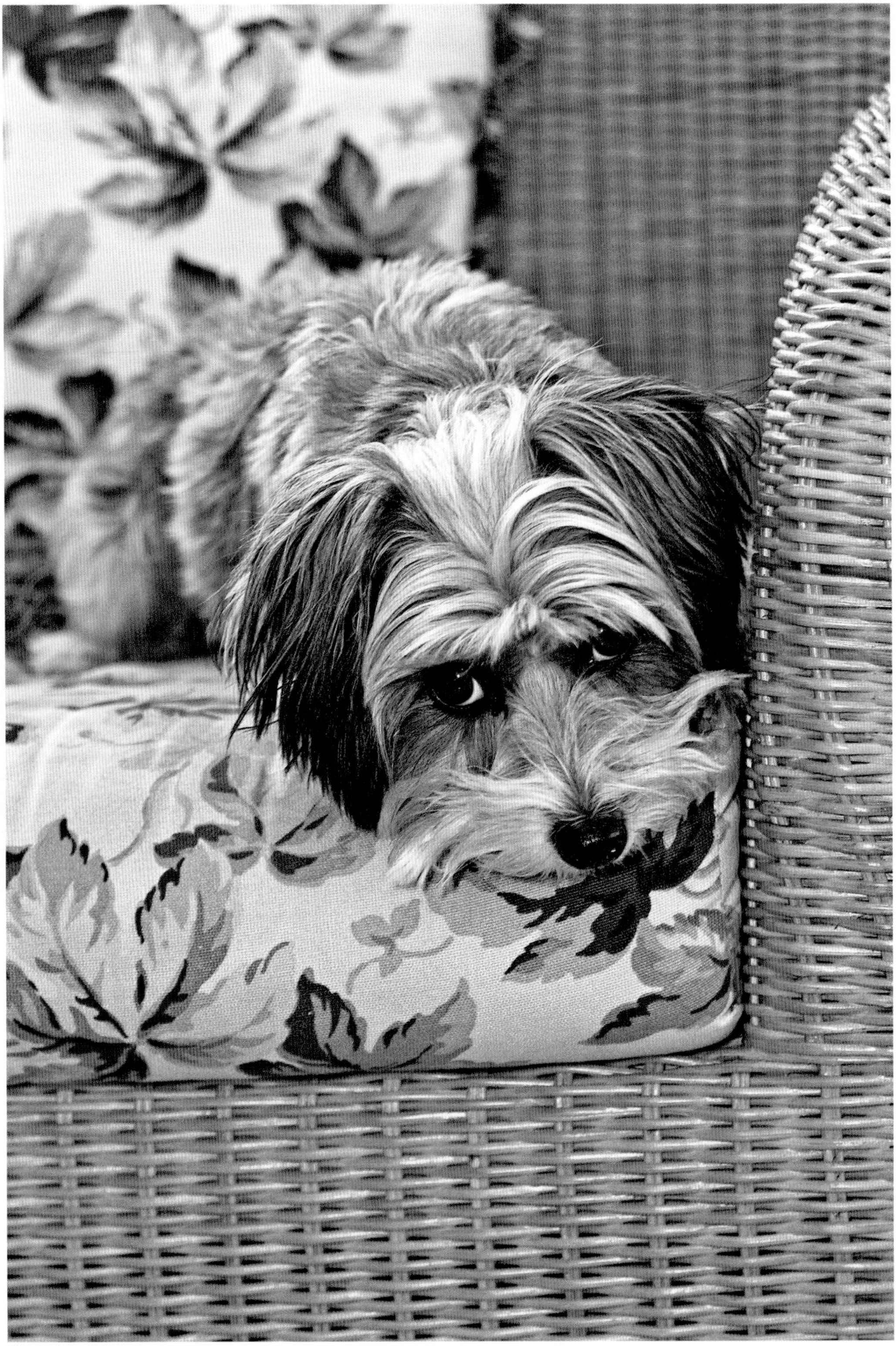

Obesity in Dogs

So MANY OF OUR pets become overweight because we use food as a reward, or we feed them just because they are cute. You wouldn't give your son a cupcake every time he said please or did his homework, but it's different with dogs. (And, oh, the way their tails wag when they get a really good treat! Irresistible.) We forget that they, too, can suffer from obesity. And obesity can create serious health problems for our dogs, just as it does in humans.

Obesity is now generally regarded by vets as the number one form of malnutrition in our dogs. Our dogs can easily become overweight, and the weight gain is often gradual. Two pounds (2 kg) here or there might not sound like a lot of weight to us, but for a 20-pound (9 kg) dog, that's 10 percent of his body weight.

How can you tell if your dog is overweight? You should be able to feel his ribs with the flat of your hand. If you can't easily feel his ribs, your dog probably needs to lose weight. You should also take a look at your pet from the side; his belly should be tucked in and look slim (however, see Day 88 to differentiate between fat and worms). If you think your dog needs to lose weight, a visit to your vet can confirm your suspicions and set you on the right path to reducing those unwanted pounds.

(See Days 66 and 79 for more tips for the overweight dog.)

> Excess weight can reduce your dog's lifespan by as much as 20 percent—for humans, that's the equivalent of fifteen-plus years. Obesity is dangerous because it can exacerbate serious medical conditions such as hip dysplasia, arthritis, diabetes, and respiratory problems. Keeping your dog physically fit requires the right food as well as proper exercise (see Day 73).

Neutering Your Male Dog

NEUTERING A MALE dog (also called "fixing," "castration," or "sterilization") requires surgery under general anesthesia. An incision is made on the front side of the scrotum and the testicles are removed. In some cases, the pet owner requests that prosthetic testicles be placed in the scrotum to keep the scrotum intact and to keep a "normal" appearance (this is generally purely for aesthetics). The male dog usually goes home on the same day of surgery and can resume his regular activity within 24 to 48 hours. In most cases, the doctor will use staples or a self-dissolving suture to close the incision.

The benefits of neutering include the following:

- Male dogs become calmer after being fixed, owing to lower testosterone levels.

- If neutering is performed early—before the time that your dog begins to lift his leg to urinate—you may be in luck: He will most likely not become a "leg-lifter." This means no marking and easier walking.

- Some scientists have made connections between neutering and cancer prevention, noting a reduced potential of your dog getting prostrate cancer because his body will not produce testosterone after the procedure.

Neutering will not affect your dog's personality or physical performance in any way. Your male dog will still be able to do everything you want from him after neutering, from being a good work dog to being a great watchdog, and he will still retrieve for you. He will maintain all the traits of his breed and at the same time will be gentler and easier to train.

Most dog rescue and adoption agencies require that dogs be fixed before adoption, which helps to decrease the number of stray and abandoned dogs.

Spa Day for Dogs

THOSE ACHING PAWS, that lackluster coat—your dog needs a day of pampering at the spa, and there are plenty of facilities that offer high-end bathing and grooming services with an option for boarding. Your pooch can go for the day and get a pet massage (see Day 347), scented bath, manicure, and stylish breed "do." The aesthetics of dog spas are essentially designed to impress owners who want to give their dogs the very best.

The same goes for dog resorts, which minimize the guilt some owners feel when family vacation time rolls around and they must leave their dogs behind. Some of the amenities you'll find at a cushy pet resort include radiant heated floors, a dipping pond for swimming pooches, skylights in kennel areas, and acres of land for running and playing.

Before making reservations at a pet spa and resort, visit the facility to ensure their claims aren't marketing fluff. (*Spa* sounds far more appealing than *groomer*—and a *resort* has to be more comfortable than a *kennel*, right? Not necessarily.) Ask your veterinarian for recommendations before taking your dog to any groomer or kennel. Interview personnel at the facility to make sure you feel comfortable dropping off your beloved.

Dogs may not enjoy the grooming process, but they know that after it's over their owners give them more attention. Dogs feel clean, itch-free, and have a greater chance of scoring a spot in the "people bed" once they are so huggably clean!

Making Your Own Dog Greeting Cards

HOMEMADE GREETING cards from your dog to your friends and family and their pets are a cute way to show you care at the holidays or for a special occasion. These memorable cards will stick out from the pack of generic greetings, and they make a great family activity.

Even the least creative of us can make a fun card by starting with a ready-made kit from the craft store. These usually include card blanks, envelopes, and embellishments for creating your card, and often include a theme, such as dogs. Everything you need is in the package—sometimes even the adhesive!

If a kit is too restrictive for your imagination, you can get blank cards and envelopes and decorate them with paper, stencils, stamps, stickers, photos, ribbons, glitter, decorative pens, and other embellishments you collect on your own. The scrapbooking aisle of your local craft store will give you tons of ideas. When I see cute paper, cardstock, ribbons, stickers, hang tags, or anything that is dog related, I often buy it and tuck it away for another time so I have a ready supply of materials to work with. If you are artistically talented, you can draw or paint on your card, too.

Advanced crafters can even fold their own envelopes out of decorative paper, using a template, or attach embellishments with special decorative eyelets.

If you want to send out many copies of your card, your local print shop or copy center will be able to make color copies and sometimes even fold them. Just be sure the size you choose fits in the envelopes you select.

Sign the card from your pet (and you, if you like) and add a "paw print" with a rubber stamp or sticker in that shape.

Old dog magazines make fun, inexpensive wrapping paper. After you're done reading them, store them in the dog pantry (see Day 208) until you need them. When you have a small gift that needs to be wrapped, tear an appropriate page out of a magazine and use it to wrap the gift. For example, use a picture of a Labrador to wrap a gift for a Labrador. For larger gifts, glue or tape the images onto larger paper, then wrap with that. This special wrapping will personalize any gift.

Why You Should Avoid Puppy Mills

PET STORE CLERKS and other sellers will never admit that their dogs come from puppy mills. And although you badly want a dog in your life, please resist the urge of buying a puppy mill dog. The myriad documented problems of puppy mills include overbreeding, inbreeding, minimal vet care, poor quality of food and shelter, lack of human socialization, overcrowded cages, and the killing of unwanted animals. How do you separate fact from fiction when it comes to puppy mills?

Pet stores cater to impulsive buyers seeking easy transactions. These stores do not interview buyers to help ensure responsible, lifelong homes for the dogs they sell. Sadly, these stores are often staffed by employees with limited knowledge about dogs and their care. Pet retailers count on the bond between owners and their dogs being so strong that the dogs will not be returned.

Be aware that certifications do not necessarily indicate a quality breeder. There are loopholes in laws where breeders can get special designations as "commercial breeding operations" and abuse the term severely. Such is the case with puppy mills. Breeders must provide food, water, and shelter, but there is no regulation forcing them to provide love, socialization, or freedom from confining cages. Even inspected puppy mills can operate under horribly messy conditions and have multiple outstanding health code violations. As a result, puppy mill pups often

have medical problems, which can lead to thousands of dollars in vet bills for you. Additionally, the poor breeding and socialization techniques at puppy mills often lead to lifelong behavioral problems.

Many unscrupulous breeders sell dogs directly to the public online and via newspaper classifieds. They typically sell multiple breeds, but will advertise each separately so as to appear to be experts regarding a given breed. These breeders are not required to be inspected by any federal agency, and in most states are not inspected at all. Likewise, purebred "papers" do not guarantee the breeder's (or the dog's) quality.

Recognize that reputable breeders care where their puppies go and interview hopeful adopters. They never sell their dogs through pet stores or to individuals they haven't checked out. Although it sounds counterintuitive, try to avoid buying a dog from a pet store—and always be wary of online and newspaper classified advertisements placed by individuals. A good rule of thumb is to never buy a dog if you cannot visit all areas of the home or breeding facility where the dog is kept.

Puppy mills will continue to operate until people stop buying their dogs, so please do your part to put an end to their practices.

Basic Training: Getting Used to a Collar and Walking on a Leash

DOGS DON'T COME collar or leash trained. The basis of teaching your dog to walk calmly on the lead is teaching him to accept the collar and lead, which means getting him used to the idea that the collar is a part of his "dog suit," and if he wants to explore the world outside of your home, the leash is the symbol of "walk." (Eventually, your dog will see the leash and make this happy association . . . and perhaps even bring the leash to you.) It is generally easier for your dog to adapt to a collar, although expect some fussing at first. He'll complain (by whining) and may rub his head on the ground in an attempt to loosen or remove the collar. He'll fast realize that the collar is there to stay, so do not remove it, despite his pitiful pleas. He'll get over it within a few hours.

Once the dog accepts the collar, put a small leash on it for your pet to drag around. The leash will seem like a toy at first—a string attached, what fun! Watch your dog carefully as he walks around the house with the leash attached, dragging. You don't want the leash to get caught on anything. Once he is used to the leash's dragging behind him, you can pick up the leash and allow him to lead you around. When a dog is confident on the leash—meaning he pulls it, as opposed to not budging or fighting it—teaching him to walk properly beside you is the next step.

Begin the walk only after the dog has sat calmly to have his collar put on and continued to sit calmly as his leash was attached.

Once the leash is attached, it is important to make the dog walk calmly toward the door. If he jumps or surges ahead, gently correct him with a tug of the leash and return him to a sitting position. Make him stay, then move on again. Repeat this process until the dog is walking calmly by your left side.

Repeat the process when you reach the door. The dog should not be allowed to surge out the door or pull you through the open door. If he begins this behavior, return him to the house and make him sit quietly until he can be trusted to walk through the door properly. Starting a walk in control is crucial to creating a well-mannered dog.

As you begin your walk, it is vital to keep the attention of the dog focused on you at all times. The dog should look to you for guidance, not take the lead himself. Every time you stop, your dog should stop. Getting into the habit of asking your dog to sit down every time you stop is a good way to keep your pet's attention focused on you.

Make sure your dog is looking at you, then move off again. If he begins to surge ahead, immediately stop and ask the dog to sit. Repeat this process until the dog is reliably staying at your side. Each time he does what you ask him to, reward him with a treat, a toy, or your praise.

If your dog pulls on the leash and you continue to walk anyway, you are inadvertently rewarding that unwanted behavior. Dogs learn whether you are actively teaching them or not, and learning the wrong things now will make learning the right things later that much harder.

Remember: It is important to be consistent in your expectations.

Helping Your Dog Lose Weight

LOSING WEIGHT IS just as hard for dogs as it is for people, but the principles are the same: reducing calories, eating healthy foods, and exercising. Your vet can help you with a specific plan for your dog that will likely include these strategies.

You can reduce your dog's calorie intake by carefully controlling what and how much you feed your pet. Your vet may recommend a dog food that is lower in calories or a specific amount of regular dog food. To prevent your dog's feeling constantly hungry, spread out the daily total in small meals throughout the day, rather than feeding your pet a lot all at once. Table scraps and extra treats can really add up, just like chips and cookies for humans, so these should be kept to a minimum and be healthy treats for your dog.

Be sure that all family members are on board with your dog's diet plan and that they understand it's for the good of your pet's health not to slip a piece of bacon when Mom's not looking.

Exercise is just as important as reducing calories and eating better. Walking, hiking, playing, and just running around will help your dog reach a healthy weight faster than diet alone. Once your dog has reached his goal weight, it's important to keep your pet active and eating well to maintain his health and his weight.

(See Days 59 and 79 for more tips for the overweight dog.)

Rabies Facts

RABIES IS A serious disease that affects animals and can be transmitted to humans. It is critical to keep your dog safe from rabies for your own protection and for the safety of other people and animals that come in contact with your dog.

The most common carriers of rabies are raccoons, bats, and to a lesser extent, skunks. These animals are nocturnal and usually come out at dusk. If you see a raccoon or a skunk out in broad daylight, it can be a sign of sickness. Stay away from the animal, bring your dog inside, and call your local animal control officer.

To keep your dog safe:

- Keep rabies vaccinations up-to-date for all dogs (and cats and ferrets)—especially if they could possibly encounter wildlife.

- Spay or neuter your dog to reduce his impulse to wander.

- Keep your dog indoors as much as possible, and keep him under your control (in a fenced yard or on a leash) when outside.

- Call your local animal control officer to remove stray animals from your neighborhood.

- Train and socialize your dog to reduce the risk that he bites a person or another dog.

Preventive measures such as vaccination have greatly reduced the risk to pets and humans of contracting rabies, but it is still a serious concern.

How to Brush Your Dog's Teeth

FIRST, GATHER THE proper tools to perform the task. You'll need a quality pet toothpaste. Human dental products may upset your dog's delicate stomach. Ask your veterinarian for recommendations. Various sponges, brushes, and pads are available to brush the teeth. Pet toothbrushes are smaller than human brushes. They have ultrasoft bristles and an ergonomic shape designed to accommodate a dog's mouth. Finger toothbrushes fit like a thimble over your finger. Dental sponges and pads are great for beginners because they are pliable. These products are a good way to introduce teeth cleaning to your dog.

The key is to introduce the toothpaste, brush, and idea of your hand in your dog's mouth well before you actually plan to brush his teeth. Begin these steps a week before the first brushing.

1. Let your dog lick some toothpaste off your finger to get a taste for it. Praise him and give him a tasty treat. Continue the paste-licking exercise for a few days prior to when you plan to actually brush your dog's teeth.

2. Squeeze a dollop of paste onto your finger and rub it on your dog's gums and teeth to get him used to the idea of your hand being in his mouth.

3. Now, introduce your dog to the dental brush. Squeeze paste onto the brush and allow your dog to lick it off. Praise your dog again and give him a treat. Continue this step for several days before actually brushing the teeth.

4. Now you can start brushing. Use a coaxing, upbeat voice and treat the process as you would a game. Instruct your dog, "Stay," and give him a treat. Squeeze the paste onto the brush and allow your dog to size it up and even sniff it. Then, insert the brush into your dog's mouth and gently brush the outside surfaces of teeth. First, brush the upper canine teeth. If your dog has had enough, stop the session and brush more teeth the next time. Increase the number of teeth you brush with each session.

Treating a Dog Bite

ALL DOGS BITE—and most bites are accidents. Puppies, in particular, tend to go overboard during play and can unintentionally nip and puncture skin. We teach our dogs not to bite with commands like "Leave it" when playing tug-of-war or fetch. But sometimes, our appendages get in the way of dogs' chompers. The bite may not be painful, but you should be sure to treat it properly so it does not get infected. For safety's sake, it's a good idea to get a tetanus shot if more than five years has elapsed since your last shot.

Clean the wound. Using soap and water, wash the bite area. Follow by swabbing on rubbing alcohol or hydrogen peroxide.

Apply pressure. If the wound will not stop bleeding, apply pressure to it with gauze, a clean cloth, or a paper towel. Hold the wound above your heart if the bite is on your hand or arm.

Cover the wound. Dress the wound with a clean bandage.

> If you get bitten by a dog you do not know, see your physician immediately to check for rabies, which can be fatal if you do not get a vaccination in time.

75

Doggy Manicure 101

SOME DOGS WILL TOLERATE nail clipping, and others will flee the room at the sight of scissors. Ideally, begin clipping your pup's nails at a young age so she will grow comfortable with the activity. Petting and playing with your puppy's paws will teach her to tolerate your touch in this sensitive area. You can take your dog to a groomer or the veterinarian to get her nails clipped, but the process is not difficult to do yourself with some practice.

Most dogs need to be restrained during nail clipping, though some will calmly sit in your lap as you trim away. Sit on the floor with your dog, hold her in your lap, or ask a friend to hold your pet on the table. Cradle your dog's head in the nook of your left arm, and clip with your right hand (vice-versa for lefties). Nails should be trimmed so they do not touch the floor when your dog steps down.

Keep tasty treats close by so you can reward your dog for her good behavior after the manicure. Pet and praise her so understands that nail clipping is bonding time with you—and what could be better?

PROPER TOOLS

Guillotine-style clippers (the nail is placed in a stationary ring and the cutting blade is squeezed down to slice off the nail)

Scissors style (be sure to clip with the blade facing you)

Nail-grinder tool (drill-like implement that gentle grinds away the toenail)

Introduce the nail-grinder tool to your dog gradually by petting her with the tool, turning it off and on so she gets comfortable with the sound.

TOENAIL ANATOMY

The **quick** is located in the center of each toenail and contains the blood and nerve supply for each nail. If your dog has white nails, the quick area is pinkish. Black nails conceal this nerve, so it's best to make several short clips, working down the nail gradually to avoid hitting the quick.

Cut toenails at a 45-degree angle about 2 mm below the quick. As you make small clips, examine the tip of the nail. A black dot indicates the tip of the quick; avoid cutting further. If you accidentally cut the quick, use flour or cornstarch to stop the bleeding. Silver nitrate products can also be purchased from your vet. Keep a bandage on hand if bleeding persists, and call your veterinarian if bleeding continues for longer than 15 minutes.

Your dog's thumb nail is called the **dew claw**, and it is attached to the leg by loose skin. This claw is easily clipped by gently bending it away from the dog's leg and using a guillotine-style clipper.

Oops: Submissive Urination

THE DOORBELL RINGS. It's your best friend, and she can't wait to greet your pup. Your dog's reaction: a puddle on the floor. For some dogs, this is not an accident—in fact, it occurs every time your pet meets a stranger in her territory, is scared, or confronted with a new and different environment. The reaction is called submissive urination, and it's a normal way for some dogs to show they're not the alpha. Even a housetrained dog—or a senior dog who is well past the puppy excitement stage—can leave dribbles or puddles when greeting you or strangers.

Submissive urination can be a sign of respect. Your dog is acknowledging that you are "in charge." Often, this behavior occurs with puppies who are still learning their place in doggy society. They may feel insecure or adjusting to their new environments. The habit will eventually pass. Abused and undersocialized dogs can also display this behavior.

How do you correct the behavior? First, avoid delayed scolding. If you notice the puddle after the fact, it is too late to say, "no." (Your dog will slink away with embarrassment, not knowing what she did wrong.) Instead, teach your dog to shake hands (paw raise) or give a kiss (hand lick), two acceptable ways for a submissive dog to say "hello."

Teaching your dog basic commands, such as "sit" and "stay," will build her confidence level so she knows how to please you (see Days 80 and 107). Next time your friend comes to the door, instruct your dog to sit and stay, then reward her. Over time, she will learn to wait for commands from you instead of "spilling" her emotions.

Exercise with Your Dog

EXERCISE IS AS important for dogs as it is for people. It helps them stay healthy and helps prevent their gaining weight. Well-exercised dogs are better behaved and less likely to test their limits indoors by chewing on furniture or otherwise acting out. Usually, those "bad" behaviors are a sign that your dog is antsy and needs a good play session or a long walk. Fortunately, exercise can be easily incorporated into your dog's routine. Here are some ideas.

- As often as you can, take your dog for a walk instead of just letting him out into the yard to do his business. It's great exercise for both of you!

- If you jog or run and your dog can keep up, take your pet along.

- Do you enjoy Frisbee? Let your dog play with you.

- Try dancing with your dog, staircase sprints, tether ball, or monkey in the middle!

- Go for a hike! See Hiking with Your Dog, Day 304, for more information.

- If you're stuck inside, try a game of fetch with a soft foam ball.

- If your own lifestyle is not all that active or your activities are restricted by your health, you can still play fetch with a ball or a stick— your dog will do most of the work.

Always remember to discuss your pet's exercise regimen with your vet before implementing it. And always make certain that plenty of fresh drinking water is available at all times during your exercise sessions.

Fleas

A FLEA IS A small, jumping, parasitic insect that lives by consuming an animal or human host's blood. Fleas used to be considered merely a nuisance, but today we know they can carry diseases harmful to both humans and animals. These include bubonic plague, pneumonic plague, and flea-borne typhus. When the flea bites its host, it can transmit whatever disease it may be carrying.

Dogs and cats aren't the only carrier of fleas, either. Squirrels, rabbits, mice, horse, chickens, raccoons, possums, foxes—and even we humans—are all possible hosts for fleas.

Fleas are similar to cockroaches in that they outlive and outlast most other insects. They are difficult to kill because of their four-stage lifecycle and because they don't spend most of their time on their host, which makes the problem of locating them and wiping them out even harder.

Fleas have four stages of life, and at every stage they can lie dormant for several months. Female fleas lay about twenty eggs per day and up to six hundred in a lifetime. Eggs can be laid in animals' fur, carpeting, bedding, and even the family couch. Even your car and vacuum bag are attractive breeding grounds for them. Flea eggs typically hatch within two days to two weeks. In the first stage, the larva, the flea is blind.

Its food source is digested blood from adult fleas' feces, dead skin, hair, feathers, and organic debris. Fleas mature within a cocoon-type sac built with pet hair and carpet fibers. In anywhere from five days to two weeks, an adult flea emerges. Now the hunt for a host begins, so it can find its first meal and begin growing.

When trying to eliminate fleas, it's not just about the animal, it's also about your living environment, your mode of transportation, and your outdoor facilities. In addition to treating your dog, you will have to pay close attention to these areas, to keep the flea situation under control.

For your car and couch at home, try sprinkling some borax powder into your carpet and on your furniture. It is most important to keep your dog's sleeping area clean and free from fleas at all times.

Be careful using do-it-yourself flea treatments. Read and understand the directions before starting. Many of these products can be harmful to you and your dog if not used correctly. If you have a severe flea infestation, hire a professional exterminator, who will be able to recommend the safest and most effective course of treatment for your particular situation, inside and out.

Safe Flea and Tick Products

WHEN CHOOSING A flea and tick product, be sure to carefully read labels on products. Some off-the-shelf formulas contain harmful organophosphate insecticides (OPs), which can be harmful to your dog. OPs are basically toxins. If ingested, the substances can affect nerve-muscle junctions and therefore impair muscle movement. There are seven types of OPs: chlorpyrifos, dichlorvos, phosmet, naled, tetrachlorvinphos, diazinon, and malathion. If any of these are listed as the active ingredient, switch to a safer formula.

Generally, products your veterinarian sells are safer. Look for active ingredients such as methoprene, fenoxycarb, pyriproxyfen, and the popular lufenuron. Such products contain insecticide growth regulators that stop the development of young fleas. They are not pesticides. Or, opt for spot-treatment products such as fipronil or imidacloprid.

Never use flea or tick medication formulated for cats on your dog, or vice versa.

Having Fun Even When Frustrated

YOUR RELATIONSHIP WITH your dog will have its ups and downs. Sometimes your dog is just having a bad day and isn't cooperating, and sometimes your pet forgets her training. She may look at you when you say "Come!" as if you are some stranger—worse, a stranger without treats. You'll say "Down," and she'll jump up. You'll coax, "Leave it," and she will not release her strong jaw-clamp on whatever it is you want to take away from her. You'll instruct her, "Stay," and she'll walk away, disinterested.

One night you'll wake up to whining noises at 2 a.m. You will rush to take the dog outside, throwing a coat over your pajamas, and you'll stand loyally by her in the dark cold. She will sniff around and growl at an animal noise, then tug on the leash in attempt to play or take a walk. She will not "take care of business." (There was no business to take care of, you realize.) And of course, she would choose to do this the night before you are expected to report to the office at 8 a.m. That's dog stuff, and we all go through it.

Your dog will puke on your heirloom rug, or at least try to gnaw on it, acting as if she's chewing on the bone in her grip as she sneaks in bites of carpet fiber. You'll hear a snapping, ripping sound from the other room and she'll look up, unchallenged by your I'm-the-boss glare—"Who, me?" She'll wag her tail, you'll play a round of ball, and the moment will be buried with the rest of your dog-frustration treasures. She'll give you a wet kiss on the face to make up for it every time.

There will be times when you think your dog is possessed by an evil spirit that wants to trash your house, ravage the pantry, and soil every surface within the four walls of your abode. That's not your dog, you must tell yourself. Yours is a sweetie. You don't deserve this (of course!). She must need a hug (we all do).

Amazingly, some attention in the form of rubbing behind the ears and your dog and you both feel better. You're in this partnership together, remember? Sometimes, you have to make the best of a bad situation. Of course, if you actually catch your misbehaving pet in the act, there are those training terms, such as the ever-popular "No!" But remember, your dog is pretending she doesn't hear. So just give her some love, and don't give up. And yes, all this fuss is normal.

Dogs are our best friends, our companions. Because we expect so much of the ones we love, it's easy to be disappointed when things don't turn out perfectly: when your dog flunks obedience class, scares a neighbor kid, or purposely pees on your couch when you leave for thirty minutes to go to the grocery store. Tell yourself, "This too shall pass." And get over it. Dogs are happy-go-lucky at heart. They want to please you more than anything. If they make a mistake, they will forget about it, and you must forget, as well.

All of these frustrations are learning experiences. We figure out how to better puppy-proof to avoid the carpet-eating temptation, and we learn that her 2 a.m. whines may be a bad dream or boredom and not a dire need to go outside for relief. We understand that even people hate to be trained sometimes, and there will be days that your dog is not a willing participant. (Surely, there are days when you're not a willing worker at the office.) So you see, we give and take, and our dogs are the ones who are always there to comfort and offer that sloppy lick of acceptance and love at the end of the day.

"Why did I get a dog, anyway?!" you huff in the heat of one of those bad times. Well, the answer is simple. Because no one will love you back so unconditionally, without reservation.

How to Adopt a Dog from a Shelter

ANIMAL SHELTERS CAN be your best bet when looking for a dog. Most have a wide selection of adult dogs, a number of puppies, and yes, even purebreds. In fact, purebreds typically account for 25 to 30 percent of a shelter's dog population. Many dogs at a shelter are there because they were obtained by a person with unrealistic expectations of the time, energy, and money required to sustain a pet for a lifetime. Sadly, many animals in shelters are euthanized for lack of adoptive homes.

Responsible shelters always assess a dog's health and temperament to make the best adoption match possible. When a dog is relinquished, the shelter staff will make every attempt to record a thorough history of that dog. While caring for the dog, the shelter's staff will learn as much as possible about the animal (as they do with strays that arrive at the shelter, as well).

Don't get discouraged on your first visit to the shelter if you cannot seem to find a perfect match. Shelters receive new dogs daily, and they typically have waiting lists and will be happy to notify you when a dog fitting your preference arrives. When picking out your dog, you can speak with an adoption counselor about whether your choice will be best for you and the dog.

In an effort to make good matches and to place dogs in lifelong homes, many shelters provide adoption counseling and follow-up help, including pet parenting classes, training courses, medical services, and behavior counseling. If they do not provide these services, they can refer you to an agency that does.

One advantage to adopting at the shelter is that their fees are usually much lower than at a pet store or a breeder. Also, the dog is more likely to be already vaccinated, dewormed, and spayed or neutered. Shelters can be found online or in the phone book under "animal shelter," "animal control," or "humane society." Many shelters have websites where they display their available dogs. Some sites offer downloadable adoption forms and information on responsible pet care.

Questions to ask about your new dog before bringing her home from the shelter:

- Is this dog suitable for a home with children?
- Does this dog chase cats?
- Does this dog get along well with other dogs?
- Does this dog exhibit any fears of men? Of women?
- How much exercise does this dog need?
- Does this dog have any health problems?
- Is this dog housetrained?
- Does this dog understand any commands?
- Is this dog crate trained?
- Has this dog ever bitten anyone?
- Does this dog bark a lot?
- Is this dog at her full adult size or will she grow larger?
- Has this dog been abused?

81

Feeding Tips for Overweight Dogs

ALWAYS REMEMBER THAT less is more. Always measure portions; you'll find that feeding out of several dishes can help with this. Start out by cutting down the amount of food your dog eats. For example, if the total is normally three cups of dry food daily, try two and a half for starters. To make the food more appealing to your pet, add no-fat chicken or beef bouillon. If your dog eats canned food, try diluting it with water.

No people food. Nearly one-third of dog owners admit to feeding their pooch table scraps on a regular basis. Stop feeding your pet from the dinner table or tossing down scraps while you cook and you will see a noticeable difference in his weight.

Cut back the snacks. Reduce the number of high-calorie treats you feed your pet each day. More than half of pet owners say they feed treats to their furry family members as a way of showing affection. There are low-calorie alternatives to high-fat, store-bought snacks. Try green beans or melon.

Use reduced-calorie formulas. Most leading dog food brands have a line for "less active" or "senior" pets. If you do switch food, be sure to do it gradually. Mix the new formula with the old in increasing amounts over seven to ten days. Be sure to consult with your vet before placing your pet on a weight-management program: Some diseases, including hypothyroidism and Cushing's disease, can cause weight gain.

Feed your pet more frequently. Give your dog smaller meals, more frequently. Three times a day is a good goal. Just as with humans, smaller meals more frequently will help boost metabolism and increase fat burning.

Try heating the food. If you have a finicky dog who doesn't like the reduced-calorie fare, try heating up the food for a few seconds, until it is warm, not hot. This will make the food smell better, and most animals really respond to smell.

(See Days 59 and 66 for more tips for the overweight dog)

Note: Do not overfeed carrots to your dog. It could lead to Vitamin A poisoning.

Basic Dog Commands

WHETHER YOU ARE training on your own or have enrolled your dog in a basic obedience class, your pet should learn five basic commands: sit, stay, heel, come, and down. These basic commands enhance acceptable dog social behavior and deepen your bond with your dog.

As you train your dog, don't scold or say his name in an angry tone. Just repeat the command and give your dog enough guidance to understand what the command means. When your pet performs as you wish, say his name affectionately and offer praise and a treat.

Dogs, especially puppies, can obey a command perfectly one day and forget it completely the next. But be patient and consistent. Avoid spending too long on a single training session: A few minutes each day is more effective than burning out your dog in a single, extended session.

Many dogs love to learn and work, especially if they can earn approval from their loved ones by doing so.

A good obedience class will also teach you and your dog hand signals to accompany the basic commands. You can start by giving both the voice command and the hand signal. Once your dog has mastered the task, begin giving only one or the other signal until your dog responds readily to either. Hand signals will also be very helpful should your dog lose his hearing later in life.

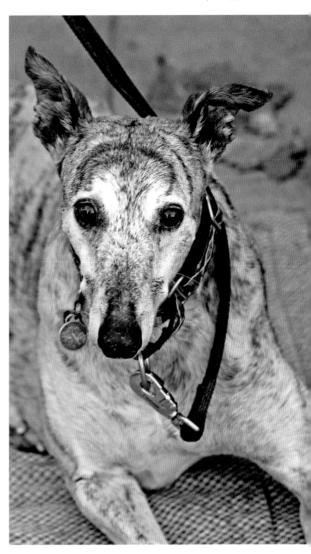

Removing Ticks

TICKS ARE SMALL parasitic arachnids that feed on animal and human blood. There are several types of ticks, including the deer tick and the dermacentor tick, which live in different areas around the world. Ticks carry a number of diseases, including Lyme disease and Rocky Mountain spotted fever, which are potentially disabling or even fatal. As with fleas, prevention is the best cure, so work with your vet to develop a plan to repel these insects before they have a chance to bite.

If you find a tick on your dog, you need to remove it right away. Follow these steps:

1. Enlist another person to hold your dog still. (See Day 333 for tips on securing your dog.)

2. Light a match, blow it out, and apply the match heat to the tick. The tick will release its head so you can quickly pull it out, head and all.

3. Deposit the tick in an ashtray or small dish and burn it with a smoldering match until you are sure it is dead. Ticks are extremely difficult to kill, and if you only remove the body and not the head, your dog may get an infection.

4. If you are uncertain as to whether you removed the entire tick, see your vet.

5. If your dog is bitten by a tick, she may start to lick herself, which can lead to hot spots that burn and hurt. You can apply tea tree oil to a hot spot or use an over-the-counter product. If the spot isn't healing, see your vet to prevent it becoming other skin conditions.

> Placing a cotton ball soaked with citronella and cedar oils in the new vacuum bag every time you change it will help kill fleas and ticks.

Planning for Emergency Transportation

IF YOUR PET has an emergency, how will you transport it to the nearest animal hospital? What if you do not own a car? If you rely on public transportation, contact taxi companies in advance of any emergency and find out if they will accept an injured dog in the cab. Then ask a reliable, nearby friend if he or she would be willing to drive you and the dog, understanding that you will use a taxi as the backup plan. (You can't expect your friend to wait by the phone.)

Make a list of the closest emergency animal hospitals and get directions to each. Do a practice run to the nearest location so you can determine the drive time and note any confusing traffic patterns that could hinder your emergency trip. Write down the hospital phone numbers and driving directions and keep this record in your pet binder (see Day 25). That way, if your pet is under the care of a sitter, the responsible party will know where to go and how to get there.

The Original Lip Smackers Cookie

THIS BASIC DOG-FRIENDLY cookie dough recipe can be modified by adding peanut butter, carob (never chocolate) chips, carrot shreds, or sunflower seeds. You really can't go wrong—it's a no-fail, fast-mix recipe that makes delightful cutout cookies for the holidays. Package them in gift baskets for dog-owner friends, or store them in an airtight container in the freezer so you always have tasty homemade treats on hand for your pup.

INGREDIENTS

2 cups (250 g) whole wheat flour

²/₃ cup (92 g) yellow cornmeal

½ cup (38 g) instant rolled oats (without any fruit or flavorings)

½ teaspoon (2.3 g) baking soda

2 tablespoons (14 g) wheat germ

2 eggs

¼ cup (60 ml) low-fat milk, or ½ cup (55 g) nonfat powdered milk

½ cup (120 ml) chicken or beef broth, or water

2 tablespoons (14 ml) olive oil

¼ cup (85 g) dark molasses (for sweetness)

1. In a large bowl, mix together the dry ingredients.

2. In a separate bowl, beat the eggs and stir in the milk.

3. Add the broth to the egg mixture.

4. Form a hollow in dry ingredients and pour in the egg mixture. Stir gently until moist and smooth. (Do not overmix.) Add the oil and molasses and continue to mix. Follow with optional add-ins (½ cup [130 g] of peanut butter, carob chips, shredded carrots, or sunflower seeds).

5. Let the dough rest for 20 minutes.

6. Preheat the oven to 350°F (180°C, or gas mark 4). Wrap the dough in waxed paper and freeze for 20 minutes.

7. Roll out the dough approximately ¼ inch (6 mm) thick and cut it into shapes. Bake for 12 to 28 minutes, until the cookies are light brown. Turn off the oven and return all cookies to the oven for "drying." (If you made several batches that are cooling, place them closely together on a couple of cookie sheets and return to oven.) Leave the cookies in the oven for at least 2 hours—or overnight.

8. Once cool, store in an airtight container.

Dogs Don't Wear Watches

WHEN WE LEAVE our dog for five minutes, we figure she will be just fine without our company and tend to worry much more if our absence will last four hours or longer. Displacing human emotion on our dogs ("She'll be so mad at me!"), we think the longer time away is surely more upsetting to the dog than that quick five-minute trip to the grocery store. (First, see Day 176 about a dog's emotional life. We are in tune to our dog's emotions, but they do not share our same human feelings.) This leaving-home scenario is a perfect example of how dogs and humans are wired differently.

Dogs do not have a precise concept of time. Whether you leave for five minutes or eight hours, your status is the same: gone. Your dog is not tapping her paw on the floor wondering, "Why is time going so slowly?" or expectantly watching the clock while you are away. Your dog does not know how long you were gone, and it will not matter unless you emphasize your exit and arrival back home. Dogs don't read clocks, but they do have sharp memories and the ability to associate past and current experiences.

If your dog seems more upset after five hours home alone than five minutes, that is probably because you react differently when coming and going for these periods of time. Your dog is not reacting to time, but she remembers what a big deal you made before leaving for hours last time, and she knows how vivaciously you will greet her upon your return. She loves that attention! When you signal leaving ("Mommy will be right back; Mommy will miss you"), the dog immediately anticipates the hearty welcome home. Therefore, your time away seems to drag. Chances are, if you step out for five minutes, leaving and returning are not a big production.

The lesson: Never emphasize your departure from home, and wait a few minutes before greeting your dog when you return. Do not act as if you were shipwrecked miles away and have painstakingly found your way back to your lost love. Coming and going is a part of life. If you treat it that way, your dog will show equal excitement upon your return from short errands and week-long vacations.

Make a Penny Can for Training

A PENNY CAN is an effective training tool for stopping bad behavior, such as nonstop barking or jumping on your guests.

MATERIALS

A clean, empty can that fits nicely in your hand

Decorative paper: wrapping paper, wallpaper, self-adhesive paper—whatever you like, cut to fit the outside of the can

Glue (unless you're using self-adhesive paper)

20 to 30 pennies or other small coins

Aluminum foil

A plastic lid that fits the can—look in the dog food aisle of the supermarket

1. Wash and dry the can.

2. Glue the decorative paper to the can. Allow the adhesive to dry.

3. Fill the can with the coins. You do not want it too full.

4. Cover the opening with aluminum foil and then the plastic lid.

USING THE PENNY CAN

As the unwanted behavior is taking place, shake the penny can and say a very firm, "No!" Your dog will not like the sound of the penny can. After only a few times of using this method, the behavior should be eliminated. If the undesirable behavior does not stop, it may be time to call in the professional trainers.

Why Dogs Fetch

A GAME OF fetch may bore a human after a few rounds of "Go get it!" and "Drop it!" Golden Retrievers are tireless fetchers, as are Border Collies and German Shepherds. For some dogs, there's nothing better than racing after a flying ball or Frisbee, capturing it, and bouncing back to the owner, who really plays the role of a human catapult. Your dog isn't shy about requesting a game of fetch. Usually, the "please" comes in the form of your dog's producing his favorite ball and dropping it by your foot or in your lap.

Why do dogs go crazy for a game of fetch?

The fetch instinct is part of dogs' DNA. In a pack, the alpha male dog would go out hunting with other senior, male dogs to collect food for the entire group. He would chase after prey, fetch and retrieve food, then return home with the bounty to share.

Fetch sparks dogs' evolutionary prey instinct to find the most basic need: food. Today, dogs get all they can eat at home and fetch is playful and a way of pleasing their owners.

Now, about those dogs who love to fetch, but have no interest in dropping the ball or Frisbee? "Drop it" is a command you must teach to your dog. Again, dating back to dog instincts of the olden days, the top dog as the "hunter" got first refusal on the meat he retrieved for the pack. The one who fetched got first pick. Since your dog is fetching one item, you as the "pack member" get what's left.

Train your dog to fetch by teaching "Go get it!" or "Go fetch!" and "Drop it," so the game doesn't turn into tug-of-war.

Diagnosing and Treating Worms

WORMS ARE INTERNAL parasites that can affect the health of your dog and your family. The various types include ringworms, heartworms, whipworms, hookworms, and tapeworms. Some live in the intestinal tract, whereas others live elsewhere in the body. It's important that you are able to recognize the signs and symptoms of worm infestation so you can quickly and effectively address the problem.

Adult dogs can contract worms in various ways. Tapeworms can be carried by fleas. Heartworms can be transmitted through mosquito bites. Some worms (and other parasites, such as giardia) can be contracted by drinking stagnant, untreated water.

The most obvious sign of intestinal worms is when you can actually see worms in your dog's feces, or—in the worst cases—protruding from the anus; they look like small grains of rice. Another possible sign of worms is if your puppy is not growing or gaining weight properly, or if your adult dog is suddenly losing weight without a change in his diet or activity. If you suspect that your dog has worms, you need to get to the vet.

Treatment for worms is best prescribed by your vet. Over-the-counter treatments are available, but may not work on the type of worms you have. Heartworm medication should be part of your dog's prescribed routine, because it is difficult to detect heartworms and they can do so much damage to your dog's health. Most puppies are born with ringworms and are de-wormed at birth and at regular intervals in their first few months. Your vet will set up a deworming schedule for you so your puppy has a healthy start in life.

Worms in dogs are transmissible to humans—especially children, who aren't always careful about washing and are casual about what they put in their mouths. Be sure to wash your hands after playing with your dog and especially after cleaning up dog waste, and have all children do the same.

Curb Carpet Licking

Your dog licks the carpet obsessively as though it's flavored like beef jerky. You wonder if there are microscopic vittles of filet mignon buried in the fibers. What is the deal? The licking is not only strange, you're beginning to wonder if your dog is sick. You haven't mentioned it to the vet because you keep thinking this carpet-licking passion is just a fling. Surely your dog will get over it.

First, your presumption that the carpet contains an appealing scent or taste could be right on. Carpet is a catch-all for food crumbs and liquid spills. Edible remains that entered the fabric years ago can live on in carpet that isn't thoroughly cleaned beyond vacuuming. Then there are carpet treatments designed to clean, and chemicals that are inherent to carpets that can smell and taste sweet to dogs. These chemicals are toxic and dangerous to your animal. Kicking the carpet-licking habit is critical.

Fill a spray bottle with 100 percent natural clove oil mixed with water until it dissolves. When your dog begins to lick the carpet, spray the area. He will not like the taste. Lead him to a safe area in the room where there is a dog bed or no carpet. Provide a toy to chew and praise your pet: "Good boy/girl."

Continue using the clove oil spray until the dog learns to stop licking the carpet. He will not want to lap up the taste of this essential oil for long; the taste is highly offensive to dogs. However, the odor is pleasant or neutral for people, so consider using this formula on shoes, table legs, and other "no chew" zones.

Journal Prompts, Part 2

- How did you celebrate your dog's first birthday?

- What incidents have occurred during walks that have made those around-the-block routines more of an adventure?

- Describe some of your dog's fun times at the dog park.

- Remember when your dog first learned to swim—on purpose, or by accident?

(See Days 41–42, 146–147, and 209–210 for more journal prompts throughout the year.)

What to Expect on Puppy's First Day Home

YOU'VE BEEN ANTICIPATING your puppy's home-coming for weeks—you picked out the dog well before she was prepared to leave the litter. That gave you plenty of time to puppy-proof the house, prepare her crate with cozy old towels (easy to wash), choose a few small toys, and stock up on the essentials: bowls, a collar, and leash. Thanks to your breeder's advice, you chose the right-size crate and are ready to welcome home your new "baby."

Call your breeder prior to picking up the puppy. When you arrive, you'll be so caught up in the excitement that you may forget basic instructions, such as how much to feed her. Make a quick phone call and set up an appointment to pick up the pup so the breeder can prepare documents, including a brief health record. Ask what type of food the breeder has been using. You'll want to keep kibble consistent at first. Take notes.

If you're bringing your puppy home in a car, be sure to have three or four clean towels with you in case the puppy has an accident or gets carsick from all the excitement and movement. (Your breeder will probably avoid feeding the pup prior to the trip, to prevent stomach upset.)

Bring a friend or family member with you to hold or watch the puppy in the car. Consider using a crate to transport the puppy in the car, which is safest. Most new dog owners can't resist cradling their pooch during the car ride. Just be sure the dog is secured.

When you arrive at home, your puppy will need to go outside. Right away, show the puppy a specific spot outside where it will consistently go to eliminate. Consistency is key as you establish a schedule for your new pet. Now bring your puppy inside and introduce her to the home. She will be exhausted and hungry after the car trip. Set out a small amount of food and show the puppy where her mealtime spot is located. Do not be concerned if she is disinterested in food. After all, this is a brand-new environment and she may be scared, or curious and ready to explore.

Feed your puppy no later than 4 or 5 p.m. and make water available only until about 8 or 9 p.m. Consider your normal meal and bedtime. If you like to turn in early but you do not feed your pup until 7 p.m., she will want a postdinner walk and playtime, and by the time she settles down, it will be 10 p.m.

Establish a reasonable meal and bedtime schedule right off the bat, and stick to it so your puppy knows what to expect. After she eats, wait ten to fifteen minutes, then take her outside and wait until she does her business.

Puppies tire easily and they sleep a lot, sometimes as much as sixteen hours a day, so once the introductions are done and the puppy looks sleepy, put her in her crate and let her sleep. A ticking clock or a radio with calming music at low volume placed in the same room as the crate can be comforting.

Those first few weeks, changing a puppy's environment may cause anxiety. Be judicious with introducing new situations and people. If a guest comes over to meet your puppy, put on her leash, even if the introduction will occur indoors. If your puppy knows you are in control of the situation and will feel protected by being on a leash, she is less likely to be anxious when meeting "strangers."

Similarly, set boundaries for your puppy regardless of whether a visitor calls. Do not allow the dog to roam every room in the house at first. This freedom can actually cause nervousness. At first, you may hesitate to retire your pup to her crate, reasoning that she is "locked up," and how can that be comforting? In fact, your pup views her crate as a safe place. A puppy that feels safe is less likely to cause trouble.

Sticking to a schedule cannot be stressed enough. Sporadic feeding times, inconsistent bedtimes, and too much freedom will make your pup feel uneasy. Dogs love structure, and they rely on their owners to provide this for them. Begin a feeding, bathroom, and bedtime regimen the first night you bring home your puppy, and do not stray from it. That way, your dog will know what to expect and will not be anxious.

Training Tips: Practice, Praise, and Positive Rewards

THE OLD SAYING "practice, practice, practice" is key when it comes to training your puppy or dog. They learn by repetition and reward for positive behavior.

Practice a little at a time, but often. Several five- or ten-minute training sessions spread throughout the day are more effective than one long session. Just like small children, puppies have short attention spans, and a bored or distracted puppy won't learn anything at all.

Who doesn't love to get a reward for work well done? Your dog is the same. Reward your dog with treats while saying, "Good boy/girl!" in a high-pitched, affectionate voice. Always reward immediately. Never wait to give an obedient dog a treat—you want to teach him that this is what you want and to keep up the good work. The more you turn the lesson into a positive and rewarding time, the better your puppy will learn.

Always end the session on a good note, going back to something your puppy has previously learned if necessary. This will encourage both of you to look forward to the next session.

Is Rawhide Safe?

RAWHIDE IS OFTEN associated with causing digestive problems and the resulting unpleasant side effects. But dogs love rawhide. It keeps them busy, cleans their teeth, and is probably one of the most popular toys in the pet store. There are entire aisles filled with various rawhide treats. Some are thin-pressed chews shaped like shoes, others are tubular pretzel knots, pressed pig ears, or "bully sticks." You can buy rawhide strips, rolls, bones, and bows. You'll find that rawhide is also more economical than other edible chews with brand names that boast 100 percent digestibility.

But is rawhide safe for your dog? That depends.

Small chunks of rawhide can pose a choking threat. Pieces of rawhide that dogs swallow are generally digested and pass easily through the digestive tract; thin rawhide sticks can potentially be swallowed whole and get stuck in the digestive tract. Although this may be rare, you should be present while your dog is chewing to watch for dangerous behavior.

Rawhide, like any toy, can pose a threat if you do not monitor your dog's chewing habits. Here are some rawhide safety pointers:

- Choose pressed rawhide, which is made of many small pieces of rawhide that are formed into tough, hardy bone shapes and last longer than loose rawhide. Limit the selection of rawhide, and avoid rawhide shoes and the bones with knots on either end. Look for labels that say "premium pressed rawhide."

- Never leave your dog alone while he is chewing rawhide. This rule follows with any dog toy, and especially new ones.

- When your dog has chewed the rawhide to the point of it getting soft, take it away and replace the piece with a new, hard chew. Allow the rawhide to harden before giving it back to your pooch.

- Avoid small rawhide chunks and shapes that can be gobbled up too quickly and cause stomach upset. Even large pressed rawhide chews can be broken down into small pieces after a vigorous chewing session.

Assemble a Dog First-Aid Kit

THERE MAY BE a time when you are on the go with your dog and she gets hurt (a cut, splinter, bee sting). As you probably won't wear a fanny pack that contains first-aid necessities when you go out on a simple dog walk around the block, you should keep a mini first-aid kit in your car in case an incident occurs while you are traveling and cannot quickly access your home kit or a vet. Here are two contents lists: one for a bare-bones first-aid kit, another for a comprehensive medical kit you should keep in your home. For both kits, choose a waterproof, or at least watertight, container. A pencil box (designed for students) can slip into a glove compartment of a car or under the seat. At home, get a container large enough to hold towels, a muzzle, and other essentials. Craft containers work well and are easy to store. Plastic is better than metal, since it won't rust and will also be lighter. Write in permanent marker on the container (or on an adhesive label) the phone numbers for your vet, the closest emergency animal hospital, and poison control hotlines, in addition to your own name, address, and phone numbers.

SIMPLE, TRAVEL-READY FIRST-AID KIT

- Sterile gauze pads, a variety of sizes
- Strips of cloth
- Bandages (including self-clinging and waterproof types)
- Cotton balls
- Cotton swabs
- Paper towels
- Resealable plastic bags
- Muzzle (an injured or scared animal may bite)
- Nylon leash
- Tweezers
- Sewing needle (for splinters and tick heads)
- Matches (to sterilize needle)
- Antibacterial wipes or pads
- Sterile saline eye solution (for flushing out eyes)
- Artificial tear gel (to lubricate eyes after flushing)

ADVANCED FIRST-AID KIT

Duplicate the travel-ready kit items for this more comprehensive kit.

- Book on dog first aid, or fact sheets on CPR, heatstroke, and other common ailments
- Copies of paperwork, including your dog's health record and medications
- Rolled sterile gauze (for bandaging, stabilizing joints, making a muzzle)
- Sterile stretch gauze bandage
- Self-adhering athletic bandage
- Roll of cotton
- Hypoallergenic cloth tape (assorted widths)
- Blanket
- Compact thermal blanket (keeps injured animal from going into shock)
- Rope (for an emergency if you have to tie up your pet)
- Bandana and/or nylon stocking (many uses, including muzzling or securing a torn earflap)
- Rubber gloves
- Nail clippers
- Eyedropper
- Rectal thermometer
- Bulb syringe (flushing wounds and giving medications)
- Hot/cold pack
- Custom splints
- Disposable safety razor (for shaving fur from around a wound)

- Mild, grease-cutting dish soap (clean skin/sticky substances)
- Hydrogen peroxide (disinfectant)
- Rubbing alcohol (Apply to skin as a body cooling agent to aid heatstroke or fever; breaks down oils, acts as drying agent between toes and skin folds. Do not use on wounds, as it can damage skin and is not an appropriate antiseptic.)
- White petroleum jelly
- Antiseptic iodine (to deter wound infection)
- Bag balm (especially useful for treating paw pads)
- Baking soda (soothes skin conditions)
- Syrup of ipecac (induces vomiting)
- Styptic powder or styptic pencil (for bleeding toenails)
- Antihistamine capsules (25 mg, for allergies)
- 1 percent hydrocortisone acetate cream (for bug bites and stings)
- Gentle pet sedative
- Milk of magnesia (for stomach upset and poison ingestion)
- Pepto-Bismol (for upset stomachs and some types of poisoning)
- Kaopectate tablets (maximum strength)
- Buffered aspirin (not acetaminophen or ibuprofen)
- Epsom salts (2 teaspoons [10 g] in 2 cups [475 ml] warm water, for drawing out infections and bathing itchy paws and skin; do not let your dog ingest)

How to Remove Pet Hair from Furniture

YOUR DOG MAY enjoy lounging on your family room sofa, but your guests probably do not appreciate sitting down in a sea of hair. Depending on the upholstery material, dehairing the sofa can be a real challenge. Even a high-powered vacuum can fail at lifting pet hair from upholstery.

If you have leather couches, the job is easy. Simply use a solution of one part vinegar to two parts linseed oil to condition the leather and safely clean the surface. Always use a soft cloth. A retired, cut-up T-shirt will do the trick.

If your couch is covered with microfiber or similar material that acts as a pet hair magnet, here are a couple of tricks. Wipe a damp sponge over the surface to lift off hair. Or, roll masking tape around your hand as if making a cast, but sticky side out, and press your hand into the couch fabric. Replace the tape and repeat, if necessary. Also convenient are sticky lint rollers, which essentially work the same way, except you gain efficiency from the rolling action and avoid the fuss of wrapping tape around your hand.

If the couch is for casual use—and if your dog sleeps on it, casual it is—take a clean sneaker and rub the rubber-soled bottom over couch cushions and seats. The rubber collects hair quickly.

Dog-Friendly Hotels

PERHAPS THE MOST complicated aspect of traveling with your dog is finding accommodations that appreciate your four-footed friend as much as you do. The good news is, locating a dog-friendly hotel is easier than it used to be. As the pet industry grows in leaps and bounds, other markets recognize that animals are part of the family and marketing their service as pet-friendly can pay off. Some cities are more geared for dogs than others (see Day 229), so you'll find a greater selection of hotels, motels, cabins, and other overnight venues that accept your dog, too. But don't plan to make reservations on the fly. Research hotels and secure arrangements before you depart home. You'll find dog-friendly hotels, highways, outdoor dining, parks, and beaches on www.dogfriendly.com.

Once you decide on accommodations, here are some questions to ask hotel/motel management before you arrive:

- Do you still allow dogs? (Their policy may have changed.)

- Do rooms have easy access to the outdoors?

- Is there a dog walking area? How often is this area cleaned?

- How close is the nearest veterinarian? Obtain the name/contact information of the animal care facility.

- Do you require all dog owners to show shot records? The answer should be yes.

- How soundproof are rooms, and how does staff handle excess barking/unruly dogs? Your dog isn't necessarily the concern.

- Will you provide a dog sleep mat/bed? Some luxury hotels will offer this perk.

How to Rescue/Adopt a Purebred Dog

MANY PUREBRED RESCUE GROUPS are devoted to finding homes for purebred dogs in unstable situations. Typically, these dogs come from failed breeding concerns, were abandoned at boarding kennels or vet offices, were rescued as strays, or were obtained from local animal shelters. Rescue groups are run by people with a deep knowledge of one particular breed. These groups keep adoptable animals until they can be placed in permanent, loving homes.

Fees for adoption vary and depend on veterinary and other costs that were incurred by the rescue group. Most of these adoptable dogs come with a mandatory spay/neuter agreement. This is done to protect the dog and the prospective owner from breeding accidents, to ensure that the prospective owner has the dog's best interests at heart, and to ensure that the person looking to adopt the dog will not turn the animal into a one-dog puppy mill.

This also ensures that possible health or genetic problems will not enter the breed's gene pool.

To find a rescue group devoted to the breed that you are interested in, contact your local animal shelter, check your paper's classifieds, or search online. (See Resources, page 318)

When you contact a breed rescue group, ask as many questions as you can to make sure this is the breed that fits your lifestyle, family, and energy level. Learn how the breed club cares for its dogs, how they decide which dogs are adoptable, and what other adoption and post-adoption services they offer. With many of these groups, follow-up counseling is often provided for a fee.

Why Do Dogs Guard the Food Bowl?

DOGS NATURALLY GUARD the things (and people) they consider important. If mealtime is a main event for your dog—and most dogs place high value on a food-filled bowl—your pet will be inclined to guard the bowl. Anyone who nears, touches, or passes your dog while he is eating will be received with a grumpy growl or bark. In worst cases, a dog may even bite. Stop guarding behavior immediately. Start when you first introduce your dog to his new home.

While the dog is eating, sit beside him and offer a treat. Put your hand in the food bowl and mix around the food. Get up, walk away, then return and repeat the exercise. Always offer the puppy a treat before fiddling with his food. This will teach your dog that you are safe, the food is not in danger of being swiped away, and he can continue the business of eating.

Practice taking the food bowl away while your dog is eating. Approach your dog while he is eating, pick up the bowl, place a treat inside it, and return the bowl to the feeding area. By always staying close to the puppy while he eats, you will help your dog understand that the food bowl area is not his territory but yours.

Occasionally hand-feed your puppy, offering kibble directly out of your palm rather than pouring it into the dish. Sit in the normal feeding area as you do this. Your dog will learn that you are not a threat—in fact, you are a friendly dining partner.

Activity Compatibility

IF YOU WOULD rather spend your Sunday afternoon beached on the living room sofa watching a football game on your big-screen television, a Border Collie's persistent requests to go for walks will frustrate you. If you're a runner who wants a companion on hikes, a Basset Hound who would rather hitch a car ride to the park may not be the best choice for you. Consider your activity level and, realistically, how much time you want to spend exercising your dog. Play and exercise are critical to your dog's health and happiness. It's not fair to skimp on walks.

BREEDS THAT NEED LOTS OF EXERCISE

Australian Cattle Dog

Australian Shepherd

Brittany

Border Collie

English Setter

Fox Terrier

German Short-haired Pointer

German Shepherd

Golden Retriever

Irish Setter

Jack Russell Terrier

Labrador Retriever

Weimaraner

Vizsla

BREEDS THAT NEED LESS EXERCISE

Basset Hound

Bulldog

English Toy Spaniel

French Bulldog

Great Dane

Irish Wolfhound

Maltese

Papillon

Pekingese

Why All the Itching and Scratching?

YOUR VETERINARIAN WILL PROVIDE a true diagnosis, but it's helpful to understand common itch-instigators so you do not allow a condition to go untreated.

FLEAS

Signs of fleas are brownish-red spots of "dandruff" that come off your dogs as they are petted or brushed. If left untreated, fleas can cause anemia. Some preventive measures are natural herbal flea collars and wipes. Chemical flea collars have been used in the past, but their proximity to the eyes, nose, and mouth of the dog has dubious chemical effects. Some veterinarians suggest feeding a dog brewers yeast (or a tablet of brewers yeast with garlic daily during flea season). (See Fleas, Day 74.)

MITES

A dog with mites shakes his head, digs at his ears with his feet, or scratches his ears. Clean your dog's ears at least once a week with an herbal preventive solution. If your dog gets ear mites, use an over-the-counter remedy or get a treatment from your vet. You will need to kill the mites first, then apply a preventive solution.

BEE STING

A dog will let you know about a bee sting by yelping, or licking and scratching the area. Bees tend to sting a dog's face. To treat, make a paste of baking soda and water (or baking soda and milk of magnesia) and apply to the site to soothe.

Remove the stinger with tweezers—don't use your fingers, or you may push it in deeper. If your dog has been stung in the mouth and you see his throat swelling, he may be allergic to bees— you need to call the emergency vet immediately. With approval from your vet, applying an antihistamine cream might help with the discomfort.

SIGNS OF ALLERGIES

Signs include flaky skin, excessive itching, redness on the body, "dog acne" around the mouth, ear scratching, and redness inside the ears. Determine the cause of the allergy, and remove it from the skin, if possible. Cedar oil is an allergen for many dogs, and some dogs may develop food allergies (or even to materials in their food dishes). Common food allergies are beef, wheat, corn, and soy. Pet acne is usually caused by an allergy to plastic in a food dish. Treatment can include steroids, or a diet change if needed.

Handle with Care: Toy Breeds

BIG DOGS CAN muscle through household bloopers such as falling off the bed or being tripped over. But toy breeds and small dogs can get seriously hurt if they trip down stairs or get stepped on by accident. Delicate, pint-size pups require additional safety measures. Basically, you must take dog-proofing (see Day 106) to the extreme, considering how heights (sofas, steps) and even clutter can be a danger to your dog. Your bed is skyscraper tall to your tiny friend. Humans are like dinosaurs with loud stomping feet. Approach dog safety from this perspective and you'll notice many obstacles at home that could harm a toy dog.

• ***Keep toy breeds off high furniture.*** The temptation to jump off a sofa or leap from a bed is too great. If they take the plunge and fall to the ground, broken bones and, in serious cases, a broken neck or vertebrae could paralyze or even kill your dog. Train your toy pup to stay off high furniture by giving her appealing options at her level, such as a cozy bed and appealing crate.

• ***Use a harness.*** Avoid tugging on the fragile neck on your toy dog or small pup and use a harness instead. You'll gain better control during walks without harming your dog.

• ***Watch your step.*** You'll get used to treading carefully around your toy breed to avoid accidentally stepping on her. Be sure to warn guests that she can wriggle into foot traffic before they know it. Teach children to handle the dog.

Teach children to hold the dog only while they are seated, and preferably on the floor. Accidents happen. The shorter distance a dog's fall is to the ground, the better.

Dog Tails: Driving Cross-Country with the Dog

OUR WEIMARANER, GRETCHEN, was just six months old when we took her on a cross-country road trip, departing our home in Ohio for a three-week, go-out-west adventure. Looking back, I realized how unprepared we were to travel with our pooch. We didn't make reservations at lodges in advance, nor did we realize how many facilities—restaurants, hotels, tourist sites—did not allow dogs. But the trip was designed to be free and easy. We camped in tents half of the time, and found dog-friendly places to stay the other half. When we took the trip eleven years ago, the hospitality industry was less welcoming to pets. Still, that didn't deter our plan to see the sights and enjoy quality time with our new "family." It was our first wedding anniversary, and Gretchen was our first baby.

We shared some of the most fulfilling and frightening times on this trip. There were opportunities to allow Gretchen to run wild and free her puppy energy in prairielike parks. She accompanied us on a hike at Yellowstone National Park, which gave her a healthy workout. The only problem occurred when she spotted wild buffalo on the walk back to our cabin. She thought they were stuffed toys and wasn't intimidated in the least—until one started charging at her at full speed. She bolted and we shut the door to our cabin just in time. The buffalo waited outside our door for two hours!

Later in the trip, we hiked the Black Hills in South Dakota. Gretchen was off-leash and loving it, running ahead of us. We soon realized why. She had her eyes on a billy goat, which had much better traction when negotiating the steep hills. Gretchen tumbled and almost flew down into a ravine. She performed a cartoon stop—screeeech—disarmingly close to falling off the edge.

Perhaps the closest call was in Montana. We rented an old ranger's station for a night perched at the top of a mountain. We drove our Jeep up the winding road for an hour and a half before reaching the top. The view was stunning, the night peaceful. The cottage was a true getaway and, of course, Gretchen was thrilled with the new environment. The area surrounding the cottage was protected by a barbed wire fence to keep out grizzly bears. (We did not know the purpose of the fencing at the time.)

Gretchen raced a few laps around the cottage, then ran head first into the fence. A huge, triangle gash on her chest bled nonstop. I panicked. I took my sweatshirt and wrapped it around her middle, and we hopped in the Jeep to find a vet. On the way down the hill, we blew a tire. Luckily, we had "fix-a-flat" in the car, so that stroke of bad luck was only a few-minute setback. Once we reached the bottom of the mountain, we stopped at several places in town before finding a vet. Gretchen was in bad shape when we arrived. My sweatshirt was sopping with blood, and she was quiet, sweetly kissing my face as I calmly convinced her, and mostly myself, "It will be okay." We arrived at the animal hospital just in time. Gretchen got stitches and before long, we were on our way to a nearby trailer park for the night. I'll always remember those adventurous times with our first baby, who has left our family with rich, warm memories.

103

Dog-Proofing Basics

DOGS ARE CURIOUS animals. When bringing a new dog into your home, it is important to create a safe environment and protect her from her curiosity. Think about the whole house, and have the house ready in advance of the new dog's arrival. If you want to get a real feel for what items in your home should be put away or protected from your dog, get on all fours (no one is watching!), and get a pup's eye view of your house. You may notice temptations you never considered: fringe on throw rugs, cords that are half hidden behind sofas (but half exposed to puppies), knickknacks on low shelves, and so forth. Go from room to room with a pad of paper and a pen so you can make a list of what to secure and protect in each room (including the garage, Day 278) and list things to look for in special areas of the house).

Here is a puppy-proofing checklist to help you cover common temptations:

- Pull cords for blinds and curtains, as well as their plastic ends, are very dangerous. Tie these up out of your dog's reach.

- Tie up or conceal loose electrical cords—dangling cords are tempting! Consider purchasing cord covers or treat cords with stop-chew solution (see Day 23).

- You'll want to block off some rooms entirely, which you won't be able to do unless the door latches securely. Make sure each door closes completely and cannot be pushed open. If you have lever door handles, which are easy for older dogs to open, consider getting baby-proof locks or mounting a strong hook-and-eye closure well above the height of yor dog.

- Keep rolls of toilet paper and boxes of tissues well out of reach of your dog unless you enjoy picking up bits of shredded paper.

- Round up loose items you don't want your dog to chew on: shoes, handbags, children's toys, crafts supplies, and so on. Stow them safely in a closed closet or out of your dog's reach.

- Stash all detergents, cleaning supplies, cosmetics, and other chemicals well out of your dog's reach, high on a shelf or in a locked cabinet.

- Likewise, store medicines, dietary supplements, and the like high up in a latched cabinet.

- Keep full laundry baskets up off the floor or in a latched closet. Elastic, zippers, and buttons are tempting to your dog and can hurt him if ingested.

- Consider adding baby-proof latches or hook-and-eye closures to all lower cabinets.

- Add a baby-proof latch to each toilet lid and train your family to keep the lid down. This way, your dog will never be tempted to drink out of the toilet and won't fall in.

- Be sure your trash cans and recycling bins have tamper-proof lids.

- Put people food away, out of reach of your dog. Chocolate is especially dangerous to dogs. Don't leave glasses/cups or opened cans of alcoholic beverages, caffeinated sports drinks, or chocolate-flavored beverages unsupervised.

- Keep plastic bags and plastic bottles, bowls, and other items out of reach.

- Find a secure cabinet for your dog's food so he can't get into it himself.

Training Tips: Building a Good Relationship

BUILDING A GOOD relationship is the secret to having a well-trained, loving pet. Relationships are hard work. They require time, energy, and dedication. (You've heard this before, but probably with regard to your "people" relationships.) You must earn your dog's respect by setting boundaries, rewarding him for good behavior, and showing him how to behave properly in the first place. In return, a dog is on a constant mission to please his owner. Your dog will want nothing more than to earn rewards and approval from you. But he cannot please you if you do not teach him what makes you happy. Just as with human relationships, we can't expect our partners to read our mind. If they don't tell us what they want, how can we please them? Yet pointing out to our loved ones what we *don't* like or want causes arguments and ill feelings. The same goes for a dog in a relationship with people. Focus on positive training methods that will help you create a strong bond with your dog and mutual trust.

Your dog will test boundaries from day one. You must commit to a basic training program from the start so you can begin building trust. Also, training provides a dog with security: he will know what to expect, how to respond, and what your reaction will be. Remember, a dog loves habit. Start when your dog is young, preferably a puppy. During this time, a dog's behavior is easy to mold and change, similar to how children learn quickly when they are young and carry those habits with them throughout life (saying please and thank-you, making the bed, and so on). Commit to puppy classes and regular training sessions to build a foundation for your relationship. Think of the classes as your quality time together—you're both learning how to communicate, and that is the key to living a long, happy life together, dog and owner.

TWELVE BASIC COMMANDS TO TRAIN

You can assign different words for these commands; such as instead of "Drop it," you can say, "Mine." Whatever cue word you use, keep it consistent. (Make a list if you think you will forget.)

1. [Dog's name] is number one!

2. "Let's go," when walking on lead or in the park

3. "Heel," any time your dog is on lead

4. "Sit," when walking or anytime you stop

5. "Stay"

6. "Okay," as a release word

7. "Calm," or any word that means for your dog to stay calm

8. "Down," to lie down

9. "Drop it," to let go of an item he has in his mouth

10. "Off," to stay off the furniture or people

11. "Come," when you want him to come to you

12. "Up," to get into the car or up onto something

13. "Go to your bed," or a similar phrase, when you put him into his crate, when the dog needs to have a time-out, or when it is bedtime

105

Recipe: Pupsicles

ICE POPS ARE PURE entertainment for pups, and they're easy to prepare and freeze. Teething puppies will appreciate the gum-soothing properties of these cool treats.

3 chicken breasts

2 (16-ounce [475 ml]) cartons low-sodium chicken broth

2 carrots, sliced

1 tablespoon (14 ml) olive oil

2 tablespoons (28 g) cornstarch mixed into a slurry with 3½ ounces (100 ml) cold water

1. Cut the chicken breasts into bite-size pieces.

2. Sauté in a skillet with the sliced carrots and olive oil. Add the chicken broth and simmer.

3. Add the cornstarch slurry and stir until the chicken mixture thickens. Turn off the heat and allow to cool.

4. Transfer the mixture into a pitcher or jug for easy pouring. Fill ice pop molds or ice cube trays, allowing ½ inch (1.3 cm) clearance at the top.

5. Remove from the molds when half frozen and insert thin rawhide chews to serve as ice pop sticks. Freeze completely.

6. To remove the solid-frozen ice pops from the molds, dip the molds into a bowl of warm water for a few seconds to loosen.

Basic Grooming: Bathing

MAINTAINING YOUR DOG'S appearance is important not only for cosmetic and overall health, but for emotional reasons, too. Your dog will feel happier after annoying hair is removed, when his paws don't hurt, and he smells good. Most important, your dog will feel good knowing that you care enough to make him feel good.

When it's time to give your dog a bath, use a shampoo made specifically for dogs. Never use dog shampoo on cats, or vice versa. Try experimenting: There are shampoos to brighten the coats of white-haired dogs and to bring out the luster of black-coated dogs, conditioners and detanglers for long-coated breeds, and medicated shampoos for dry coats, to name just a few.

Before bathing, brush out all knots in your pet's coat. Protect your dog's ears from collecting water by gently placing a cotton ball with a dab of mineral oil into each ear so that it may be easily removed.

Use a nonskid rubber mat on the bottom of your tub, so your dog will have secure footing. Follow the shampoo's label directions and always rinse your pet well. Be careful to dry your dog thoroughly when bath time is done.

If you start regular bathing habits when he is young, your dog will adjust easily. If you have an older dog who is not used to regular baths, it's best to introduce him to bath time gradually. Begin by playing with him in an empty bathtub, giving him his favorite toys or treats. After a few play periods, if your dog appears relaxed, repeat the process but place a few inches of water in the bottom of the tub. Continue this procedure a few times. When your dog seems comfortable, add some more water. Continue until any fear he had of the tub, water, or bathing subsides. Only at this point can you give your dog a full bath.

Curbing a Garden Digger

YOU LOOK AT your rose garden and see a fragrant, delicate display of hard-won beauty. (Roses are not easy to grow!) Your dog eyes up that bed and sees opportunity—a chance to dig, to keep food warm and babies safe. Wait a minute—this is not prehistoric times, and your dog has a perfectly cozy bed—several of them, actually—and babies, well, he's been neutered. This is one of those everyday situations when our dog's innate behaviors intrude on our modern lifestyles. If your Scottish Terrier historically dug for varmints and helped control rat populations, good luck changing the past. It's in his DNA. Same goes for Dachshunds, which were also bred for digging game like badgers, foxes, and otters. These breeds are born to dig. Your garden could be chock full of them, you never know. Your Scottie will find out.

Basic instinct results in many ruined flower beds. Take care to protect your garden and flowers by closely monitoring your dog's outdoor time. If you have a fenced-in backyard and allow your dog to roam the area freely, consider fencing to block off beds. You can use the same mesh fencing material designed to keep out deer and rabbits. Another solution is to use a tether lead and be sure the dog cannot reach the beds. Use rudimentary training commands to correct bed-digging behavior. If you catch your dog in the act, say "No," and retrieve him from the bed. Give him a toy or chew and praise him. Use positive reinforcement to help your dog choose other options than bed-digging for entertainment. And when training loses out to basic instinct, joke to yourself that at least your dog is stopping to smell the roses.

♥ Your Role after a Pet Loses His Owner

THERE'S A CLEAR grieving process that humans experience after the death of a pet (see Days 167–168). But what happens when the dog outlives his owner? How can the new owner, whether a godparent or trusted friend/family member, help the dog adjust to different surroundings, smells, and a life without his No. 1 companion? The transition isn't easy.

Dogs grieve just like humans. They get depressed, they mope. The dog may jump up and bark if he sees or hears a car drive by that he thinks might be his owner returning home. The dog will look around his new home for the late owner, and if you say the owner's name in conversation, his ears will perk up. Expect this behavior in the beginning, and give the dog time to work through the difficult time. In severe cases, you might talk to a vet about antidepressants and homeopathic solutions to help the dog work through a serious bout of depression.

Ease the dog's transition to his new life with you by surrounding him with all of his familiar personal belongings: bed(s), crate, toys, chews, food and water bowls, leash, collar, and any other item the dog associates as "his." Place the bed in a comfortable area for the dog to sleep. Allow him to immediately establish his safe zone so he knows where to find privacy and comfort. Find an appropriate spot for food and water dishes (see Day 2). Although you will want to spoil your new family member with toys from the pet store, he'll reach for items that have meaning for him. Don't toss the old ones, even if they look battered.

Dogs need companionship. As you become caregiver and friend to your inherited pet, he will rely on you for the necessities, love, and comfort. Give the dog time to respond to you. Do not expect him to immediately replace his "mommy." But over time, and for some dogs rather quickly, he will adjust to his new home and love you the only way dogs know how: unconditionally.

Taking in Brothers and Sisters

When a pack of dogs loses their owner, whether or not they came from the same litter, they share a sibling bond that is best not broken in a time of tragedy. It would be difficult enough to separate dogs that "grew up" together under perfectly normal circumstances. Following the death of an owner, if the pack is broken up, the dogs will grieve doubly, for the loss of their pals and their den leader. If at all possible, keep a "family" of dogs together. In their new home, they will help one another transition to their new environment.

Recipe: Low-Fat Veggie Biscuits

SERVE TO YOUR dog only if she is not allergic to any of the ingredients; dogs, like human, may have a sensitivity to gluten, which would put these grains out of the running.

4 cups (500 g) rye flour

1½ cups (120 g) whole rolled oats

1 cup (235 ml) water

2 eggs, slightly beaten

¾ cup (90 g) shredded carrots

¼ cup (15 g) minced fresh or dried parsley

2 garlic cloves, minced

1. Preheat the oven to 350°F (180°C). In a medium-size bowl, stir together the flour, oats, and water until well blended. Stir in the eggs and add the carrots. Add the parsley and garlic and mix well.

2. On a lightly floured surface (using rye flour), knead the dough, adding more flour if sticky.

3. Roll out to ⅛-inch (0.3 cm) thickness. Cut out ½-inch (1.2 cm) wide biscuits, using a pizza cutter or sharp knife.

4. Place on a lightly greased baking sheet and bake for 25 minutes. Transfer to wire rack to cool.

5. Store in a sealed container in the refrigerator.

Yield: 48 to 60 treats

Let's Trade

YOUR PUPPY IS clenching a dress shoe, or any number of items that are off limits. The laundry basket is full of treasures—even those little plastic screw caps at the base of a toilet are removable and chewable, your puppy has learned. The point is, the dog has got her mouth on something that you need to extract from her pointy clenched teeth. With bare hands, the task could get ugly.

Teach your puppy to "trade" the off-limits item for a treat, bone, or safe chew toy. Although the prospect of wanting what one can't have will discourage your puppy from giving up the shoe at first, she will quickly learn that trading for a treat is not a bad deal.

Here's how to teach her to trade: Choose a play toy that the puppy isn't terribly attached to and offer it to her. Say "Drop," then give her a tasty treat when she obeys. Repeat this several times in a row with the same toy. Next, offer your puppy her favorite chew toy. Improve the treat accordingly—offer jerky rather than kibble, for instance. The dog will not be as willing to trade her favorite toy.

Practice the trading exercise several times. Finally, progress to using this command sporadically, always keeping tasty treats on hand. If your dog picks up a stick or piece of garbage during a walk, offer to trade and reward with a treat. Eventually, you will be able to ask your dog to "drop" any item because she will understand that she will win a treat in exchange.

110

The Best Activities for Your Breed

DOGS HAVE NATURAL talents for hunting, chasing, and swimming that we should encourage so they will enjoy exercise. Try tethering a German Short-haired Pointer to a suburban backyard and asking her to play ball. She'll do all she can to break loose, and before you know it you'll be chasing her full-speed through neighbors' yards. This dog was born to run. Retrievers love nothing more than a game of fetch—and watch out for that swimming pool. They love a dunk and are skilled swimmers. Tap into your dog's talents and establish an exercise routine that focuses on activity and play he prefers. Doing so will prevent your dog from becoming stir crazy, which can result in bad behavior.

What type of workout does your dog really want?

AGILITY

Australian Shepherd

Belgian Sheepdog

Border Collie

Miniature Schnauzer

Mixed breeds

Papillon

Shetland Sheepdog

Standard Poodle

SWIMMING

Flat-Coated Retriever

Golden Retriever

Labrador Retriever

Newfoundland

Portuguese Water Dog

FETCHING

Border Collie

Chesapeake Bay Retriever

German Shepherd

Golden Retriever

Labrador Retriever

JOGGING

Dalmatian

Irish Setter

Pointer

Rhodesian Ridgeback

Vizsla

Weimaraner

FLYBALL

Australian Cattle Dog

Border Collie

Canaan Dog

Jack Russell Terrier

Mixed breeds

Shetland Sheepdog

Whippet

TRICKS AND OBEDIENCE

Bichon Frise

German Shepherd

Golden Retriever

Labrador Retriever

Papillon

Toy Poodle

111

Soothing Teething Woes

YOU PROBABLY DO not recall the achy discomfort you felt in your gums and jaw when your adult teeth pushed their way into your mouth. A more recent memory may be the pain following wisdom teeth removal. The point is, toothaches are miserable, and your puppy suffers through a mouthful of pain between ten and twenty weeks of age, when those pointy pearly whites fall out and duller, stronger adult teeth grow in. You can relieve your pup's distress with these homemade frozen washcloth treats.

MATERIALS

Low-sodium chicken- or beef-flavored broth

Mixing bowl

Washcloths

1. Fill the mixing bowl with the broth.

2. Soak the washcloths in the broth, allowing the cloths to become saturated with the liquid.

3. Gently squeeze out excess the liquid.

4. Tie each washcloth in a simple knot.

5. Place the washcloths in the freezer on a tray. Once frozen, serve to your puppy. She will be most appreciative of the flavorful, chewable variation on an ice pack.

Note: Be sure your pup doesn't run off to an heirloom carpet to chew these treats, as the thawing washcloth may leave behind a damp spot that stains.

Clean Drinking Water
Is Important for Dogs, Too

DID YOU KNOW that the average dog should drink about 1 ounce (30 ml) of water per pound (.5 kg) of body weight? A 70-pound (32 kg) Lab should have about 70 ounces (2 L) of fresh water over the course of a day—even more on hot days. Equally important, the water she drinks should be fresh, cool, and clean.

Water from ponds, streams, puddles, and ditches may contain chemical contaminants, dangerous bacteria, and parasites, such as worms or giardia. Infected animals may have been in that water and left behind things we do not want our dogs to drink. A good rule of thumb: If you wouldn't drink it, your dog shouldn't, either.

Signs that your dog may have ingested dirty water are vomiting, listlessness, droopy eyes, diarrhea, flulike symptoms, difficulty coordinating, or constant sleeping. If you think that she may have had dirty water, call your vet right away. Kidney failure, liver failure, and in some cases death can result from exposure to some water contaminants.

Chlorine, which is used in water treatment, isn't good for dogs, either. In some water supplies elevated chlorine levels create an unpleasant taste and/or odor, too. Consider running your drinking water through a water filter before giving it to your dog. Several kinds of filters are on the market today, from pitchers to faucet-mounted units to filters that build right in to your plumbing system. Or, look into a pet fountain, which is a dish that circulates the water continuously through a filter.

How to Build a Doghouse

A BRIGHTLY PAINTED doghouse can be a backyard accessory but it still must be a practical home. Think about your pet's habits. Does your dog like to sleep on top of the house? Adding shingles is not required, and will be uncomfortable for dogs that crawl on top of the roof. Finish the roof instead with a weatherproof, nontoxic (very important!) preservative, such as linseed oil.

Also consider size and location. Is your dog large or small? Adjust the proportions of this project to cater to your dog. Place the doghouse in a safe area, away from the driveway or high-traffic areas.

This project is a fair-weather doghouse, not one that will keep your dog warm in winter. Your dog will appreciate the shelter from moderate summer sun. A proper four-season doghouse is just large enough to fit the dog, since its main warming system is your pet's body heat. To prepare a doghouse for winter, it must contain a baffle door and insulation.

Carefully measure and pencil in parts on the plywood before cutting. Refer to the Parts Diagram, which is laid out to make best use of the 4 × 8-inch (10.2 × 20.3 cm) sheet of exterior siding. Cut through the wood with a circular saw or table saw.

MATERIALS

Circular saw or table saw

Goggles and hearing protection

1 (4 x 8-inch [10.2 x 20.3 cm]) sheet of 5/8-inch (1.6 cm) exterior siding

1 (8-inch [20.3 cm]) -long two-by-four, to be cut into two-by-twos

1 (10-inch (25.4 cm) -long) two-by-four

Nails (16d for base, 8d for house, and short roofing nails for shingles)

Hammer

Square (for measuring angles)

Sandpaper

Shingles or siding (optional)

Paintbrush and exterior paint

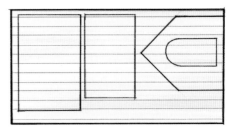

Cutting Diagram

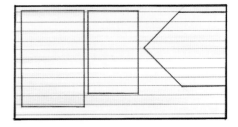

1. Consult the cutting diagram for dimensions for the siding.

2. Wearing the goggles and hearing protection, use the saw to cut the pieces to form the dog-house platform from the 10-inch (25.4 cm) -long two-by-four, as follows (using the square to make sure the corners you are cutting are right angles):

2 Platform Sides: 22⁷/₈ inches (58.1 cm) long

1 each Platform Front and Back: 20³/₄ inches (52.7 cm) long

4 Platform Legs: 6 inches (15.2 cm) long

3. Assemble the doghouse platform **(Figure 1)**. Nail the legs on each end of the long side pieces. Attach the front and back pieces to the side ends, using 16d nails. The front and back pieces will overlap the side piece ends.

4. Align the first floor panel on top of the base you just built. Be sure all ends line up, then nail in the platform. Stack the second panel on top of the first, nailing it in place. You now have a sturdy foundation for your doghouse **(Figure 2)**.

5. Begin building the house. Nail the frame elements flush against the short edges of the sides. You will leave a 3½-inch (8.9 cm) space at the bottom of the sides to allow for the platform.

6. Next, attach the remaining wood for the frame elements to inside roof line of the front and back panels. The pieces should meet at the top and extend, leaving 2½ inches (6.4 cm) of space between the roof line and side pieces.

7. Assemble the structure. Nail one side to the platform at the bottom. Repeat for other side. Attach the back of the doghouse, aligning it with the side. Nail it first against the platform, then into the frame elements in the corners. Repeat for front panel **(Figure 3)**.

8. Before attaching the roof, be sure all nails are concealed and the wood is smooth (use the sandpaper to smooth it) so the home will be comfortable for your pet.

9. Nail roof panels in place. Nail a 22-inch (55.9 cm) two-by-two against the inside edge of one roof panel. Place this roof panel and nail it to the frame. Nail the second roof panel in place.

10. Finish the doghouse by adding shingles, or siding that matches your own home. Paint as desired.

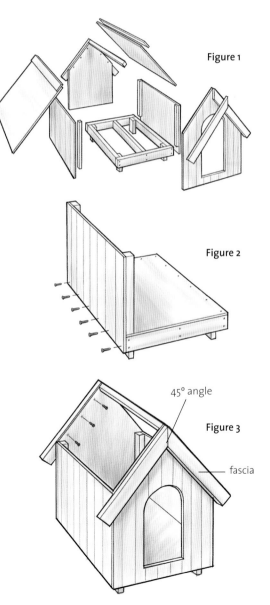

Figure 1

Figure 2

Figure 3

45° angle

fascia

Health Concerns:
Purebred vs. Mixed-Breed Dogs

ALL DOGS FALL into one of two categories: purebreds or mixed breeds. Purebreds conform to a breed standard consisting of physical and behavioral characteristics specific to each breed type. Mixed breeds, or "mutts," have ancestors from more than one breed.

Purebreds are appealing to some owners because of breed physical characteristics or reputation. Because breeding is overseen carefully to preserve hereditary traits, there is a measure of predictability purebreds offer, and this generally extends to temperament, such as being good with children or loyal guard dogs. We say generally because dogs are like children in some ways. Their dispositions cannot always be carefully calculated, no matter how "pure" the breed. Upon adopting a purebred dog, you will receive registration papers from the relevant breeder's organization that certify that indeed your dog is purebred and detail her lineage. This type of information is important for individuals who want to breed or show their dogs.

Keep in mind, though, that registration papers do not *guarantee* the dog's health and temperament; they simply certify the dog's ancestry.

Unfortunately, purebreds are more likely to suffer from genetic defects as a result of inbreeding. Some examples of these genetic problems are hip dysplasia, epilepsy, cancer, thyroid imbalances, and eye problems. For instance, many German Shepherds today are genetically predisposed to hip dysplasia, and Scottish Terriers are known to suffer from cancer of the bladder. Mixed-breed dogs are less likely to exhibit these problems because their genes draw from a wider pool.

If you are considering a purebred, you'll need to weigh the risks of common health problems in that breed against the desire for a particular appearance or temperament and the desire to show or breed the dog.

A Doghouse Welcome

YOU BUILT A stylish doghouse for your pooch. It has siding, just like your "real house," and colorful shutters. It looks like a barn-style shed that was shrunk down to just the right size. (Learn to build your own in Days 118–119.) It's a beauty! Surely your dog will be impressed and bound through the doggy door to settle right into her brand-new abode.

Not so fast. How do you expect your dog to know the house is hers? To your dog, the doghouse is a strange new structure that her owner is awfully excited about. She will not realize that this is her doghouse unless you introduce it to her properly.

Here's how to welcome your dog to her new backyard home:

- Set a chair by the doghouse and relax there for an hour or so while your dog sniffs out the house.

- Try placing a favorite toy and an old shirt or towel with your scent on it in the house.

- Crouch near the entrance and call her name.

- Place a tasty "good treat" (see Day 164) inside the front door of the doghouse.

- Don't force her to enter. Let her take the time she needs—hesitation is okay.

- After a while, if she still isn't interested in going inside, crawl into the doghouse yourself (even if just your head and shoulders will fit). Show enthusiasm over its interior.

- Try placing her meals inside the house.

- While playing fetch, toss the ball or toy into her doghouse. Once she goes inside and stays, praise her. Feed her a treat while she is in the house to reinforce the behavior.

Entertaining a Lonely Dog

DOGS CAN GET lonely if they don't spend enough time with humans or other dogs or are left alone for long stretches of time. They can also feel lonely after the loss of a companion dog or owner. They sometimes express this loneliness by tearing up the house while you are gone. You can help prevent this loneliness by taking him for a long walk just before you are going to be gone for a long time and making sure that you are doing some training a couple of times a day to stimulate his mind and body. But when you can't be there for your dog, there are a few things you can do to help comfort him.

For a young puppy, place a hot water bottle in a soft, plush cover. A hot water bottle will stay warm for a while after you leave, and he'll enjoy snuggling up to the warm "fur." This will make the puppy feel as if he has a warm body next to him. Or, wrap the hot water bottle in one of his blankets (for how to make your own dog blanket, see Day 38). Even when your dog is a little older, it's always good to have a couple of blankets for him to lie on. The familiar scent is comforting.

A chew bone with a meaty or chicken-flavored interior inside is a treat for your dog and will help occupy him while he waits for you to get home. You can also purchase a safe toy that has a cavity to hold a treat. Chewing on approved bones and toys is excellent busywork for dogs.

Dispensing Ear and Eye Medication

WHAT HAPPENS WHEN your dog gets an infection and needs medication for these sensitive areas? It's difficult enough to put eye drops in your own peepers, let alone squeeze liquid into your dog's eyes. Before you leave the veterinarian's office, ask for a quick lesson so you can watch the process before you have to perform it. At home, be sure to thoroughly wash your hands before giving medication, and plan dosages for times when your dog is calm or tired. The trick with eyes and ears is that there are two of each. The second dose is always more difficult because your dog is aware that the feeling is uncomfortable and probably less willing to comply. Reward your dog with a treat after each eye or ear application.

Ears: Liquid, gel, and cream medications must penetrate deep into the ear canal. Clean your dog's ears, then insert the tube (or dropper) into his ear. Squeeze out an appropriate drop or a dollop, according to the directions for the treatment. Lightly pinch the ear together to close it, and gently rub the ear for a few minutes to be sure medication distributes evenly.

Eyes: Kneel on the floor, facing your dog, and hold his head gently, using your thumb and first finger to open his eye. Place the eye drop or gel dollop of the correct dosage into the corner of the eye. Gently close the dog's eye (he may do this naturally) to disperse the medication.

Moving to a New House

MOVING TO A new house can be just as stressful for your dog as it is for you. Your dog has grown accustomed to his cozy sleeping spot by the front window. He knows where he dines, plays, and finds all of his toys. Your home is his territory, and when you pack up and move out, the process itself is traumatic because of the boxes and chaos, and the result is a new, strange place that doesn't feel like home—yet. There are several ways to ease the dog's transition.

The first order of business is packing. As you begin deconstructing each room of the house, your dog will probably slink around and nervously evaluate the situation, perhaps initiating some drama by barking or acting out. Create a safe room for him to stay in while you're packing and unpacking and the movers are taking items in and out of the house. This room should have his bed, food, water, a few familiar blankets, toys, and a chew toy. Keep disruptions to a minimum in this room.

On moving day, play some low-volume music in the dog's safe room to mask the unfamiliar noise of moving. Put a "do not open" sign on the door and be sure it is latched properly so your dog won't get lost in the confusion. Try to have his new ID tag on his collar already, just in case.

Upon moving into your new home, immediately establish your dog's key living spaces and begin establishing new routines.

You may want to confine him to one room at first, then open up new rooms to him one by one over a period of a few days. Hide toys or treats throughout the house to make exploration fun. Avoid washing his bedding or blankets until he's settled into the new house. Familiar scents will help him get acclimated faster.

The first night in your new home, resist the urge to leave the mess and go out to dinner. Order in and spend the time getting settled. By staying with your dog these first hours in the house, he will understand that this strange place is not so bad, and that you are not abandoning him in this new, unfamiliar place.

If you are moving to another country, consider enlisting in the help of pet movers/relocators. These professionals have years of experience, know all local rules and requirements, and are licensed, insured, and bonded. They can even help acquire travel documents and monitor your pet's movements from curbside pickup, through flight tracking, and on to customs clearance and quarantine.

Travel Bags: An Alternative to Carriers

TRAVEL BAGS CAN be a stylish, lightweight alternative to hard-sided travel carriers. These bags come in a wide variety of styles and colors. There are designer bags, sporty sacks, and backpacks that can hold your pooch.

Travel bags can be divided into two categories: crate alternatives and doggy day bags. Crate alternatives are generally soft sided and lightweight. They can be collapsible, but their purpose is to replace the permanent crate at home while your dog is en route or on location somewhere other than home. Larger crate-style carriers can double as a doghouse. They're portable but not something you would carry through an outdoor market while you shop.

Doggy day bags are carriers that sometimes resemble handbags, and other times look like infant slings used to keep a baby close to Mom, while Mom goes hands-free. The backpack and sling-style carriers are appropriate for toy and small breeds. These carriers are always with the owner—they're carryalls.

Before you invest in a dog carrier for travel or everyday use, consider these purchase pointers:

- If you travel a lot by airplane or train, check with the airline or rail company to see what their policies and size restrictions are before purchasing a travel bag for your dog.

- Buy the right-size carrier for your dog. She should be able to stand up, turn around, and lie down in the bag.

- Get your dog used to the carrier well before your trip. Leave the carrier out and open and invite her to explore it by leaving a treat inside. Take her on short, local trips in the carrier, in the car, or on public transportation (if it is allowed) so that the carrier won't be one more stressful surprise on the day of the big trip.

- Consider starting with an inexpensive travel bag until your dog is used to it, in case she has an accident in it or chews on it.

Establishing a Mealtime Routine

Dogs thrive on routines, especially when it involves feeding. Once you've decided where and how you will feed him, stick with the plan. If you must make changes, introduce them gradually.

Find a feeding spot that is out of the main traffic flow of your house, and then always feed him there (see Day 2). He will learn where to expect food. Once your dog is housebroken, water should be available 24/7 at the "canteen." Make sure your dog understands where his food and water are. When he takes his first drink and nibble of food, praise him so he begins to develop positive associations.

Unless your dog is particularly finicky (see Day 303), he'll remember where his bowls are and be ready to eat when it is time. Talk with your vet, breeder, or animal shelter about when and how much to feed your dog. Use the same word or phrase every time to call him to eat. Before long, your dog will recognize the crumpling noise of the dog food bag or the shaking noise of a plastic storage container when you scoop in for his portion. He'll come tail-wagging and hungry to his food spot.

Now, a couple remarks on mealtime routines and begging. One of the reasons why establishing an eating zone for your dog is so important is because he will learn that eating happens there—not under your family's dinner table, out back by the grill, or at any other place where human food is present and people are eating (and he is not). Avoid offering your dog scraps while you are eating, and if he suggests (by whining) that he wants a taste, do not give in. Do not look at him. You can offer him a morsel after the family is finished at the table. Put that "treat" in his dog bowl at his feeding station. Ask everyone in the family to follow the "don't feed the dog" rule. Consistency with meals, training, and everything in a dog's life is crucial.

> If you're traveling with your dog, it's important to set up his water and food bowls immediately and make sure he knows where they are. Keep to his established feeding schedule as much as possible.

Obedience Training

Dogs, BY NATURE, are pack animals. As you and your family become your dog's pack, your new dog will look to you—the leader of the pack—for guidance. Keep in mind that it is unrealistic to expect the dog to abide by the rules of the household without teaching appropriate behavior. Much like people, every dog is different. Regardless of these differences, training is necessary for all dogs and beneficial to your entire family. Several types of training are available.

PUPPY CLASS

A developmental training course for the three- to five-month-old puppy. A puppy class emphasizes socialization with people and other puppies. Instructors usually offer information on housebreaking and problem-solving and teach basic household commands.

BASIC CLASS

This is a basic training course for dogs five to six months and older, aimed at training you to train your dog. The basic class emphasizes the essential training commands needed to make a dog a good companion: heel on a loose leash, sit, stand, down, stay in position, and come when called. This basic training is important in keeping your dog safe.

CANINE GOOD CITIZEN (CGC) CLASS

CGC is an American Kennel Club certification program that is designed to reward dogs that have good manners at home and in the community. Your dog will need to know the commands and exercises taught in a basic training class to qualify for a passing score on the CGC test. Dogs that pass the CGC test receive a certificate from the AKC and are recorded in the AKC's Canine Good Citizen Archive. (For international equivalents, see Resources, page 318.)

TRAINING CLASSES FOR COMPANION EVENTS IN COMPETITION

A variety of classes are available that prepare owners and their dogs for competition in obedience, agility, tracking, and other competitive events. When you attend classes with your dog, instructors will show you how to teach her and will expect you to practice at home. The basic novice obedience level of competition begins with exercises that attest to the dog's good manners: walking on a leash at the owner's side, standing to be touched by a stranger, sitting and lying down with distractions, and coming when called. Advanced obedience levels demonstrate the owner's ability to train the dog to do a variety of "tricks": fetching a dumbbell, jumping different obstacles, obeying commands in an instant whether given by hand signal or voice, and finding items touched by the owner. At this level of obedience training you build a working team, a partnership with both human and canine working in sync. Utility dog is another level of obedience competition. The dog must respond to hand signals that direct her to go down, sit, come, and return to heel; find two articles handled by her owner out of a pile of several placed on the floor; retrieve one of three gloves as directed by the owner; and perform a high jump and a bar jump at the owner's direction.

Reviving Mr. Squeaky

YOUR DOG'S FAVORITE squeaky toy is her No. 1 form of entertainment and your primary reprieve. It keeps her busy for at least an hour. Although its high-pitched squeals are somewhat agitating, you can tune it out because your beloved is never happier than when playing with it. Surprisingly, you didn't celebrate the peace and quiet that resulted from Mr. Squeaky losing its voice, thanks to an especially rough play session that flung stuffing from the plush toy all over the living room and extracted a clear, plastic squeaker unit.

Fortunately, you captured that plastic squeaker before your dog got her mouth on it. Those mechanisms are dangerous choking hazards. On your kitchen table are the remains of Mr. Squeaky: plush, slobbery exterior; fluffy stuffing; and the voice box.

Is there a way to revive Mr. Squeaky?

In fact, yes! And you can even install a less dangerous noisemaker so, if your dog rips apart the toy again, she'll be in a safer position.

Follow these steps to bring Mr. Squeaky back to life, and to restore the joy of your anxiously waiting pup. (She really appreciates this, you know.)

- *Replace the squeaker with bells.* Buy a bag of small, decorative round jingle (or cat collar) bells at a craft supply store (or in bulk from pet supply catalogs). These bells are less risky than the plastic squeakers.

- *Restuff and sew.* Replace polyfill stuffing and add additional filler if necessary. Insert the jingle bell or squeaky replacement. Using cotton thread—not nylon, which can cut dogs' gums—hand-sew together the burst seam.

- *Toss and treat.* Mr. Squeaky is back, and so is your dog's favorite pastime. What a treat!

Skunked!

DURING AN EVENING walk, you spot a skunk slinking by, out of the corner of your eye. The white "warning" stripes on its mink-black coat are a clear indication that the critter you hear is no squirrel. Before you can steer your dog away from the area, the skunk freezes, stomps its feet, and sprays its yellow musk. Your dog is covered in the stench, and it will not wash out with regular shampoo and water. In fact, many groomers advertise emergency skunk odor removal services. If a skunk sprays into your dog's eyes, rinse eyes thoroughly with water and a mild eyewash. Then, follow this home remedy for eliminating skunk odor:

1 quart (1 L) 3 percent hydrogen peroxide

¼ cup (18.4 g) baking soda

1 teaspoon (5 ml) liquid soap

Bathe dog with the solution, careful not to allow the mixture to come in contact with your dog's eyes. Rinse thoroughly. The soap will break up skunk spray oils, and the hydrogen peroxide and baking soda will neutralize the thiols that cause the offensive odor.

Fixing Yellow Spots on the Lawn

THERE'S NO HIDING where your dog's "area" is located. The yellow spots and dead grass are tell-tale signs. You avoid using lawn care products, but the unsightly area is getting out of control. Rest assured, there's a formula to prevent urine-related lawn burnout. The best treatment is prevention (you've heard this before), which means neutralizing urine before it even touches the lawn.

Tomato juice is known to lessen the acidity of urine that burns turf. Not all dogs are interested in lapping up the vegetable juice, so you may try special tablets you feed to your dog to neutralize urine. Look for "dog urine neutralizer" on packaging. The supplement is harmless to your dog and will protect your lawn.

For curative treatment of urine spots in your lawn, try spray products that are applied to the browned-out area. These biodegradable formulas contain plant extracts and plant enzymes that break down dog urine and convert it into nutrients. They also neutralize soil beneath the spot to promote grass growth.

To avoid yellow patch spread, designate one area of your lawn for bathroom activity. If preserving your curb appeal is important, begin potty training your dog in a discreet location. He'll make a habit of returning to that less-visible spot to do his business.

Dog Tails: Beagle Bagel Run

SIMON, OUR BEAGLE, is an excellent escape artist. He was constantly devising new ways to break out of our fenced-in area, and he succeeded regularly. We always knew he would return home, and he never wandered far—usually to the cemetery in our backyard, just beyond the fence. That was a thrill, until he discovered the coffee shop down the street.

One morning, after searching for him on foot and by car, we eventually went home and waited for his return. His absence was longer than usual. After a few hours, he trotted up the driveway nonchalantly with a whole bagel in his mouth. He walked right into the house and into our bedroom, jaws still tightly gripping that bagel, and he attempted to bury it underneath the pillows on our bed.

Simon must have special radar for bagels. On another occasion, he was rooting around in the midwinter snow and dug up a bagel bit. We're not sure where it came from, but leave it to Simon and his keen sense of smell to unearth edible rewards. I have a feeling that the coffee shop was missing plenty of inventory over the years, thanks to Simon's taste.

125

Essential Supplies for Your Dog

IT'S EASY TO become overwhelmed or go overboard when shopping for dog supplies. The shopping list of essentials can grow quite long if you're starting from scratch. You will need to have the basics for training and care of a new dog, but you don't want to purchase too many unnecessary items. This list will give you a good foundation . . . and doubles as a maintenance checklist throughout your life with your dog.

Water and food bowls: You'll need two: one for water and one for food. (See Day 2 for choosing bowls.)

Collar and leash: Every dog needs a collar and a leash for walks and outings. A harness can be a good alternative for smaller dogs or dogs who tend to pull at their leashes. (See Day 44 for selecting a leash.)

Identification: Every dog should have an ID tag with his name and his owner's contact information.

Food: Select a dog food program that is within your budget and appropriate for your dog. Many varieties of commercial dog foods are geared toward dogs of a certain age and size.

Bedding: Your bedding choices will depend on your dog's age and your personal preferences for household décor. A puppy will need a crate for housetraining. Older dogs can use anything from a quilted blanket to a dog bed complete with mattress and frame.

Grooming tools: Plan on buying a brush, flea comb, nail trimmer, small toothbrush, and dog toothpaste.

Treats and chews: All dogs should have toys and treats to keep them occupied and entertained. Pick a handful of toys that are size appropriate for your dog, as well as real or synthetic bones for chewing. (See Day 3 for selecting toys.)

How to Stop Door Scratching

Is YOUR DOG a door scratcher? The behavior may be a helpful reminder that he needs to take care of business, or it could be an insistent request to go outdoors for a walk or playtime. Door scratching is also a symptom of separation anxiety: You leave, and your dog wants out of that door to find his number one.

The scratching is innocent, but it can destroy your door. If your dog won't give up the habit, try these preventive measures to save yourself from sanding down and repainting the surfaces.

Train your dog not to scratch. Attach a training mat (called a Scat Mat) along the area where the dog scratches. These battery-operated plastic sheets or strips discourage scratching by delivering a safe yet uncomfortable electric charge when touched by the dog's paws. After the dog realizes that scratching leads to discomfort, you can remove the training mat.

Install a pet door. Dogs are happy when they can come and go as they please, provided the outdoor area is safely fenced. Pet doors are available to suit every style: a standard wooden door, a glass slider, French doors, and so on.

Install door covers or shields. For dogs who scratch on the door after you leave the house, prevent damage by using self-sticking door covers or protective plastic door shields.

Hide existing scratches. A commercial scratch remover for wood will cover the damage. Look for wax crayons and wood putty pencils that match the door color.

Playing Hide-and-Seek

PRACTICE THE "COME" command with this child-hood game that offers your dog physical and mental exercise. Begin the game when your dog least expects it. Hide in a closet, behind a door, or behind a sofa or chair near the room where your dog is lazing around. Call your dog's name and say "Come!" Let him search the house for you. Praise him when he finds you and give him a tasty treat—one of the "good" treats you save for training sessions, such as a piece of jerky or a chicken-flavored chew.

For a variation of the game, take one of your dog's squeaky toys and steal away to a hiing spot. Squeak away until he finds you, then reward him with a treat. With practice, your dog will become a supersleuth. Involve other family members or friends in the game. The mental stimulation and excitement of finding you (and the treat reward) fulfills three important needs: bonding, training, and exercise.

Variation: Hide the Treat

Your dog looks bored. She's milling around the house, potentially headed for trouble unless you direct her toward a constructive activity to keep her busy. Sweeten her day by hiding a favorite treat in the house. Ask her, "Where's the treat?" Use a word she associates with a yummy reward, whether that is *cookie, biscuit, treat*, or some other word. Let her run the house, and help her search. Eventually lead her close enough to the tasty reward so she can find it.

Say the command "Come!" one time. If you give your dog the order as a string of comes—"come, come, come!"—how will he know when to *really* respond? Keep it short, say it a single time, and wait for your dog to obey the command.

Caring for the Canine Surgical Patient

DOGS HAVE SURGERY more often than you might think. They often begin their lives with spaying or neutering; later in life, surgery is common for dental problems, hip dysplasia, and other conditions. Life's little accidents can mean surgery, too, such as stomach surgery to remove a mistakenly swallowed item.

If your dog's surgery is elective and not emergency, be sure to prepare for it by following your vet's instructions, which will probably include no water or food (including treats) for a number of hours beforehand.

Your dog will probably be a little confused by the change in routine and sense that something is about to happen, so be sure to give her extra love and affection to help reassure her.

After surgery, you will need to keep her quiet and calm—no playing or running—for the period prescribed by your vet, usually at least twenty-four hours after surgery (and typically more). Her crate comes in handy here. You may need to use a cone collar to keep your dog from licking and chewing at the surgery site.

A Remedy for "Wet Dog" Smell in Your Car

SWIMMING IS A fun activity for you and your dog to do together, as is a long walk in a rainstorm or a romp in the snow at the park. The downside is that your dog isn't always completely dry when it's time to get back into the car, which can leave the car quite fragrant. This simple homemade cleaning solution will help eliminate that odor from your carpets and upholstery.

¼ cup (60 ml) white vinegar

¼ teaspoon (1 ml) liquid glycerin soap

4–6 cups (1–1.5 L) hot water

1. Mix the ingredients and pour into a spray bottle.

2. Test a small, hidden area to make sure the carpet and upholstery are colorfast and won't be damaged by the solution.

3. Lightly spray the carpets and upholstery.

4. Rinse the carpet and upholstery with a clean rag and a bucket of clean, warm water. Wring out the rag well; you don't want to soak the fabrics.

5. If you have a wet/dry vacuum, you can use it to help remove some of the moisture so the washed surfaces will dry faster.

6. Leave the doors open until everything is completely dry. A fan can help, too.

7. If desired, lightly spritz homemade air freshener in the car (see tip below).

8. Allow further air-drying.

Recipe:

All-Natural Spray Air Freshener

For a quick and easy natural air freshener, mix three drops of your favorite essential oil (such as lavender or citrus) in 8 ounces (235 ml) of hot water in a misting-style bottle. Shake well, then spray lightly. If you prefer a heavier scent, use more oil; less scent, less oil. Avoid spraying on painted surfaces and test fabrics for colorfastness before spraying on them. This will store for a couple of days in the refrigerator.

Involving Your Dog in Your Wedding

You wouldn't think of leaving your best friend off the guest list for your "big day." Why should your dog be shipped to the kennel for the nuptials? More dog owners include their pooches in wedding ceremonies than ever before, assigning them special jobs, such as ring bearer or usher. Still, there are drawbacks to involving your pet in the pomp and circumstance.

If you decide to create a role for your dog in the wedding, first consider these practical wedding planning tips:

• **Prepare for the unexpected.** If you decide to invite your dog to the reception, the buffet is a sure target for mischief. And there is always the chance that your four-legged bridesmaid will not saunter down the aisle as you had hoped. There will be lots of new, exciting smells and people to greet, after all.

• **Choose an appropriate role for the dog, depending on his age and temperament.** Your Jack Russell Terrier will probably need an escort (and leash) for his walk down the aisle. A calm, off-leash Golden Retriever can handle transporting the rings. Older dogs will likely sit quietly through a ceremony, but frisky puppies will find too many distractions.

• **Dedicate a "spotter" for your dog in case she gets out of hand.** The bride and groom should not need to wade into the crowd to correct bad behavior. Ask a member of the wedding party to be on dog watch during the ceremony. Or, hire a pet sitter.

• **Primp your pooch for the big day.** Make an appointment with a groomer well in advance of the wedding day. Plan to have your dog bathed the day before the ceremony so her coat will be free of dander. Some guests may be allergic.

• **Plan the wedding attire.** You can purchase pup-size tuxedos and dresses, tiaras, and special ring-bearer pillows that strap to your dog's back. If you order these items online, allow plenty of time for shipping (and for order mistakes—you never know).

• **Fast on wedding morning.** Not the bride—the dog! Do not feed or give your dog water prior to the ceremony, thus decreasing the likelihood that she will need to make an emergency exit, or may not make it in time. You do not want accidents in the wedding video.

• **Is this really a good idea?** You must feel confident that your dog's presence will enhance rather than add stress to your wedding day. The event is already overstimulation central for humans—imagine how dogs will react. Deciding to include your dog means ensuring that she has the care she needs, is well monitored, and will be escorted to a quiet place if she becomes scared or frightened. While the wedding is "your day," pet ownership responsibilities are still in effect.

Creating a Cool Sleep Spot in the Yard

IF YOUR DOG is an incessant backyard digger, the reason may be that burrowing for varmints is in her DNA (terriers are famous for this). Or, perhaps your dog is simply looking for a cool place to rest. Problem digging could be your dog's way of creating a comfortable nest to protect her from the summer heat. The ground temperature is cooler than a grassy surface scorched by hot sun. Your dog's solution is to dig below the surface and cull out a sleeping spot.

Prevent the dig-fest by creating a cool flop spot for your dog. The area should be cooler than the soil in your flowerbeds, and cleaner.

MATERIALS

Shovel

Concrete mix

Wheelbarrow or large container

Trowel

Screwdriver (any type)

Playground sand

Tarp

1. Dig out a shallow pit (depression) sized to fit your dog comfortably. Think: nest.

2. Use the trowel to mix the concrete in a wheelbarrow according to the package instructions.

3. Pour the concrete into the pit and smooth out with the trowel until the surface is completely and evenly covered.

4. As the concrete begins to set, poke holes in the bottom of the pit, using a screwdriver. These drainage holes will ensure that the sleeping pit doesn't turn into a pool after rainfall.

5. After the concrete dries, pour playground sand into the pit. Sprinkle water on the sand to keep it cool, and cover it with a tarp when not in use to dissuade stray cats from mistaking the sleeping spot for a public restroom.

Stop Problem Barking

BARKING IS AN instinctive behavior and used to communicate all sorts of messages, from "The house is burning" to "I am lonely." However, your dog's barking habits may make your neighbors want to smack you with a rolled-up newspaper!

Many pet stores sell "bark collars" that provide mild electrical shocks or other stimuli to stop barking. Although these devices may stop the barking, they do not address the underlying cause, which more often than not will manifest itself in some other inappropriate behavior. Before you correct the behavior (see Bark Stoppers at right), determine the reason for your dog's barking. Following are some common bark triggers:

Isolation and boredom: If your dog is home alone for long periods at a time, problem barking can be a sign of boredom or loneliness. Try to provide lots of safe, interesting toys and rotate them occasionally to keep your dog interested. Make sure to exercise and play with your dog every day. Consider hiring a dog walker to come during the day to provide some "excitement," or, if you have the finances, try one or two days per week at the local doggy daycare.

Territorial protection: Train your dog on a "quiet" command: interrupt his barking with a noise like a handclap, or by shaking pennies in a can (see Day 86) and then say, "Good quiet" and provide a treat and some affection as soon as the barking stops. You can also try some simple dog behavior modification. Ask a friend (but not someone the dog knows well) to work with you by walking by your house while you train your dog to ignore the person, using the "quiet" command. Additionally, spaying or neutering can also cut down on territorial behavior.

Fear of loud noises: When thunderstorms or fireworks cause barking fits, try not to coddle your dog: This will only teach the lesson that barking at noises yields extra attention.

Instead, turn on some kind of "white noise," like a fan, to lessen your pet's startle response—and always remember to reward your dog for obeying the "quiet" command.

How to Stop the Barking

Keep in mind, barking is not all bad. It can warn you that a stranger is approaching your home, or that something is out of the ordinary. But unwanted barking can be annoying, both to you and to your neighbors. These techniques will help solve the problem of unwanted barking.

1. A blast from an air horn when your dog starts to bark for the wrong reasons usually does the trick. Dogs are more sensitive to sound than humans, and will stop in their tracks when they hear this. Follow it up with a firm "No" and a "Bad girl" to reinforce the message. Remember, use your dog's name only in association with good behavior.

2. Nonshock collars are available that spray citronella or lemon oil automatically when your dog barks. Dogs don't like either of those scents around their face, and soon will stop the unwanted barking.

Don't use either of these training tools in situations where it is good for your dog to bark. If she is barking for the right reasons, let her bark and give her praise. Soon she will learn when it is appropriate to bark and when it is not.

133

Make Your Own Minted Tennis Balls

YOU CAN PURCHASE minted tennis balls that freshen your dog's breath during play, but making your own is inexpensive and easy.

These inexpensive homemade balls are a win-win for both dog and owner: They love to play ball, and you get to enjoy their fresh breath!

Note: Some mint flavors are not safe for dogs to ingest—choose peppermint or spearmint.

MATERIALS

1 tablespoon (14 ml) peppermint or spearmint oil (culinary grade, from the natural foods store)

2 tablespoons (28 ml) fresh parsley juice (puree fresh parsley in the blender; optional)

4 cups (1 L) very warm water

Blender

6 plain, pet-safe tennis balls

Large stainless-steel bowl

Cake cooling rack

Lidded airtight plastic tub to store your finished tennis balls

Regular tennis balls can be dangerous for dogs. Sometimes there is lead in the paint used to make them fluorescent. The polyester felt can be hard on teeth and can come off easily and get caught between teeth. The dye is not always colorfast, which can lead to stains on your carpet. Also, they don't hold up well to aggressive chewing, and tend to come apart in small pieces that your dog could swallow. Always use pet-safe tennis balls, which are available in larger pet stores and some sporting-goods stores.

1. Blend the mint oil, fresh parsley juice, and warm water on high speed to emulsify.

2. Place the tennis balls in the stainless-steel bowl. Pour the mint mixture over the tennis balls and mix well.

3. Place the wet tennis balls on the rack to dry.

4. Once they are dry, store them in the lidded tub.

When You Need to Get to the Vet

IT CAN BE difficult to know when your dog's illness is run-of-the-mill and when you need to get to the vet right away. This checklist will help you decide. Call your vet if your dog has these symptoms:

- Elevated temperature for more than 24 hours
- Change in skin temperature
- Change in skin color
- Change in tongue color
- Eyes are not bright; he appears dazed

- Abrupt or prolonged changes from his normal behavior, such as irritability or hyperactivity
- Sluggishness or drowsiness for long periods
- Unexpected changes in his bowel movements
- Blood in his stools
- Severe or prolonged constipation or diarrhea
- Urinating too much or cannot relieve himself at all
- Tenderness around his genitals
- Vomiting over a prolonged period
- Forceful vomiting after every feeding
- Refuses to eat for more than a day, or paws at his mouth
- A prolonged cough
- Difficulty breathing, especially if the breathing is noisy and rapid
- An open wound or a swelling
- A bite from another animal, or a sting or scratch that looks inflamed
- Difficulty keeping his balance, walking, or standing
- A limp that does not improve after a day or two

If your dog has any of the above symptoms, don't hesitate to call the vet's office. It doesn't hurt to make a phone call, and you just might save your dog's life. Your vet will never fault you for asking health questions.

Dog Hair . . . Everywhere!

IT IS A FACT of life: If you own a dog, you have dog hair, and if you have dog hair, you have shedding. Dogs usually shed twice a year, in the spring to get rid of their heavy winter coats and in the fall to get ready for winter. Just like we shed our coats and jackets, our dogs also shed theirs. Blowing coat, as it is sometimes called, is an issue that every dog owner deals with.

Here are some tips and ideas for dealing with all that extra hair.

- **If you have a long-haired breed,** a slicker brush or pin brush will help you get a lot of the hair out. You can use a long-tooth comb before you brush to get out any tangles.

- **For short-coated breeds,** a shedding blade, sisal mitt, or rubber hound mitt can really make a difference.

- **If the weather is warm or you live in a warm climate,** brush your dog outside. The birds love the hair and will use it in the construction of their nests.

- **If it is cold outside and you can't go out,** pick a room, such as the bathroom, that has a tile or linoleum floor that is easy to clean. This will make it easy to sweep up the hair and dispose of it.

If you knit or crochet and have a long-haired dog such as a Samoyed, Alaskan Malamute, Husky, or Saluki, you can have the shed hair spun into yarn. The finished product will be beautiful and keep you warm, and it's a great way to recycle. Check online and at your bookstore for more information about this.

Journal Prompts, Part 3

- How does your dog sense when you are down and comfort you?

- What nicknames do you call your dog? (Which ones are just between the two of you?)

- Describe your first out-of-town trip with the dog.

- Draw (or describe) a map of your dog's favorite walking routes. Write a story for each route.

- Describe a time when your dog was scared, met another doggy friend, or made you laugh at one of his antics.

- What happened when you introduced your dog to other pets at home? Describe the interactions you observed. What tips would you share with other owners?

- What are your dog's favorite foods? (Yes—it's O.K. to include people food, too.) If your dog could send you to the grocery store with a list, what would she request?

(See Days 41–42, 90–91, and 209–210 for more journal prompts throughout the year.)

Creating Proper Pet Tags

PET TAGS ARE like drivers' licenses. They identify your dog by name, breed, owner's address, and phone number. Like people, your dog should have multiple forms of identification. You may opt to have your dog microchipped (see Day 289), in which case you will be given a tag containing his microchip identification number. Microchipping is wise because if your dog gets lost and his collar and tags are removed, he is still identifiable. The tiny microchip in his body is like an internal GPS tool so the microchip provider can identify and track the location of your dog. On the other hand, someone who finds him without a collar may not know he has a microchip embedded. To be on the safe side, always double-tag by including a basic, metal tag that contains your vital stats. If you are wary about putting your address on your dog's tag, give a phone number. The idea is to make it extremely easy for someone who finds your dog to return him safely to you.

You can get a basic ID tag with your dog's name and your contact information made at a pet store—many of them have stamping machines and can process the tag on site. You can also obtain mail-in order forms for tags at your veterinarian's office, or at the Humane Society office, or order a tag online. If your dog is irritated by the jangling sound of a dangling tag hanging from his collar, choose a silent slide-on tag that fits along the collar. Or, you can have identification information embroidered directly onto a collar.

Additionally, your vet will provide a rabies vaccine tag that contains the veterinary hospital contact information and serves as verification that your dog has been immunized. If your dog socializes in dog parks, this alerts other dog owners that your dog is a safe playmate.

Tucking into Bed Together

YOUR SPOUSE SAID it first: "The dog will not sleep in our bed." You agreed completely. You both resisted the urge to cuddle your puppy to sleep for months. Crate training went smoothly; your dog learned to love its safe zone. Still, at night she wants to crawl under the covers with her best friends (you). The doggy bed on the floor does not have the same appeal as the tiny bit of real estate at the end of your bed—or between your and your partner's pillows. Before long, you give in, your spouse caves, or both of you decide that nothing would be sweeter than bonding with your "baby" in bed.

That is, until your dog begins treating your mattress like turf and starts digging holes as if there must be groundhogs underneath the bed. Or, she romps around and plays with the covers like a wild teenager at a pajama party. Wait a minute. Whose bed is this, anyway?

Inviting your dog into bed is fine, as long as you treat the situation just so: as an invitation. Your dog is a guest in bed. She should be on her best behavior while in bed with you, and if not, you must correct the bad manners. Here are a few pointers:

• Walking a tight, prenap circle is okay. That's the cozying-in motion dogs make before nestling down to sleep. But if the activity becomes playful rather than restful, remove your dog from the bed, set her down in a crate or on a doggy mat, and give her a toy to chew. Say, "Sit. Stay. Good girl." When she settles down, invite her back to the bed and try again.

• Keep a doggy mat or crate by your bed. This is your dog's safe zone, and a place for your dog to have time out if she cannot behave on the bed.

• Curb late-night activity. Feed your dog and walk her hours before bedtime. Chew-time is best during the afternoon, not minutes before you want to retire for the night. Allow your dog that necessary winding-down time to laze around so when she tucks into bed with you, she's tuckered out and not likely to play games.

Activity Compatibility

OLDER DOGS STILL love to play, but even a healthy dog will slow down as he ages. He might not be able to walk as fast or as far as he could in the past or be able to scramble over things like he used to. You'll need to adjust your activities for his abilities. Sidewalks can be hard on an older dog's joints and pads, too. Slow your pace, shorten your walks, and choose a soft, easy path.

If your dog loves to be outdoors and moving but cannot walk far, depending on the dog's size you can consider a carrier that attaches to your bike or a dog stroller for when he gets too tired to go on. Toy and small dogs can fit in pouch-size carriers that you strap on to your body, similar to a baby sling. Bike carriages that hold dogs are best for small to medium breeds. Large dogs can still be pulled in a stroller, but check the equipment's weight limits.

Swimming and water play can be a great exercise for older dogs, because it is non-weight-bearing and easier on his joints. If he's not a good swimmer or doesn't have the stamina to swim for long, playing at the edge of a lake or pond or in a shallow children's pool will let him keep his feet on the ground while getting some of the benefits of swimming.

Older dogs need mental stimulation, too. You can help keep your dog's mind sharp and ward off depression by continuing to play such games as hide-and-seek and teaching him simple new tricks. (Don't listen to the adage: Old dogs *can* learn new tricks!)

Foods for Sour Stomachs

YOUR SWEETIE IS sick, poor thing. She's not interested in kibble, and after a day of her not eating, you're concerned. She has barely touched her water bowl, and she's doing her sick mope: slinking with her tail between her legs, not even barking at the mailman. You want her to eat so she can gain strength and feel better, but her regular diet is not the answer. Instead, choose from this menu containing items that are kind to sour stomachs. Let all cooked foods cool before serving to your dog.

Cooked, plain white rice

Cottage cheese

Boiled chicken, white meat

Boiled turkey

Scrambled egg

Boiled egg

Boiled or baked potato

A plain-and-simple diet is the best thing for your pooch when she's sick. These options will be more appealing to her than kibble. Monitor her behavior, and watch her stool—a no-fail sign of a dog's health. If stool is not firm after 24 to 36 hours, see the vet immediately.

> To help rehydrate a sick dog, mix water with an electrolyte drink.

Paw-Print or Photo Coasters

COLORFUL PAW PRINTS or photos sandwiched between glass make fun coasters for your own home or for a gift.

MATERIALS

8 (1/8-inch [3 mm] -thick, 3 1/2-inch [9 cm]) glass squares with smooth edges (two for each coaster; buy these ready made or have a glazier cut and smooth them)

Glass cleaner

Paper towels

Clear-drying craft glue

Binder clips (large)

1/4-inch (6 mm) -wide silvered copper-foil tape (found at many art or craft supply stores)

Sharp scissors

Pencil or bone folder

FOR PAW-PRINT COASTERS

1 sheet colored paper

Paw print rubber stamp

Stamp pad

FOR PHOTO COASTERS

4 color copies of your dog's photo, sized and cut to fit the glass

1. Clean and dry both sides of each of the glass pieces, using the glass cleaner and paper towels. Avoid leaving lint or fingerprints behind.

2. If you are making the paw print coasters, cut four pieces from the sheet of paper to fit the glass, ink the paw print stamp, and stamp the paper. Allow the ink to dry.

3. Position a paw print or photo on one pane of glass. Use a tiny dab of glue on the back of the print or photo to adhere it to the pane. Continue with the remaining three prints or photos. Allow glue to dry before continuing.

4. Carefully place a second pane on top of each piece, sandwiching the photo or print between the two panes. Align the edges exactly.

5. To seal, hold the panes together with binder clips, moving the clips from one side to another as you tape. Place the end of the metal tape along an edge of the glass, and wrap the tape around the entire perimeter. Overlap the ends slightly, and then snip the tape with scissors.

Step 5

6. For a tight seal, rub the tape thoroughly until the edge is smooth, using the side of a pencil or bone folder as a burnishing tool.

7. If necessary, clean the coasters with a soft cloth or paper towel and glass cleaner. Do not submerge coasters in water because the tape does not produce a watertight seal.

Make a Doggy "Passport"

CREATE A DOG passport to organize your pooch's important papers—health certificate, vaccination record, microchip ID number—so you can easily keep track of his "vital stats" when you travel abroad. You can use an envelope-size portfolio or a large wallet (checkbook size) to hold the papers. A zippered vinyl case with dividers also does the job so you can conveniently tote your pet's information along with your own.

Your dog's "passport" should include:

- Current health certificate

- Vaccination record

- Visas, if needed (see Days 237–238, on traveling abroad)

- An ID card for your dog with his name, photo, and notes about any special markings, along with your contact information (you can make this yourself)

- Registration and/or license number

- Microchip ID number (see Day 289, on microchipping your dog)

- Vet's name, address, and phone number (home and at your destination)

- A bright-colored card listing your dog's feeding schedule and amounts, medication schedule and amounts, allergies, and any peculiarities (such as aggression toward people in uniform)— whatever would be useful for a stranger to know about handling your dog

- Emergency contact and next-of-kin information

Dog Breeds Ideal for Your 9–5 Work Schedule

SOME DOGS ARE better suited to their owner's nine-to-five lifestyle because they can handle being home alone for more than nine hours at a time. If you feel that your schedule and lifestyle will still accommodate a dog, consider one of the dog breeds that will adapt easily to being home alone for long periods. A few breeds that are independent and thrive well alone for long periods of time include French Bulldogs, Irish Wolfhounds, and Pugs.

French Bulldog: This is a loving breed that truly enjoys being around people, but is perfectly self-sufficient (once trained) when spending the day at home. The French Bulldog needs minimal grooming, and is therefore a low-maintenance choice for busy individuals who don't want to fuss with combing, brushing, and carting their dog to get frequent haircuts. A short walk and some playtime each day will be enough exercise to keep your French Bulldog content.

Irish Wolfhound: Although these are larger dogs, they have a sweet disposition and they spend an incredible amount of time napping. This breed is the opposite of your always-wired Jack Russell Terrier. Training is a must for this breed, but a few walks each day and getting to run off-leash a few times a week will be sufficient for this gentle giant.

Pug: This quirky, sturdy dog is friendly and requires little exercise. Pugs function well alone during the day if they are trained properly and given boundaries. Also, pugs are well behaved with children, although care should be taken to make sure younger ones are gentle around this breed. Watch out for hot days, because pugs have a low heat tolerance.

What to Do If Your Puppy Is Jumping and Biting

JUMPING AND BITING are attention-seeking behaviors that you'll want to nip in the bud. You want to teach your puppy that jumping and biting are not appropriate behaviors for getting what he wants.

If you know that company is coming over or if children are running about, keep a short lead on your puppy. If he tries to jump up on people, pull him back with the lead and say "Off!" or "Down!" Command him to adopt a sitting position, then reward him with enthusiastic praise and a treat when he behaves.

Clove oil, hot sauce, homemade stop-chew oil (see Day 23), or commercial products made to stop chewing can also be used to stop biting. The two problems are quite different. Biting is a single, snap action, usually in response to a stimulus, such as a hand reaching down to pet the puppy's head. Chewing satisfies an urge of some kind—to alleviate teething pain, burn energy because of lack of exercise, or keep occupied if a dog is bored.

Puppies like to bite hands, so apply the product of your choice to your hands. When your puppy starts to chew on your hand, firmly push down your thumb under her tongue and your index finger under her chin and say, "No chewing!" With the nasty taste and pressure on those pressure points, it shouldn't take too long before she stops nibbling on your hands.

To stop your puppy from biting the hand of someone else, who does not have stop-chew substance slathered on her fingers, first ask the person to not put her hands near the puppy's mouth. Explain that you are training him not to nip at "foreign objects" (i.e., hands). If a bite occurs, firmly say "No." Give your dog an acceptable chew toy and when he begins gnawing on it, praise him by saying "Good boy," and offering him a tasty treat. Rewarding your dog for biting on approved items will help him understand what is okay to bite and what is not.

Why Does My Dog Yawn after Playing?

AFTER A LONG, vigorous walk or an intense play session, your dog yawns repeatedly. Of course, you figure, the dog must be tired, completely worn out. Yawning is her way of saying, "Time to take a nap." Not necessarily.

When dogs yawn, the inhalation of oxygen helps lower blood pressure and calms the body. Your dog may be yawning to catch a second wind, or if she participated in rough play with a more dominant dog, the yawn may be in response to a stressful situation or overstimulation.

Essentially, dogs and people yawn for the same reasons: boredom, fatigue, stress, excitement, and so on. Knowing this, if your dog yawns, plops on the couch next to you, and gives you a coaxing look, she wants you to entertain her, play with her. She's bored. If your dog yawns after a long walk, she's likely catching her breath after exerting lots of energy.

Addressing the question of yawn contagion—you yawn, the person next to you yawns, someone else in the room follows—can your dog's yawn cause you to also yawn? (That's a lot of yawns!) The answer is, perhaps. As man's close companion, dogs are highly attuned to our behaviors, and we also respond to our dogs' body movements and mannerisms. Who's to say that we can't catch a yawn from our dogs, and vice versa?

Careful! Chocolate Can Be a Killer

MANY THINGS THAT humans eat can be dangerous to dogs. Chocolate is among the worst, but it is also attractive to your dog because of its sweet smell and delicious taste.

Chocolate contains theobromine, a chemical in the same family as caffeine, which is toxic to dogs. Some types of chocolate contain more theobromine than others, and some dogs are more sensitive to it than others, but even what seems like a small amount can be enough to be deadly. Never give a dog chocolate, and be sure any chocolate you keep in the house is stored securely away, out of your dog's reach. Be especially vigilant when entertaining and at holiday time, when candy dishes are out or a guest may bring chocolates as a gift.

If your dog ingests chocolate, call your vet immediately. If your vet is not available, contact a pet poison hotline. The vet may tell you simply to watch the dog, or may suggest that you bring him in right away, depending on the type and amount of chocolate the dog has eaten. The vet may also suggest that you give him hydrogen peroxide to make him throw up (see first-aid kit, Day 95).

If your dog seems to have a taste for chocolate, carob is a harmless alternative that is often used in "chocolate-flavored" dog treats. You can find carob chips and carob powder at the natural foods store to use if you are making your own dog treats.

A Pet Buddy System

THERE WILL BE times when a situation will call you out of the home for longer than your dog is used to staying alone. Maybe you must work late one night. Perhaps you have car trouble. The list of possibilities is endless. In any case, you want your dog to be safe while you are gone—and to get a potty break and some dinner.

Make arrangements with two or three neighbors you trust or family members who live close by. Give them a house key, show them where you keep food, the leash, a first-aid kit. You should prepare a brief instruction sheet to keep in a doggy notebook, along with your vet's contact information and important details about medications. This notebook is a valuable resource for others who care for your dog.

If you have a security system, show your "pet buddies" the code. (This speaks to the level of trust you must have in the people you assign this role.) Program their contact numbers into your cell phone so you can reach them on the go. Ideally, you can return the favor by serving as their main contact for pet care in case they have an emergency at home.

Dinner Party Etiquette

YOU'RE HOLDING A dinner party at your house. As you scurry around the kitchen prepping side dishes and performing a fast cleanup in the dining room, your dog can sense that something big is about to happen. You notice by her clingy behavior in attempt to get your attention. When the guests arrive, she realizes that all of this fuss must have been for her. Friends have come over to play! Many dogs love a good people party and view it as an opportunity to score more lovin' (hugs, treats, and playtime). Other more timid dogs are completely frightened by the noise, activity, and strangers.

Whether the gathering is a casual dinner party or an all-out celebration, your dog needs special attention to ensure that her antics—timid responses such as peeing upon guests' arrival, or boisterous hellos such as jumping and scrounging for dropped food—do not interrupt your event or your dog's health and happiness.

If your dog is overwhelmed by this type of scene, provide a safe, quiet place for her to retreat. Consider taking her to a dog-sitting friend's home or board her at a kennel for one night. Although many owners view boarding as the last resort, the option is far more desirable for dogs than being frightened and intimidated by a night of too much action at home.

If your dog is allowed to mingle with guests, make sure all dangerous foods are out of reach. Politely discourage generous guests from feeding your dog tastes from the table. Let her know there are boundaries. Crate time will be important to calm her down if her playful party behavior becomes overbearing. For kids' parties, watch the floor for spilled cake, dropped party favors, stray shoes, and candy. Remember that some children are frightened by dogs and may not welcome your pet's tail-wagging excitement.

A Dog's Calendar for the Seasons

January: Schedule a visit to the veterinarian. Start off New Year's Day with some doggy yoga. Find a dog-friendly superstore or indoor mall and walk around for some warm indoor exercise.

February: Take a break from the winter doldrums. Enroll your dog in an indoor agility class. Give your dog a massage for Valentine's Day.

March: Spring cleaning. Throw out old bedding and weathered toys. Go with your dog to a big pet-supply store and restock the toy bin. Find an empty public swing set and hit the slides with your dog. Practice obedience training with some biscuit hopscotch: Your pet must wait patiently for the biscuit while you hop the course.

April: Shop for components of and pack a first-aid kit (see Day 95) for car and home. Play bobbing for tennis balls in a large puddle or in a tub of water. Head into the city for an on-leash weekend walk around people and stores.

May: April was wet and rainy; invest in a new collar and lead. Volunteer at an animal charity or host a rescue dog. Shop at a large garden center with your best friend—so many trees, so little time.

June: Purchase some floating dummies, and practice water retrieving. Shoot flower-laden pictures of your dog. Save the best picture for your winter holiday cards. Go to an outdoor restaurant. Take your dog on a postdinner promenade.

July: Schedule a visit to the veterinarian. Hire a professional trainer for an obedience refresher. Take your dog for a joyride.

August: It's the dog days of summer. Head out for some cool lake swimming. Have a doggy sleepover and invite a favored playmate. Find a dog-friendly hotel and go on vacation.

September: Beaches start opening to dogs. Walk on the shore and dig in the sand. Last chance for an outdoor bath. Go to a dog show to learn about your dog's specific breed and pick up tips from breeders and vendors.

October: Build a leaf pile for your dog to play in. Visit the pumpkin patch. Bake some homemade pumpkin dog biscuits. Take your dog trick-or-treating with the kids.

November: Order a cold-weather coat. Gobble, gobble. Go on a post-Thanksgiving hike looking for wild turkeys that got away. Try painting your dog's portrait.

December: Gift wrap some special presents, and let your dog open his own gifts. Build a snowman with your dog. Plan your pet-related New Year's resolutions.

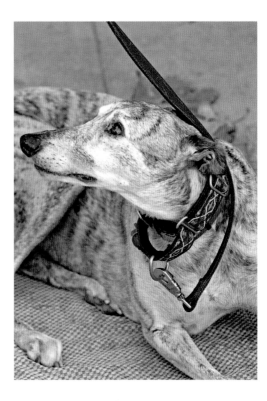

Trick: Clean Up Your Toys

IF YOUR DOG already knows how to fetch, you can teach her to clean up the mess of toys that, by end of day, litters the house. We show our children how to clean their room and put away toys. Dogs are equally capable of learning to pick up after themselves.

1. Take your dog's favorite toy and hide it for a couple of days. (Your dog will not forget about this favorite toy.)

2. Recover the favorite toy to teach "fetch" and "drop it." Reward with food when your dog retrieves and drops the toy. Play fetch and drop it for a while with this toy.

3. Decide on a new command (such as "Go get it,") and place the toy away from your dog. Do not throw the toy; the point is for him to bring it to you rather than chase it. Once the toy is placed a distance away from your dog, point to the toy you want him to pick up and return to you. Say "Drop it," then reward with a treat.

4. Repeat this process with all of your dog's favorite toys. You can name the toys as you train your dog, such as "Go get squeaky!" or "Get Mr. Bunny!" Your dog will learn what toy to retrieve as you gradually take away and reintroduce each toy.

Rewarding with Treats

FOOD IS AN important reward for many dogs. Although play-driven puppies prefer a wild game of tag, and clingy dogs want affection, food by far is the No. 1 signal to dogs of a job well done. They hear the jangle of the treat jar, or recognize the crunching sound of a cellophane wrapper being removed from a favorite edible bone. Their radar for treats is supersensitive—foodie dogs won't miss an opportunity for a snack.

But not just any snack will do for training. Break out the chicken-flavored, bacon-infused, cheesy, meaty, fatty snack your dog will do anything to earn. You'll only reward her with a nibble. The "good treats" are especially important to use when teaching your dog new tricks or more advanced commands. What constitutes a good treat? These are the snacks that instigate a Pavlovian effect as soon as your dog can smell them. Your dog will eat them as if she hasn't been fed in a month. The nose knows.

Training treats often look like jerky, and small bite-size pieces can be broken off. Tuck a training treat in your pocket for walks. Keep treats tucked away in every room of the house. Because you'll be teaching your dog to perform commands in different environments, you need to be prepared.

Once your dog catches on to a trick or command and can perform it several times in a row, dial back to less extravagant treats such as kibble. Because you'll conduct training sessions before mealtimes and during walks—up to five times per day—you can't dole out the dessert-caliber snacks every time. You may need to adjust your dog's meal sizes depending on how many treats you feed during the day. Use common sense.

Managing Dog Diabetes

YOUR DIABETIC DOG can live a normal, healthy life if the disease is properly managed. Type 1 diabetes, diabetes mellitus, is the inability to produce or properly use insulin, which regulates glucose levels in blood. If diabetes is not managed, dogs can go blind or suffer from life-threatening complications. The disease can be controlled by adopting habits that also benefit humans with type 1 or 2 (adult onset) diabetes: proper diet, exercise, and constant monitoring of blood glucose levels. The difference is, not all humans with type 2 require insulin shots to manage the disease, whereas dogs that develop this disease need the injections. Because their body can no longer produce insulin, they must rely on an outside source.

Diabetes is usually identified in older dogs, with typical onset between ages seven and nine. The disease is two to four times more common in females. As in humans, obesity is also a risk factor. Symptoms of diabetes include excessive thirst, urination, and loss of appetite and weight. Eventually, dogs may become lethargic and lose interest in food completely. Your vet will diagnose diabetes based on clinical signs, medical history, and lab results that indicate elevated glucose levels in blood and urine.

Managing dog diabetes involves a four-pronged approach. When owners commit to the program and practice consistency, their dogs can live a happy, long life.

Administering insulin: Your vet will prescribe the proper dosage based on your dog's weight. Twice-daily insulin shots are best given after mealtime. If your dog expresses disinterest in eating, only administer one-quarter to one-half of the injection. Be consistent with injection time.

Maintaining diet: Provide your dog a consistent, high-fiber diet of quality dog food, which will regulate blood sugar levels. Limit snacks to 10 percent of total daily calories. Offer such low- or no-carb treats as carrots, popcorn, or meat. Feed your dog twice a day at the same time.

Exercising regularly: Give your dog regular, consistent opportunities to exercise and avoid sporadic/strenuous activity. In such a case, your dog could potentially suffer from a fatal drop in blood sugar.

Monitoring the disease: Regular visits to the vet for glucose testing are critical. Establishing proper insulin dosage may take several months. As you monitor your dog at home, watch for signs of hypoglycemia, which is triggered by insulin overdose, excessive activity, or a missed meal. Keep food or corn syrup handy.

Safely Confronting an Aggressive Dog

Even a familiar walking route can present unanticipated dangers. When an aggressive dog comes out of nowhere and threatens you and your dog's safety, how should you react? Our natural reactions are to freeze up, to yell at the dog, to yank our dog's leash and run home. These behaviors could cause the dog's aggressive greeting to escalate into harmful action. If you confront an aggressive dog head-on, first drop the leash. Otherwise, you'll end up with a tangled mess and you could prevent your dog from defending himself or running away to safety.

Following are some tips for safely handling the confrontation:

Tune in to surroundings. Keep an eye out for open garages, alleys, open gates, and other places an aggressive dog may bolt from.

Cross the street. If you see danger ahead, cross the street and continue walking. Do not panic. Turn a corner to get out of sight. Protect toy dogs by tucking them under your coat or shirt.

Change your route. Drive to a safer location if the area by your home poses too many threats.

Stand still. Be quiet, and place hands down by your sides. Do not look the dog directly in the eye. Act calm and if the aggression continues, sternly say "No!" and take a few steps backward. Continue backing away to safety.

Break a lunge. If the dog lurches toward you, offer him a sweater, purse, backpack—anything you have that the dog can mouth besides you or your dog.

Identify protection. Look for sticks, rocks, trash can lids, or other protective items to defend yourself in a worst-case scenario.

Curl and cover. If the dog knocks you to the ground, curl into a ball with your hands over your ears to protect your head, neck, and stomach. Try to shield your small dog underneath you. Allow your larger dog to run or to retaliate and protect you.

Visit your doctor. If you were bitten or scratched in an aggressive dog confrontation, or if your dog suffered a blow and some bites, visit your veterinarian immediately.

Coping with the Loss of Your Dog

When your dog dies, it is normal to feel overwhelmed by sorrow. Understanding how we grieve and finding ways to cope with your loss will bring you closer to the day when memories of your loyal friend bring smiles instead of tears.

We love our pets and consider them family members. We celebrate their birthdays, confide in them, and carry their pictures in our wallets. Our dogs provide companionship, acceptance, emotional support, and unconditional loyalty and love during the time that they share with us. If you understand and come to terms with this bond between us and our dogs, you have taken the first step toward coping with pet loss: knowing that it is okay to grieve when your pet dies.

COPING STRATEGIES

Don't try to stuff your feelings or minimize your grief. Not allowing yourself to go through the grieving process can be detrimental to your overall emotional as well as physical health. Allow yourself to take time off from work to make necessary arrangements.

It's okay to think and talk about your pet. Remembering the antics, favorite toys, and activities of your pet brings back happy memories and allows you to grieve. Research has shown that positive and happy thoughts cause chemicals to be released in your brain and body that are soothing and relaxing.

You don't have to "get over it" right away. Rather than "getting over" the death of your pet, think about how you can learn to live with the loss as well as the changes in your life due to the loss. Change isn't always a bad thing. Once you move to this phase, your grief will start to resolve and you can reflect on your relationship with fewer painful emotions.

Obtain closure. Every pet owner needs to say good-bye their own way. Some pet owners choose to have a full burial in a pet cemetery, others choose to cremate and keep the ashes in a special urn, and others choose a more symbolic route such as writing a story or a poem about the animal. There are a number of "in memoriam" websites for dogs where you can create a loving tribute to your dog. Whatever suits your relationship with your pet and your needs is okay. Sometimes making a donation in your pet's name is enough.

Seek additional support. If you experience prolonged grief, episodes of crying, difficulty sleeping, impairment in social or physical functioning, or inability to concentrate, you may be experiencing pathological grief and should seek help from a mental health professional. Consider looking into pet loss groups as well as pet loss hotlines

153

Barks in Different Languages

WHETHER YOU'RE expressing it as "woof, woof"; "wo, wo", "; or "voff, voff," the way we mimic a dog's bark probably doesn't translate to the dogs themselves. Study up on these "bark" equivalents before you travel overseas. Foreign dog owners will be impressed that you know the language, even if their dogs think you're speaking nonsense.

Albanian: *ham, ham*

Arabic: *hau, hau; how how*

Cantonese Chinese: *wo, wo*

Catalan: *bup, bup*

Czech: *haf, haf*

Danish: *vov, vov (or waf, waf/woef woef)*

English: *woof, arf, bow-wow*

Estonian: *auh, auh*

Finnish: *hau, hau (or vuh, vuh)*

French: *ouah, ouah (or ouaf, ouaf)*

German: *wau, wau (pronounced "vow")* or *wuff, wuff*

Greek: *ghav, ghav*

Hebrew: *hav, hav*

Icelandic: *voff, voff*

Indonesian: *guk, guk*

Irish: *amh, amh*

Italian: *bau, bau*

Japanese: *wan, wan*

Mandarin Chinese: *wang, wang*

Korean: *meon, meon (or mong, mong)*

Lebanese: *haw, haw*

Nigeria (Calabar area): *wai, wai*

Norwegian: *voff, voff*

Polish: *how, how*

Portuguese: *au, au*

Russian: *gav, gav*

Serbian: *av, av*

Spanish: *gau, gau*

Swedish: *vov, vov*

Tamil: *bou, bou (rhymes with how, how)*

Thai: *hoang, hoang*

Trick: Flip for a Treat

IF YOUR DOG knows the commands "Stay," "Hold it," "Leave it," and a release word ("Okay!"), he can learn how to flip a treat off his nose. The fun, circuslike trick is a show-off move for your pooch. Here's how to teach him to balance a treat on his nose and flip it. (Eating it is the easy part.)

1. Coax your dog into a sit-and-stay position. Reward him with praise.

2. Lay a flat dog cookie or bone-shaped treat on the flat bridge of his nose. Instruct your well-mannered dog to continue staying. At the same time, reward him with a tasty treat—cut-up hot dogs are a favorite. Leave the cookie on his nose for 5 seconds, then remove it.

3. Gradually increase the time you leave the cookie on his nose, constantly praising and rewarding him with a hot dog or a tasty treat when you remove the cookie.

4. Your dog will naturally "flip" his nose to try to remove the cookie. Immediately click your clicker or say "Yes" to show your approval for the "wait" and "flip." Reward with a treat. Gradually build the cue "flip" into the routine. (See "Bow Down" in Day 226 for a similar example of multistage trick training.)

5. Eventually, you will be able to place a cookie on your dog's nose; tell him to "leave it" and allow it to sit there for a while, then instruct him to "flip" the cookie off his nose—and eat it.

Tidy Up! Training Tip

JUST AS WE teach our kids to pick up their toys, you can teach your dog to pick up his toys, too. Follow these easy steps and soon your dog will be wagging his tail every time you ask him if he wants to pick up his toys.

1. Place the toy box in a designated area. Once you decide on a location for the box, don't change the toy box location for a while.

2. Bring your dog to his box with a favorite toy, and give him the toy.

3. Snap your fingers over the box. When your dog leans his head over the box, tell him, "Drop, tidy up," and offer him a treat at the same time. This should encourage your dog to drop the toy to accept the treat.

4. Repeat the drop-in-the-box step four times.

5. Repeat these sessions once or twice a day.

6. As your dog catches on, try giving him the toy farther and farther from his box.

7. After he catches on to this step, go near the box again, but this time leave the toy on the floor and encourage your dog to pick it up.

8. You can increase the number of toys he picks up. Start by rewarding only a two-toy drop. Then initiate a three-toy drop, then four. Soon he will be wanting to play this game every day.

Human Holidays, Doggy Disasters: Fireworks

FIREWORKS CAN BE very scary for our dogs. For any holiday where there will likely be fireworks nearby, whether a big commercial display or a few firecrackers in the neighborhood, plan to keep your dog indoors. Try to leave a radio or TV on louder than the fireworks outside, especially if you are not going to be home. Before festivities begin, take your dog on a long walk or engage her in a vigorous play session so she is tired once the fireworks show begins. You may also consider giving her calming aid tabs, which are available at pet stores. Read dosage information carefully and discuss this option with your vet first.

During fireworks, keep an eye out for signs of stress. Look for the three P's: panting, pooping, and pacing. Loss of hair, hiding under the bed or couch, not wanting to go on walks, and not eating for more than one day are other signs of stress, as are excessive licking and behavioral changes, such as constant tail chasing. These behaviors are normal in stressful situations, but if they last more than a day, seek your vet's advice.

Pool Safety

YOUR BACKYARD POOL is center stage during summer months. The whole family enjoys weekend afternoons lounging by the water, grilling out on the patio, and splashing around in the water. Naturally, your dog wants in on this action. Whether or not your dog is a good swimmer (learn to teach him in Day 241), take these poolside precautions so the area is secure for your pooch.

Supervise. This goes without saying, but do not ever allow your dog to enter the pool area without you.

Fence in the pool area. Aside from privacy benefits, a self-closing fence will keep puppies (and children) out of the vicinity when there is no supervision. Your backyard may consist of a fence-within-a-fence if you have fencing along your property line and around the perimeter of the pool. This setup will allow you peace of mind, and your dog the freedom to enjoy the backyard (poolside or not) safely.

Mark the exit. Your dog will easily recognize the exit if you mark it with a flag, flowerpot, or lawn ornament of some kind. If your dog becomes disoriented for any reason, he'll know where to leave the pool area.

Install a pool alarm. There are various alarms on the market. Some include collars that are programmed so a device sounds when the dog enters or exits the pool area. These tools are handy if your backyard has a pond or creek that isn't fenced in. With an alarm, you'll know when your dog is near water and you can supervise him.

Dog Tails: Edward the Ultimate Retriever

OUR GOLDEN RETRIEVER, Edward, loved to please and be rewarded. He would do anything for a biscuit and a rub behind the ears. He was also very obedient and receptive to training. Our family depended on Edward to fetch the morning paper from the box at the end of our driveway, and he took this job seriously. That's because when he returned with the paper, he always earned a tasty biscuit. At the time, we lived in a new neighborhood and our home was one of the first built. As neighbors' houses were completed and more families moved in, Edward continued his morning routine of gathering our paper. But he became acutely aware that more mailboxes were going up, and there were more papers—which translated into golden opportunities for more treats.

Several days in a row, Edward left our front door in the morning to retrieve the paper and returned dragging several paper bags with his teeth. Edward figured the more papers, the more biscuits. Smart dog! We returned the papers one by one to our neighbors' homes. Through Edward's "collection services," we gradually met people who moved to our block.

Your Dog Is Not Human

MOST DOG LOVERS treat their pets like children. When they grow older, their dogs become best friends—companions. Dogs are loyal, they listen, and they're always on your side. You can pour your heart out to your dog, and he won't tell a soul. If you feel down in the dumps, he'll lick you on the face and wag his tail, fetch his ball for some playtime, and before you know it you're laughing and romping around the backyard together. Dogs curl up at your feet while you read quietly, and they're right by the door waiting for you when you get home. If only people could be so considerate and attentive! But the fact is, dogs are not human.

We tend to project human values on our dogs. We interpret their sympathetic looks as though they are reading our minds. In reality, dogs do not feel the way humans do. They do not hold grudges, and they do not understand why you worked late and did not feed them at normal dinner hour.

Dogs do respond to your emotional needs because they have keen senses. However, projecting human emotions onto your dog can interfere with training efforts and prevent you from really connecting with what your dog needs to be happy in your household.

When training a dog, it is critical to understand what is really going on in your dog's head. Dogs are motivated by attention, treats, and play. Dogs love to please. They work to gain your approval, and your companionship is just as important to them as theirs is to you. Do not allow contrived emotions to derail training efforts. Concentrate on house training, teaching your dog basic commands, and socializing your dog so he can be the best friend and respectful housemate you've always wanted.

Stop for Traffic

WHETHER YOU LIVE in a suburban neighbor-hood or on a busy main thoroughfare, the most important term you can teach your dog while walking is "wait" (or "stay"). The choice in terms is up to you. Begin this behavior by training your dog during walks to stop when you stop.

Stop walking: Prompt your dog to "heel." Then you stop. The dog should "heel" next to you. When your dog obeys, give him a little snack or lavish him with praise. Remember to take turns rewarding with treats and praise. You don't want your dog to expect a snack every time he stops on a walk, which could be frequently.

Stop at intersections: As you practice "heel" and your dog becomes accustomed to stopping when you walk, advance to teaching your dog to always stop and "wait" at an intersection. When you approach a curb, slow down your pace and stop walking. Your dog should also stop. Look at your dog and say "Wait." You look both ways for cars. Then make eye contact with your dog again and say "Let's go" or "Okay"—whatever release term you use consistently. Repeating this exercise at every intersection will teach your dog to automatically stop, wait, look, and then cross the street with you.

On the run: The "wait" command is also critical if your dog runs out the door unexpectedly. If you call out "Wait," he should stop immediately so you can bring him back to a safe zone. You train this safely indoors, first asking your dog to "sit," then rewarding his success. Then ask your dog to "wait." Do not make a move. Once your dog begins to stir, say "Good boy," and give him a treat. He will recognize that waiting earned him a treat. Gradually increase the wait time period. Then, try the exercise outside in the backyard while your dog is on leash or tethered to a lead. If you call out "wait" and your dog does not respond, as long as he is within eye shot and safe, do not bolt after him. He will think you are playing chase. Approach him slowly, calling his name in an enticing manner, as if your pocket is full of treats just for him. If he is truly on the run, call neighbors from a cell phone if you have one on hand and alert them so you can increase your odds of bringing him home safely.

When Is Your Daily Walk Too Long?

WALKING WITH YOUR dog can be great exercise for both of you. But do you know when it is time to stop walking?

Consider your dog's size, age, and health when planning your walks. Large, younger dogs will be able to walk much farther and much faster than small, older dogs. A dog that has been sick will likely be slower and have less stamina, too.

When walking with her on a summer day, avoid the hottest part of the day by going early in the morning or in the evening. She will get warm quickly if it is a hot, humid day, just as you would. A dark-coated dog will heat up more rapidly than a light-coated dog, because her coat will not reflect the sunlight back but will absorb the heat.

Some signs that it is time to stop walking are when she begins to lag behind and isn't stopping to sniff the flowers or pee on a fire hydrant. If she begins to pant or drool, or if she walks off the path and tries to find some shade, these are indicators that she is too hot and it is time to stop the walk.

In the wintertime, a dog has to expend more energy to keep her body warm, which may leave less energy for a long walk. A dog coat can help keep her warm and avoid hypothermia. Still, she should not be kept out too long in very cold weather, as she could develop breathing problems.

Keep an eye on your dog when going for your daily walk, and take her home if any of these signs develop.

Human Holidays, Doggy Disasters:
Candy Overdose

HOLIDAYS MEAN LOTS of treats and buffets, family gatherings, and opportunities for your dog to snatch a few of those goodies set out on the table for guests to enjoy. We tend to let our guard down during the holidays, when the environment at home goes from calm to chaos. Meanwhile, our dogs treat themselves to a potential case of food poisoning.

Raisins and chocolate (see Day 323) are toxic to dogs in any quantity. Sugar in large quantities isn't good for your dog, either. Taffy can get stuck in dogs' teeth, and hard candies can get lodged in their throats and block the airway. Keep all candy away from the family dog— no exceptions.

You can still treat your dog with healthy alternatives. Many doggy bakeries and pet stores sell holiday cookies for dogs; get some extras to hand out to any dogs that visit your home.

Tether Safety

A TETHER IS a stake-and-lead device that allows your dog 360 degrees of freedom while being leashed to a stable anchor driven into the ground. Tethering your dog is helpful if you are both outdoors, your dog is not trained off-leash, and you want to allow your dog some romp time without you holding on to him. Never tie up your dog and leave him outdoors without supervision.

There are several reasons why. First, your dog is vulnerable and cannot run or protect himself should an intruder (animal or person) enter the yard. Second, there is always the chance—even if it is minute—that a driver or passerby with bad intentions could steal your pup. Pet-nappings are not unheard of, and unfortunately, some people make it easy by tying up and leaving their dog in the yard. Third, your dog can get into all sorts of mischief while you are not watching: eating potentially dangerous plants and flowers, digging, barking incessantly. A tether can be dangerous if an excited dog that doesn't yet know his boundaries sprints off to capture a squirrel and gets yanked back by the lead. He can snap his neck, sprain his back, or break a leg.

Tethers are ideally used in a protected area of the yard within sight of your supervision. They can be perfectly safe and allow the dog to spend enjoyable "free" time outdoors without being leashed by your side. However, take precautionary measures and carefully examine the area your dog will be roaming before you stake the tether into the ground. (Position it so that the dog cannot reach flower beds and other no-dog zones.) A tether is not a dogsitter. Always, always watch your dog while he is outside.

Careful with That Collar

Choke chains and pinch collars are appropriate for walking and training dogs only. Replace the choke chain with a traditional collar when tethering your dog, or while your dog is at rest. Dogs have hanged themselves by pulling too hard while tethered, or even snagging the collar on something in the house. These collars should only be in use when your dog is taking orders from you.

Volunteer Opportunities to Help Dogs

YOUR LOCAL ANIMAL shelter is a terrific place to volunteer and make a difference in the community and in the lives of many dogs. There is much more than paperwork involved in these volunteer opportunities. If you are an outgoing person, you can greet potential dog owners, and as a dog lover you'll have no trouble voicing the benefits of pet ownership. If you cannot commit to a regular volunteer schedule, sign up to help with one-time events, such as adoption days. Consider your skills and how they can help the shelter: writers can create press releases, designers can help with the website, business-minded individuals may lend a hand with bookkeeping tasks, and so on. You won't know unless you ask what kind of services the shelter needs!

Here are just a few things most shelters use volunteers for:

- Walking and playing with dogs
- Updating the shelter's website
- Taking photographs of new dogs up for adoption
- Writing articles for and/or designing the shelter's newsletters
- Greeting visitors
- Helping out on adoption days or at adoption events
- Bathing dogs
- Transporting dogs
- Cleaning cages
- Filling water bowls
- Helping with administrative tasks, such as recordkeeping, bookkeeping, and answering phones
- Working at fund-raising drives and events
- Fostering dogs

All of these jobs help keep a shelter working so that more dogs can be helped. And volunteering benefits you, too, by introducing yourself to new people and dogs, learning new skills, gaining experience, and building confidence in yourself. Call your local shelter and see how your skills match up to their needs.

165

Why Do Dogs Chase Cars?

ON A LEISURELY walk on your quiet street, a ruby red two-seater convertible buzzes up the street. Your dog goes nuts and breaks out into a full sprint, pulling you right along with her. It's not the sports car, nor is it the color red. On high-traffic roads, your dog pays little attention to the hum of cars constantly coming and going. That scenario lacks the "chase" effect; constant traffic is less antagonistic to a dog.

Not all dogs chase cars, but those who do treat it like a sport. And they probably chase kids on bikes, cats, small animals, and other dogs. (Sound familiar?) So why the heated chase? Why the freak attack when a single automobile whizzes by?

Even socialized, well-behaved dogs have a natural instinct to some extent to hunt down prey. Predatory instincts are hardwired into their brain. Some dogs chase down cars for territorial reasons: They view the car as an intruder. You should discourage this "prey drive" and reinforce positive play as a way for your dog to release "chasing" energy.

Well-adjusted dogs playing together express prey drive by playing tag. They take turns being "it." The fun is not in reeling in the catch—the thrill is in the chase. Throw a Frisbee or ball with your dog so she can exert that pent-up prey-driven energy. Then when you go for walks, she'll be less interested in chasing cars because she knows she can get her "fix" at home during play.

Posture-Perfect Feeder

AN ERGONOMIC FEEDER ensures that dogs won't strain their necks while reaching for food. Small breeds can comfortably dine from bowls set on the floor, but larger or elderly dogs may need a lift. Rather than purchasing a pricey stilted feeder, make your own using a potting bench. You choose the paint, the bowls, and the base for this custom feeder.

MATERIALS

2 stainless-steel dog bowls with rims

Paper and pencil

Wooden potting bench

Jigsaw

Sandpaper

Rule

Nontoxic paint

1. *Trace and cut out bowl pattern.* Place two dog dishes on the paper and trace around the bottom perimeter of each. Cut out the two circles to use as a pattern for holes to be cut in the wooden bench.

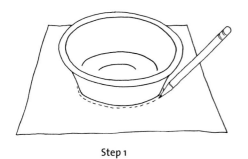

Step 1

2. *Place the cutouts on the bench and trace.* Use a ruler to be sure the circles are equidistant from the edges of the bench. Allow at least 4 inches (10 cm) between the bowl holes for spillage; otherwise water will slop into the food dish, and vice versa.

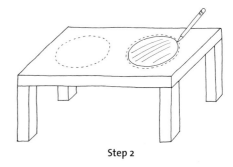

Step 2

3. *Saw circle shapes.* Using a jigsaw to cut through the bench, cut along the outside of traced circles, cutting ¾ inch (2 cm) beyond the traced line.

4. *Sand rough edges.* Concentrate on the areas just sawed, and smooth over the entire wooden structure, to remove rough patches and establish a polished surface for painting.

5. *Decorate with nontoxic paint.* Be creative with color and design. You can draw shapes on the bench or even paint your dog's name on the feeder. You can sponge-paint the surface for a faux-finish look, or use an antique painting kit for shabby chic appeal. Be sure the piece is fully dry before you allow your dog near it.

6. *Set the stainless-steel bowls into the holes.* The rim of bowls will prevent their sliding through. You may consider attaching no-slip adhesive pads underneath the four corners of the base so the feeder sits securely on a slippery kitchen floor.

Creating Your Own Dog Run

A DOG RUN IS a dedicated, safe place for your dog to exercise, and you can train your dog to use only this area to do his business. You don't need a lot of room to set one up; a small side yard will do, if that's all you have.

Find a suitable place that you can fence in on all sides. If you can site it against a wall or an existing fence, you won't have to buy as much fencing to enclose it. The area should be big enough for your dog to play in; a space 6 feet (1.8 m) wide and 12 feet (3.7 m) long is a good size for a medium- to large-size dog. It should have some shade areas (if you don't have natural shade there, you can create some with an awning or other structure). A nearby water faucet to make cleanup easy is a good idea, too.

Before beginning, check with your city's building department and your neighborhood association, if you have one. Many areas have restrictions on the styles and heights of fences that can be used, and some require permits. Once you're cleared, arrange to have the fence and a gate installed.

Measure the total area of the run. You'll need these measurements for purchasing materials at your local home improvement center. Consult with someone in the building materials department there, who will help you figure out how much of each material you need for the area you're covering.

MATERIALS

Peat moss to cover the area to a depth of 1 inch (2.5 cm)

Ground lime powder, approximately 10 ounces (280 g) per square foot of area

Pea gravel to cover the area to a depth of 2 inches (5 cm)

Urine sticks, one for each dog (available at pet stores)

Nontoxic dog run cleaner (available at pet stores)

1. Cover the the area with 1 inch (2.5 cm) of peat moss.

2. Sprinkle lime over the peat moss at the rate of 10 ounces (280 g) per square foot. The lime helps with odor absorption and drainage.

3. Lay pea gravel down over the peat moss and lime to a depth of 2 inches (5 cm).

4. Place the urine sticks where you want them. They will encourage your dog to urinate on them, not elsewhere in the yard.

5. Wash down the dog run at least once a week with nontoxic dog run cleaner to help eliminate germs and odors.

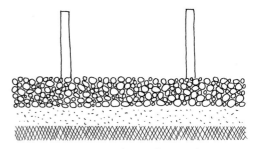

Cross section of ground materials

If your dog must have grass to do his business, by all means get some grass to put in your run to help give her incentive. However, note that with use the grass dies and must be replaced. Gravel is much easier to clean and keep fresh.

Human Holidays, Doggy Disasters: Costumes!

MANY PEOPLE DRESS up their dogs for Halloween and other holidays. You can purchase a costume at your local pet store or online at any number of websites dedicated to togs for dogs. Even special "hair" dyes are available for your pet's coat, if you want to change their hair color to match the festivities.

When buying a costume for your dog, take him with you if you can to fit the costume; this saves a return trip to the store if the costume doesn't fit. You want it to go from the dog's neckline just below the collar, down to his rump, just above where his tail starts. Make sure it fits snugly—not too tight and not too loose. You can also choose a costume that doesn't fit the whole animal for those dogs who won't stand for a full-body costume. You want him to be comfortable in it so he won't chew at it to get out of it. Also keep in mind how the costume hangs around your dog's stomach: You want to make sure that there is enough clearance for him to relieve himself if he will be in the costume for any length of time.

Check for and clip any loose strings or trim that your dog might be tempted to chew on. If the costume comes with a mask, make sure the eyeholes are large enough for him to see through. If they aren't, use scissors to make them larger.

Regardless of the costume you choose, it's a good idea to walk your dog before getting him into his costume. And don't forget to take pictures for your dog scrapbook or journal!

If you are taking your dog out trick-or-treating with your children, take some extra treats along for him. Be sure not to plan a route that is too long for him, and head home if the stimulation from all those children in costumes becomes overwhelming.

Stopping the Front Door Dash

AN OPEN FRONT door is a ticket to freedom for dogs who see the ready exit as an exciting opportunity to explore the outdoors. If your dog makes a habit of scooting out the front door to greet the pizza man and then follows him to the car, or bolts out the entry as soon as you crack it open to greet a guest, you should teach her that the open door is "no big deal." Dogs that escape in a frenzy can be hit by cars, attacked by other dogs, or lost. Prevent the behavior with this desensitizing exercise:

• Expose your puppy or new dog early on to the door opening and closing. Do it twenty times a day during times when traffic is light.

• Ask friends to knock on the door, and enter and exit your home without fanfare.

• Do not egg on your dog by excitedly saying, "Daddy's home!" or "Friends are here!" Remember, the front door is no big deal.

Eventually, your dog will grow used to the front door activity. If desensitizing is ineffective despite your best efforts, use baby gates to create a dog-safe zone in your house so she cannot access opening doors.

Why Do Dogs Wag Their Tails?

BARKING AND TAIL wagging are the two ways our dogs communicate with us and other dogs.

Welcome home: Broad, medium to fast sweeping motions. The happier he is, the faster his tail wags.

Curiosity: Mostly horizontal but not stiff. This wag is to signal, "I am interested, I would like to get to know you, but I am not challenging you or being aggressive."

A challenge: When the tail is fully horizontal, a duel is offered up to another dog or a human.

Leader of the pack: The tail is held up and over his back.

Relaxed: The tail is lowered, but not between the legs.

In fear for his life: The tail is between his legs and shaking.

Top dog: Tail up but not vertical lets you knows he is confident and in control.

Confusion: Slow wagging signifies confusion over whether he is encountering a friend or a foe.

Aggression: A bristling tail signifies aggressive intent.

Don't mess with me: The tail is held high and stiff and wagging fast.

Don't be fooled by the smile: An excited tail wagging combined with aggressive signals say, "I may be friendly to some dogs and some people, but not all the time." Do not trust.

Home Alone for the Night

IF YOU LEAVE home for one night or several, you must make arrangements for your dog. Some options include boarding him at a kennel, taking him to a reliable friend or family member's home, or leaving your dog in his own environment and enlisting in a pet sitter for walks and feeding. Not all dogs can handle being home alone. Before you cancel the kennel reservations, consider the pros and cons of leaving your dog in an empty house.

Home is a sanctuary for your dog. He has lots of cozy sleeping spots, toys, and family members to play with him. He expects you to leave for work daily, but you always come home. When you do not return for dinner, walktime, or prime-time television/chew bone hour, he gets nervous. It's dark. No one is home. Sure, a friend stopped by and filled up the food bowl, but where are his mom and dad? The night ticks by, morning comes, and your dog is wondering what the deal is. Still no one home.

Some dogs can handle this independence and are happier in their own home than being boarded at a kennel. If you have more than one dog, leaving the "pack" at home may be preferable because they can stay in their own environment and keep each other company. Some dogs simply don't mind if their owners are gone, and they know that the family will return eventually. (See Day 85.) If this describes your dog, enlist in a reliable pet sitter to visit your home regularly while you are gone. Be sure this person knows your dog's routine, and prepare a dog care binder (see Day 25) containing vet contact information and other emergency numbers.

The decision to leave your dog home alone during the night depends on your dog's personality, expectations for a "normal day," and the all-important trust factor. Never leave a puppy home overnight. First be sure your dog is potty trained and understands his boundaries at home.

Being a Good Neighbor

GOOD NEIGHBORS MAKE strong communities, and part of being a good neighbor is making sure you and your dog are considerate of others living nearby. If you live in a condominium or apartment complex, your close quarters demand attention to dog obedience. That includes teaching your dog to not bark excessively, picking up after her, and not allowing her to run loose or trespass on neighbors' property. This is tough if their property is within arm's reach of your front door—but it is possible with training.

Basic obedience training will teach your dog to walk quietly at your side on a leash and to not lunge at or jump on strange people or other dogs she may meet in the neighborhood. A barking dog can annoy your neighbors. (See Day 142 for dealing with barking.)

Many communities have "pooper scooper" laws that require owners to clean up after their dogs. Even if your community doesn't have a law, cleaning up after your pet is still a good idea and reflects your consideration for your neighbors.

A fenced yard is the best way to keep your dog from soiling or digging in a neighbor's yard. If you don't have a fence, use a tie-out. Two of the most popular are a swivel stake or a tree trolley. Swivel stakes are anchored in the ground; tree trolleys fasten to a tree but allow a dog to run around the tree without the chain becoming tangled.

Dogs should wear collars with an ID tag as well as have microchip or tattoo identification. Proper ID will enable someone to contact you if your pet wanders far from home.

Exercise and Your New Dog

IF YOU ARE THINKING about going on an active outing with your puppy or dog, there are a few things you should consider. First, puppies require frequent spurts of exercise, and you should take care that their play and walking is limited to soft surfaces at first, such as grass, dirt, or even your home's carpet. A puppy's tissues are still soft and his bones are still growing. Remember that too much exercise can be stressful on your young pup's growing body. As your puppy matures, he will be able to handle more vigorous exercise on a number of surfaces, including hard pavement. What if you walk your dog on the sidewalk? Just be careful and mind your puppy's young joints. A short up-and-down trek in front of your home is enough to get your puppy used to his leash. Then engage in a fun play session on the soft grass or indoors.

A dog's size and breed affect the level of activity he needs: A large Doberman will require more exercise than a petite Lhasa Apso. Here are some guidelines for the right amount of play for a few common breeds at the puppy stage.

Toy dogs generally need less activity. Approximately 5 minutes of interactive play a few times daily will suffice.

Terriers typically require medium to high activity levels. Allow 10 to 20 minutes of interactive play, two or three times daily.

Retrievers and scent hounds are high-energy dogs. They need 15 to 20 minutes of interactive play, two or three times daily.

Be sure to give your puppy enough playtime to ensure his health and happiness, but don't overdo it.

Holiday Overeating

HOLIDAYS ARE JUST the time to enjoy a few culinary indulgences, and while you're enjoying the pumpkin pie, you can share a little of the feast with your dog.

However, dogs can overindulge, just like people, so be sure to limit her holiday mealtime treats to small tastes mixed in with her regular kibble. Be sure your guests know not to feed your dog from the table. Remember that dogs should *never* have chocolate (see Day 158), onions, raisins, or bones from the turkey, and keep alcohol out of her reach, too.

Small bits of lean turkey, duck, or ham make a tasty addition to mealtime. Remove any bones or skin. Top with a little bit of gravy diluted with warm water. Green beans, peas, and carrots in small amounts are all fine for your dog, as are little dollops of mashed or sweet potatoes—just a teaspoon or so. Avoid stuffing, since most stuffing has onions in it. It's a good idea to spread these special treats out over a couple of days to avoid overfeeding.

When your feast is over, be sure all the food is put away and take out the garbage. The post-Thanksgiving trash can is a big temptation even to dogs who are generally well behaved—all those bones and scraps.

Sanitize Dog "Disposal" Containers

THE "DOO" YOU collect, bag, and dispose of into trash containers is out of sight and mind—until the odor begins to reek, especially in hot weather. There's nothing pretty about poop-scooping, and you'll probably cringe just reading about it. As a dog owner, you are fairly desensitized to the business of cleaning up, but it's not dinner conversation. It's a chore. So we'll keep this entry short and snappy. Write down the following recipe for a super-"doo"per cleaning agent for trash cans where soiled bags are tossed. Clean containers make cleanup and disposal less, should we say, stinky?

MATERIALS

6 cups (1.5 L) very hot water

3 tablespoons (42 g) borax

6 drops tea tree oil

Rubber gloves

Scrub brush

Citronella oil

1. Pour the water into the dirty (empty) trash can.

2. Add the borax and tea tree oil.

3. Wearing rubber gloves, stir the borax mixture and use the brush to scrub the inside of the trash container. Let the mixture sit for 5 minutes.

4. Pour out the mixture into a mulched area or outdoor spot that you do not use for growing plants. (It is not harmful, but it's best not to drench landscaped areas with cleaning substances.)

5. Rinse the trash can with hose water. Finish by adding a few drops of citronella oil to the bottom of the trash can. This will keep the container smelling fresh and deter flies.

Gifting a Dog—Not Always a Joy

A PUPPY FOR Christmas; a Valentine's Day dog for your sweetie; a four-legged, furry birthday surprise for a lonely parent: The joyful recipient will surely thank you profusely for such a *cute* gift! Or not.

Movies portray the rustling box under the Christmas tree, a faint whimpering sound muffled by wrapping, and, perhaps, a wet box corner where the "gift" had an accident. Who wouldn't be thrilled to open this gift? It's a puppy!

What the movies do not show is the child's dissipated excitement a few hours or days later when the puppy messes on the floor and needs to be fed, walked, played with, and trained. An only child may not appreciate the addition of an attention-demanding new "sibling." And the same story goes when older children give their empty-nester parents a dog, figuring their mom and dad surely want to fill the gap left by children who moved out. (The children missed the "freedom, baby!" memo.) Unfortunately, the children often do not ask their parents whether they want to be tethered to their home to care for a puppy. In the early months, puppies can be as much work as babies.

Giving a dog to someone is the equivalent of playing stork and dropping a baby off on that person's front porch. They are now obligated to care for and love that puppy for the rest of the pet's life.

Resist the temptation to give a friend, family member, or spouse the gift of dog ownership unless he or she is fully expecting the "surprise." While your intentions are sincere, the long-term responsibility may not be the type of gift your loved one wants. Many dogs become shelter orphans because their owners could not, or did not want to, fulfill the task of parenting a dog. A dog is a family decision. It's a choice a couple makes together. Dog ownership indeed is a gift—but it certainly is not a last-minute present. If your friend has been talking for years about getting a dog, give him or her a book containing breed information and puppy training tips. Then let the person decide when the time is right to adopt a "baby."

177

Bringing Home a New (Human) Baby

A NEW BABY means a big change in your routine—and in your dog's. It's important that your dog get used to the sights and sounds of a baby before the real one arrives to make the introduction go smoothly.

Expectant parents can bring a baby doll home well before their due date. Cuddling with it and talking to it will help your dog get used to the idea of someone else sharing the attention.

If a friend has a newborn, or even older children, ask if you can bring a tape recorder to her home to record the sounds of baby's crying and children playing and laughing. Play the tape recording several times a day for your dog at least three to four months before you bring home your new baby.

When the baby is born, have someone bring home one of the baby's swaddling blankets for your dog to smell. It helps to have your own personal scent on the blanket, too. The idea is to try to help your dog become familiar with the new baby's scent before they are officially introduced.

On the day you come home with your new baby, have a loved one assist you with the introduction; this will help with blending. Have the friend hold the newborn while Mom and Dad walk in first and greet the dog. Bring the baby in and pass her to Dad. After a few minutes, pass him to Mom.

So long as Mom and Dad still give as much attention to the dog, he will learn to love the baby and accept the new pack order. Don't be surprised if he does something to protect the baby when you least expect it. Congratulations on your newest family addition!

How to Stop Counter Grazers

YOUR DOG IS only a jumper when there is people food involved, and when that food is within a tempting distance of his reach. One whiff of dinner-in-progress and he lurches up onto the counter, front paws on the surface as if he's leaning at a bar waiting for service. That tongue of his extends and he *almost* gets a taste of the pot roast left cooling. Even squat dogs will surprise you with their counter-surfing abilities. Basset Hounds are short, but their long bodies, when in vertical position, are tall enough to give their chops full-on contact with food that's near the edge of the counter.

How do you stop your dog from "shopping" the counter for treats? First, consider your dog's perspective. He doesn't normally jump (you've taught him better), but the rewards can be heavenly if his counter surfing is successful. If he gets a taste of what's out of reach just one time, that success is just enough to keep him coming back for more. Begging at the counter while you prepare meals is annoying, and your dog will be persistent. If your dog is fairly skilled at this sport, and you tend to leave food on the counter unattended, several tasty wins will ingrain the behavior and you'll have a difficult time breaking the habit.

Finally, some advice on preventing counter jumpers, and how to correct the behavior before it gets out of hand.

Prevent it: Defrost frozen meat in the fridge or microwave oven—never leave it on the counter for long periods of time where it will be an easy target. Do not feed your dog morsels of the meal-in-progress. He will think he deserves a snack every time you begin preparing food. If you deny him, he'll jump up to the counter to serve himself. Be careful not to leave food too close to the edge of the counter. Keep the counter clear of food between mealtimes. Ask your family to clean dishes, put away leftovers, and wipe up the crumbs. (Dogs sense even the smallest nibble.)

Correct it: Use clicker training (see Day 359) to teach your dog "down" when he jumps on the counter. Be consistent. Consider purchasing a motion-sensitive alarm that sounds when your dog jumps up to the counter. These are handy for jumpers who conduct countertop investigations while you are gone. Alarms should be used as a part of training, not independently.

Boat Safety for Dogs

SOME DOGS ARE natural swimmers. They'll plunge into the water without coaxing. Other dogs are landlubbers that tiptoe around the smallest puddles during walks. Regardless of your dog's tolerance for swimming, he should always wear a "float coat" on a boat. Dogs that fall overboard accidentally can tire quickly, especially in a strong current. They can drown before you notice they are missing. Shallow water or deep, it doesn't matter.

Boating with your dog is pure enjoyment— bonding on the open water, or lazing around on the deck of a docked vessel. Before you cast off, consider these important safety measures.

• Make sure there is adequate shade for your dog, and ensure that the floor is not too slippery or hot for him to walk on (both common with fiberglass-bottomed boats).

• If you anchor your boat in open waters and let your dog swim, attach a lightweight doggie boat ladder to the diving platform (at the stern). This will make helping your dog out of the water much easier.

• Consider purchasing a boat alarm, which comes with a remote dog collar that sounds if the dog falls overboard.

• Monitor fishing gear. Dogs will smell bait and be tempted to nose through dangerous tackle boxes that contain hooks and other items they can choke on.

See Resources, page 318.

Human Holidays, Doggy Disasters: Christmas

SEVERAL THINGS TYPICAL to the winter holiday season can be dangerous for dogs: the Christmas tree (the needles, the stand, tree preservatives, ornaments, and tinsel), the food (chocolate), and the plants (poinsettia, mistletoe, and pine boughs). These tips will help ensure a safe holiday for the entire family.

TREE

Pine tar from a real Christmas tree is toxic to dogs, and the needles can puncture your dog's intestines if swallowed and not digested. A lightweight stand could easily allow the tree to tip over. Commercial tree preservatives can contain harmful chemicals. Ornaments and tinsel can be hazards, too—what dog wouldn't want to stop and play with all those shiny, dangly things? Broken ornaments and tinsel can be ingested and cause stomach or intestinal problems.

If you can't place your tree in a room your dog can't access, use a sturdy stand and consider adding stones with the water to add weight so he can't knock it over. Use sugar water (about 1 part sugar to 3 parts water) as a tree preservative, rather than chemical solutions, and consider buying a stand with a covered water receptacle. Place delicate and breakable ornaments out of his reach—remembering that dogs will stand on their hind legs to get at something they want—and consider nixing loose tinsel altogether. Keep an eye on your dog and train him to stay away from the tree using a stream of water from a spray bottle or a shake of the penny can (see Day 86) and a firm "No."

FOOD

Remember that chocolate, raisins/grapes, and onions can be deadly to dogs, and follow the same procedures with your holiday food and drink as described in Day 193. Be especially careful with gifts under the tree—it's not uncommon for owners to find presents chewed open when their dog smells chocolate or other treats inside. If you suspect a wrapped gift might contain chocolate, store it somewhere safe until it's time to open presents.

DECORATIVE PLANTS

Poinsettia and mistletoe are poisonous, as are bulbs forced indoors. Keep them out of reach. If your dog seems distressed and you suspect he has gotten into these plants, call your vet immediately.

Recycling and Dog Products

WE ALL KNOW to recycle our own used, discarded items, but have you ever thought about recycling your dog's items? Consider the following:

- When you walk your dog, bring a biodegradable bag to carry dog waste.

- When you shop for dog food and treats, look for items packaged in paper, aluminum, or recyclable plastic, rather than foils.

- Choose dog toys, beds, and clothing made with recycled or sustainable materials, such as hemp, recycled cotton filler, or fleece made from recycled plastic bottles.

- Pay attention to packaging and stay away from nonrecyclable plastics and over packaged items.

- Seek out companies that make a public commitment to the environment by recycling their packaging materials and waste products.

- Walk your dog in your neighborhood if possible, rather than using fossil fuels to drive to a dog park. (An added benefit is that if your dog ever gets loose, your neighbors are more likely to know who her owners are.)

A Travel-Ready Backseat

WHETHER YOU ARE planning a cross-country road trip, a day adventure, or simply running errands around town, you want your pooch to ride safely, comfortably, and securely. Dog kisses are sweet, but not when your 100-pound (45 kg) Golden Retriever horses into the front seat, completely blocking your peripheral vision. When your dog rides shotgun, you risk getting into an accident. (Sure, we're all guilty of allowing our pup to enjoy the prime seat, but it's just not the safe way.)

Thankfully, there are bundles of backseat bedding products on the market to convert your backseat, hatchback, or open trunk area (in minivans, station wagons, and SUVs) into cozy accommodations. No matter the size of your car—surprisingly, the back of a Volkswagen Beetle offers great visibility for a pup on the go—you can outfit the vehicle with a bed.

Assuming your dog is obedient enough to handle not riding in a crate, here are some alternative options.

For backseats: Some doggy seat belts come with a line that secures across the backseat ceiling. A harness and strap attach to the lead and restrain your dog while allowing some freedom to move. Other harnesses attach to existing seat belts or fasten to cargo hooks. A seat cover will protect the upholstery and prevent nails from scratching leather or vinyl. Hammocklike covers create a U-shaped den. Aside from pure comfort, the hammock prevents your pooch from sliding onto the floor if you make a quick stop.

For hatchbacks/trunks: You can purchase custom, quilted, and fleece beds that fit a hatchback or open trunk area in a minivan or SUV. Just as easily, you can measure the area and purchase similar material from a fabric store. You can easily toss these covers into the washing machine. If your dog is prone to accidents or carsickness, first lay down a potty training bedsheet you would purchase for a toddler. On top, layer old towels for comfort.

Introducing a Second Dog into the Family

DOGS RELY EXTENSIVELY on smell, so it helps to introduce the dogs to each other's scent before bringing the new dog home, if possible. Once you have picked out your new dog, bring home a blanket that your new dog has been playing with at the breeder's or the rescue center, and vice versa. Allow each dog to sniff their future sibling's towel. Offer the towel like it is a toy or treat—something special that the dog will want to sniff and love.

When you bring your new dog home, introduce the dogs outdoors—not in the house, where the "older sibling" is in charge. Place the new one in front of your dog gently, and say, "Look! For you!" or a similar cooing phrase. Then, give your dog a treat and praise her. Lead her to believe the new puppy is just for her. This will assure her right away that she is the big sister, and the "alpha" of the two.

The first few days in the home, confine your new puppy to a crate or special room, and be sure to allot special play and feeding times to both your dog and the puppy. They each need their own time with you. Allow your new puppy to adapt to her new surroundings, get used to her bedding, and learn how she fits into the family. Gradually, for a few minutes each day, introduce your first dog to your new addition.

Once your new puppy has adjusted to her crate or special room, your next step is to bring her out on her leash into the main room of your house while your first dog is confined to another room. This gradual introduction to the home is important so your dog does not feel threatened, and your puppy can learn her surroundings and feel comfortable. Let her wander around without the fear of being attacked by the first dog. After about an hour, slowly introduce both dogs. They will show interest in each other; let them smell each other and get to know each other. If you see any aggressive behavior, step in, separate them, and start all over again. If there is no aggressive behavior from either dog, keep a close eye and hopefully you will see the beginning of the bonding process and a lifelong friendship.

Feed each dog separately until you know that they are safe and comfortable with each other. Even after they are comfortable, you should feed them in the same room, but don't set their bowls right next to each other. Talk with your vet for additional suggestions on what to watch for to make this as smooth and easy a transition as possible.

Multiple dogs are no harder to take care of than just one, and you are not only giving another dog a home, you are giving your dog a playmate to help keep him young and an additional outlet for his extra energy.

People Food for Dogs

FEEDING YOUR DOG certain vegetables, proteins, and omega-3 fats can supplement a diet of high-quality kibble. Go ahead and give your dog guilt-free apple slices and carrots—raw or steamed, and cut into bite-size pieces. Dogs love sweet banana, too—when you lop off slices for your morning cereal, save a taste for your pooch.

When feeding your dog healthy people food, follow the same rules of moderation humans should adhere to at mealtime. Introduce new foods slowly. You can give your dog too much of a good thing. Don't feed your dog chicken scraps, fatty meat portions that you rejected from your own plate, or any food with seasonings. Dumping your tenderized steak leftovers (the fatty ones) into your dog's bowl after dinner will not do your pooch any favors.

Following is a list of people food selections that dogs can enjoy, too:

- Banana
- Apple slices
- Carrots, steamed or raw, cut into bite-size pieces
- Plain yogurt
- Cooked chicken, turkey, salmon, liver, or other meat (avoid skin, fat, and sauces/seasonings)
- Steamed green beans
- Hard-boiled egg
- Sardines (bones and skin are fine)
- Peanut or almond butter
- Canned solid pumpkin or cooked butternut squash
- Blueberries
- Baked sweet potato

Summertime Tips

HERE ARE A few simple reminders for you and your dog to have a healthy and fun summer.

- Make time to take your dog to the groomer for his summer haircut or simply to help with the shedding of winter fur. The groomer can help the shedding process along, which means less hair all over your house, and also cut his nails and clean his ears.

- Summer is travel time for many people, so it's a good time for a wellness visit with your vet to make sure your dog is healthy for traveling and to get a health certificate if you need one. Your vet can also advise you about any precautions you should take for potential dangers at your particular destination, such as Lyme disease.

- Most people spend more time outdoors in the summer, which means more opportunity for your dog to wander off and get lost. Check his collar to be sure it's in good shape and his ID tags to make sure they are readable and up to date. If you will be spending time at a summer place, consider having a tag made with that address and contact information, too.

- Fleas and ticks are much more abundant in summer, so be sure to keep up with your dog's flea and tick prevention regimen.

Investing in Pet Insurance

YOUR DOG'S MEDICAL BILLS can really add up, and most owners are not prepared to cover the high cost of veterinary care—especially when emergency procedures are necessary. Because pet insurance is a topic usually discussed when your dog is a puppy, it's easy to discount the importance of coverage and justify that, "Our dog is perfectly healthy!"

But accidents happen. If your dog swallows a tennis ball, you could shell out $2,000 (£1,408) to get it removed (see Murphy the bulldog's story, Days 300–301). Aging dogs may need cancer treatment or expensive medications. Insurance packages are available to cover various kinds of coverage.

Monthly premiums are relatively low, but can vary widely depending on the plan you choose as well as your dog's age, breed, and where you live. Plans range from accident-only to premium plans that include everything from vaccines and wellness exams to chemotherapy and complex surgeries. A few things that are not usually covered are congenital, hereditary, or preexisting conditions. For more information about pet insurance, ask your veterinarian to refer you to reputable providers.

Create a Doggy Drop Spot

HAVE YOU EVER felt that your dog's supplies and accessories were slowly taking over your house? Consider consolidating them in one designated area of the home. A dog drop-spot (or pantry) is a place for all of your dog supplies, from pet food to chew bones and your pooch's important health documents. Keeping everything together in one space—anything from a storage box to an entire room, depending on how much gear you have—will ensure that you can find essentials at a moment's notice. Because you will amass quite a few dog goods, keeping them organized will prevent other storage areas from becoming cluttered. Also, you won't overbuy on pet goods because you will know exactly what inventory is stocked at home. (It's surprising how many bones, toys, treats, and other goodies you go through in a month's time!) A designated dog pantry is also helpful in case of emergency: you'll know exactly where to go to find health documents or veterinarian information.

Now, let's organize your dog pantry. Following are some items you'll want to store in this dedicated space:

- Your dog's first-aid kit (see Day 95)
- Health certificates and medical records, kept in a labeled file folder
- Your dog journal
- Pet food and treats
- A few backup toys—always good to keep them handy in case your aggressive chewer destroys Mr. Squeaky (see Day 129 for revival methods) and needs another diversion
- Chew bones
- An extra leash and collar
- Grooming supplies
- Optional: pet or pet-themed craft supplies

Journal Prompts, Part 4

AS YOU CONTINUE to fill your journal with amusing anecdotes and pet owner insights, consider writing entries on these topics:

- What tricks does your dog perform well? How does he like to show off in front of friends?

- How have you celebrated holidays with your dog? What were your favorite moments about those times?

- Describe the most fearful moment you have experienced with your dog. Did he run away from home? Did he hide for hours before you found him? Has he had a medical emergency? How did you feel when you realized your best friend was in danger? How did that change or develop the owner-dog relationship?

(See Days 41–42, 90–91, and 146–147 for more journal prompts throughout the year.)

Adopting an Older Dog

WHEN YOU ADOPT a dog, you are saving a life; this is especially true of older dogs in shelters. There are many older dogs in shelters who need a good home, and sometimes adopting an older dog can be preferable to rearing a puppy.

Most adult dogs have already had training of some kind, although you may have to give them a refresher course. They have all their shots and have usually already been spayed or neutered, so you won't have those costs to worry about, and a fixed dog will be less likely to wander. They have worked through all of their puppy phases, such as chewing.

People don't always consider adopting an older dog, thinking they may be inheriting someone else's problems. But older shelter dogs are not always problem dogs. An older shelter dog may have been picked up on the street as a stray, or her owner may have died and not had an estate plan for her, or she may have come from a puppy mill. These days shelters and breeders make sure that all the dogs in their care are adoptable.

They are tested for temperament, how they get along with other dogs, how they get along with other species of animals, and how they get along with people. If there is a reason that a dog cannot be adopted for temperament issues, the shelter will bring in a trainer or as a last resort will euthanize her.

When you bring home your adult dog, you will still want to confine her in the beginning, until she gets the hang of being in a new place. Put her bed or crate in a high-traffic area so she gets used to you and doesn't feel abandoned. Get her to the vet within the first week, and let the shelter know if any health problems are found. Most shelters have a return policy that covers health problems or unforeseen behavioral problems.

What better way to start a new chapter of your life than to save another life?

What's Your Dog's Training Type?

BEHAVIORIST TRAINER Kathy Santo asks, "How do you treat yourself after a hard day? Do you indulge in a favorite dessert, buy a new outfit, splurge on a gadget, or is the best reward feedback from your boss that you did an A-1 job?"

If you'd like a fancy dinner out, you're a "treat" personality. Those who splurge on a gadget or perhaps a new lipstick are "toy" people. And if nothing pleases you more than lavish compliments, you're a "praise" responder.

Now, consider what personality type applies to your dog. Does he go for the biscuit or chew toy? Or does he want to crawl into your lap for special attention? You're thinking: All of the above! But narrow the choice to just one. What reward does he value the most? By tuning in to his favorite reward, training becomes more productive.

Think about it this way: If you know you'll earn dinner out at your favorite spot—and you could take or leave that shiny new gadget—then you'll be sure you do what it takes to get that fabulous meal. If the gadget is your boss's thank-you and you are preoccupied with other projects, you may not bother to do the work to earn the reward. Same goes for your dog and those training commands.

So think about it; what does your dog *really* want? Make that his grand prize, and he'll work harder for you during training sessions.

What to Expect from a Doggy Daycare

MANY DOGS ARE left home alone during the day while their owners go to work. Some dogs adjust well to the alone time and find constructive ways to keep busy. Depending on the dog's age and the setup at home, he may have access through a doggy door to a fenced-in backyard and, if he is trustworthy, the run of the house. But not all dogs can handle this freedom—or the eight-hour stretch of independence. Dogs who miss their owners' company say so by chewing furniture, barking nonstop, messing in the house when they know better, or climbing up on forbidden couches and beds.

If you can't adjust your schedule, you must change the circumstance at home to set your dog up for success. Many doggy daycare facilities are cage-free, safe, and stimulating environments for dogs. A caring staff supervises play, and your dog will come home well exercised, fed, and socialized. Usually, daycare facilities contain a large play room with toys, even couches, agility "playground" sets, and areas for dogs to rest and have quiet time. Dogs should be separated by size, and puppies should not run with the big dogs. (Ask about this when you visit the facility.) The daily fee will vary, depending on where you live and the facility's amenities.

Some questions to ask the doggy daycare manager before enrolling your pet:

- Is there a vet on premises or close by, in case of emergency?
- Do you have separate playrooms for big and small dogs?

- What water source is used for drinking, and how often does staff refresh water bowls?
- Are playroom floors cement? (Dogs can rip up padded floors.)
- Are all dogs evaluated for aggression?
- Do you have proof that all dogs received shots before their stay at the daycare?
- Do you have Web cameras? (This is a perk rather than a necessity, but it is fun to watch your dog at play while you are at work.)
- Do you provide grooming and/or private training services? (These are conveniences, not essentials.)

Not all dogs respond well to a daycare environment. If your dog is timid or aggressive, the group play environment is not beneficial for your animal or others in the daycare. Although daycare can be rewarding social time for many dogs, the experience can be damaging if you force into daycare a dog that is not comfortable in rather lively circumstances. Consider your dog's personality carefully before making the daycare choice.

189

When is Vomiting a Cause for Concern?

AN OCCASIONAL UPCHUCK is completely normal. Isolated, infrequent episodes of vomiting can be due to swallowing rawhide (this does not agree with every dog's stomach; see Day 94) or drinking too much water too quickly. You can generally chalk the occasion up to the old "input-output" rule. What a dog puts in her stomach is not always pretty, and nastiness occasionally needs to come out.

WHEN TO WORRY

Is your dog pacing or restless? Is she panting or breathing inconsistently? These mannerisms generally indicate pain and could be an indication of bloat. Bloat occurs most commonly in large breed or deep-chested dogs. Call a vet immediately if your dog shows these symptoms or continues to throw up. If your dog collapses because of sudden loss of strength, the fall might indicate loss of consciousness. The cause might be heatstroke or any number or ailments that you should rely on a veterinarian to identify. If in doubt, call the vet.

CLEANUP

Sometimes your dog's vomit is bright yellow, and other times it is all saliva. That bright yellow is coloration from stomach acid. Clean up vomit by first removing all liquid by blotting with a paper towel. Do not wipe; press towels into the carpet (or hard floor surface) and allow the towel to absorb the moisture. Create a paste with 1 tablespoon (15 g) borax, ½ teaspoon (2.5 ml) lemon juice, and ½ teaspoon (2.5 ml) water. Allow this mixture to sit in a bowl for 10 minutes so it forms a thick paste. Then, rub the paste into the stain. Follow with cold water and repeat if necessary.

TEA FOR TOTO

Peppermint tea is an old remedy for upset stomachs. Brew a strong cup of tea, *let it cool,* and serve small portions (serve ¼ cup [60 ml] at a time). to calm your dog's stomach. Or, turn to an old human standby: Pepto-Bismol (the trade name for bismuth subsalicylate). Call your vet for advice on dosage.

Dosage Requirements

Give your dog an oral dose of 3 percent hydrogen peroxide (see dosage at right) by using an oral syringe or turkey baster, or mix it with a small amount of milk. If your dog does not vomit within 15 minutes, you can repeat the procedure up to three times, waiting 15 minutes between doses. Take your dog to the veterinary hospital in the process. (Put a towel and an all-natural cleaning solution in your car to manage upsets en route.)

WHEN TO INDUCE VOMITING

If your dog swallows a toxic substance, you may need to induce vomiting. Always call your veterinarian or the poison control hotline first because in some instances, inducing vomiting can be dangerous. Also know that inducing vomiting is a quick solution that will buy you time until you arrive at the animal hospital; it is not a cure. Never induce vomiting if the toxic substance is caustic (bleach, cleansers), sharp, or if the dog shows signs of lethargy, convulsions, difficulty breathing, seizures, shock, uncoordination, or unconsciousness.

If you observe none of these characteristics, with your vet/poison control's blessing, you can induce vomiting to clear your dog's system of the harmful substance. Never use syrup of ipecac. It is no longer advised by veterinary professionals.

Dosage Ratio

For every 10 pounds (4.5 kg) of body weight: administer 1 to 2 teaspoons (5 to 10 ml) of 3 percent hydrogen peroxide

Dogs and Construction:
When You Are Remodeling

HOME REPAIRS, construction, and redecorating are stressful for the entire family. You may be microwaving dinner for the family in the basement or sleeping on the couch, and your dog will notice that things just are not normal at home. That's especially true if you must shift his eating area or sleeping spot during renovations. By anticipating your dog's needs, you can help him get through the upheaval of home repairs—and be just as happy in your redone home.

Renovations can require lots of outside help, and that means people entering and exiting your home—potentially leaving doors or gates open. To be safe, keep your dog in an enclosed area during construction: a "safe" bedroom or area of the home that is not being impacted by change. Equip that space with your dog's favorite blanket and toys—to instill a sense of security. Never put a frightened dog in an area with a large window, as he might try to break through the window to avoid noise.

After the workers leave for the day, your dog—like your children—still needs supervision. There may be sharp tools, nails and screws, paint and paint remover, wood preservatives, or other harmful items lying around, or a wall or refinished floor may need time to dry thoroughly. Scour the work-in-progress zone of your house for potential hazards, and aim to contain your dog in untouched areas so you can assure his safety.

Scrapings or dust from the removal of lead-based paint presents another hazard; dogs can get lead poisoning, too. If possible, have the paint professionally removed and keep your dog away from the area. Be certain that all flaking paint or paint dust is promptly removed.

When bare wires are exposed, your dog can get shocked or even electrocuted. Close off any rooms with bare wires.

If your construction project is only a one-day job, get your dog out of the house: Take him to the groomer, a doggie daycare service, or visit a friend. If the project is an extended one, you may want to board your dog—or at least give him his own area in the house that is outside the remodeling area.

Try to maintain as many daily routines as possible, including grooming, exercise, and playtime.

Travel Tips: What to Pack for Your Dog

PACKING FOR A trip is as important for your dog as it is for you. As you check off the do-not-forget items on your packing list, refer to this packing list for your dog so you remember his essentials. Don't be caught short—make sure you bring the following items to ensure a pleasant trip for the whole family, including your dog. Depending on your destination and the length of your trip (afternoon excursion or overnighter), adjust this packing list to suit your needs.

- Extra leash and collar
- Any medication your dog may be on
- Food and water dishes
- Your dog's preferred brand of food, in case it's not available where you're going
- Bottled water from home—you don't know what's in the water on the road, and it might upset your pet's stomach
- Treats
- Cooler with ice—pets are very susceptible to heatstroke
- Health certificate
- Vet's name and number
- Favorite toys
- A recent photo and written description, including name, breed, gender, height, weight, coloring, and distinctive markings, in case your dog gets lost while you're away from home

- Flea and tick repellents
- First aid kit
- Premoistened wipes with no alcohol
- ID tag with two numbers—one for home, one for where you are staying
- A dirty blanket from home, to give your pet the smell of home and makes him less nervous
- Grooming supplies
- Crate

What to Expect on Puppy's First Night Home

YOU HAVE MADE it through the first day with your new puppy, and now the whole family is exhausted and ready for bed. Take the dog outside one last time and wait until she relieves herself. Although most puppies tire easily, if she has a lot of energy, take her for a short walk to help make her tired.

Put her in her crate while saying the phrase you want to associate with bedtime, such as "time for bed" or "night-night," and giving her a small treat. Close the crate door and make sure the sheet is covering everything but the door, to give her a feeling of security. You can place a hot water bottle and/or a ticking clock in the crate with her for comfort; a radio with soft music on low volume nearby can also be comforting.

The puppy will cry the first night by herself in the crate. Resist the temptation to take her into your arms (or bed) and coddle her. The ideal setup is for her crate to be by your bedside. When she cries, stick your finger through the crate-door grates and let her lick you, while offering assurance in a calm voice: "It's okay." Then, remove your hand and stop speaking to her, and go back to sleep. You can comfort her the first few times she cries, but it has to stop sometime—you need to sleep. Let her "cry it out" a bit and she will eventually stop. She knows you are by her crate-side because you have comforted her. She knows she is not getting out of her crate.

She will settle down. Expect this crying the first few nights at home. The puppy will eventually learn that "night-night" means that she is safe, you are nearby, and she is to stay in her crate.

You will notice that there are different cries for hunger, outside, and attention. If you ignore cries for attention once you've put her to bed, the puppy will soon learn that they don't work and will stop.

Your puppy will need to relieve herself a couple of times during the night. As a general rule, a puppy can hold her bladder for the number of hours that she is months old—for example, a four-month-old puppy should be able to hold it for four hours. Set an alarm clock if you think you may sleep through the dog's "gotta go!" cries. Once she has done her business, put her back in the crate to sleep more. Put a chew bone in the crate with the puppy to keep her occupied if she isn't sleepy right away and you need your sleep. You need to establish the routine and show the dog that nighttime is quiet time.

Plan a Safe Beach Outing

A BEACH DAY is an opportunity to expose your water-loving dog to an exciting environment with lots of new smells and sights. But the sun, sand, and surf can pose threats to your dog if you aren't careful. Conside these factors before you depart:

Sport a float coat. Your dog should always wear a flotation device. Some dogs are experienced enough to ride the waves on their own, but err on the side of caution.

Check water conditions. A strong current can be dangerous even for seasoned canine swimmers. The undertow can quickly drag you and your dog out to sea. Stay on the beach until the tides calm.

Watch the weather. Weather conditions change quickly on the water. Keep an eye on the sky, and listen to weather reports before departing for the beach. Watch for signals from lifeguards (if present), and do not take chances. If the sky looks dark and the water is placid—well, you've heard about the calm before the storm.

Rinse off. Saltwater causes itches. Be sure to bathe your dog after saltwater swims. Also, do not be surprised if your dog has loose stools after a beach day from the saltwater and sand. If the condition persists, then contact your veterinarian for a checkup.

"Can I Pet the Puppy?"— Meet-and-Greet with Strangers

IT'S A FAMILIAR SCENE: You are walking your dog at the park, and a child with his mother points at you—well, your dog—from a distance. "Can I pet it?" the child exclaims, racing across the grass to greet your pup. His mother, footsteps behind, calls out, "Wait! Ask permission first."

You can instruct your own children to never rush up to a strange dog, and to always ask permission before petting a dog. You can't always intervene, however, when someone else's exuberant child breaks free to greet your pup. When this happens, calmly ask the child to stand very still, explaining that your dog may show excitement by jumping. Not all dogs can tolerate attention from a child. Know your pet's personality around children, and ask the child not to pet your dog if he is not trained to "sit" and "stay," or has never been socialized with children.

If your dog will gracefully accept a pat on the back from a child:

- Ask the child to slowly extend his hand, fingers curled in, so your dog can sniff it. Explain that this is like shaking hands with your dog.

- Watch your dog's body language during the hand sniff. She will tell you whether she wants to meet the child. A tail wag is yes. A quick, uncomfortable sniff is a timid yes. Backing away or barking is a clear no.

- If your dog is eager to interact with the child, tell the youngster to avoid touching your dog's eyes and ears—and not to pet the top of your dog's head. While it's our natural tendency, dogs much prefer a chin or back rub. Show the child how to pet the dog—in gentle strokes, not pats.

After the novel interaction, praise your dog for her good behavior.

195

Reduce Shedding

SOME DOGS SHED A LOT, others like the American Hairless Terrier do not shed at all. Most dogs shed to some extent, and you can reduce airborne fur (and resulting allergies) by taking good care of your dog's coat. Good, old-fashioned regular grooming is the key to reducing shedding. Simply put, the more hair you remove from your dog by grooming (bathing, brushing, combing), the less hair will end up matted to your sofa or drifting in tufts across your hardwood floors.

Tune into your dog's shedding nature. Some dogs with double coats, such as Golden Retrievers, shed a layer of fur during warm seasons. Be diligent with grooming during this time to "catch" fur before it becomes airborne. Brush your dog daily to reduce the amount of shedding.

Evaluate your dog's diet. A malnourished pup will show it in her coat, just as human's skin suffers when diet is compromised. Premium pet foods contain essential nutrients to maintain your dog's overall health, including her fur coat.

Note: If your dog is losing more hair than normal (and it's not because of sweltering summer temperatures), call your vet. Excessive shedding can signal underlying health concerns.

Cure in a Bottle

You may have seen no-shed pills at pet stores—treats that promise they will reduce your dog's shedding. Bottled formulas that promise the same result: stop shedding! The reality: Don't count on it.

Feng Shui for Dogs

FENG SHUI, WHICH literally means "air" (or "wind") and "water," is the Chinese art by which, through the precise placement of objects, one creates balance, health, wealth, and harmony. Apply the teachings of feng shui to enhance your best friend's life and reap the rewards of good health, harmony, and fortune. The principles of feng shui teach you how to live harmoniously with your environment by recognizing that everything around you is alive, connected, and changing.

Through feng shui, one balances the extremes of yin (feminine) and yang (masculine). Examples of yin characteristics are objects that are cool, dark, ornate, floral, and curved, whereas yang qualities are hot, straight, large, light, or plain. Objects innately possess different yin and yang qualities. Additionally, one must consider the five elements of earth, metal, fire, water, and wood. These five elements encompass the building blocks of everything in your environment. Like yin and yang, the five elements carry qualities of shape, material, and color and must be optimally balanced to optimize chi (also known as qi). Chi, which means "cosmic breath," is the invisible energy that circulates as the source of prosperity, health, and harmony. Through the principles of feng shui, you can optimize the flow and accumulation of chi energy in your dog's life. Your dog, who spends most of his time indoors, will benefit from good chi in the home.

Since your best friend spends a lot of time sleeping, his snoozing quarters should have good chi and should be weighted toward yin qualities.

Here is a feng shui checklist for your home:

☐ Do not place your dog's bed under a window or in a corner where chi can stagnate.

☐ There should not be any water elements in the room, since the sound of water can disturb your dog's sleep.

☐ Do not place the bed directly across from an open door or at the end of a long corridor where chi can travel too quickly.

☐ There should not be any heavy objects above or behind the bed, such as lighting, shelves, or cabinets.

☐ Minimize mirrors, which could reflect light and movement and frighten your pet.

☐ Avoid using bedding made of synthetic fabrics that distribute negative chi.

☐ Place your dog's bed against a solid wall away from any door that could swing open.

☐ Consider placing the dog's bed on the opposite side of the house from the active front door or garage, to prevent his being disturbed.

Get a Social Life

THE SOONER YOU expose your puppy to new people, places, sounds, and situations, the better adjusted she will be in the long term. It's difficult to cohabitate with and care for a dog that is scared of people, barks incessantly at anyone in a uniform, tucks her tail between her legs at the sight of large trucks or bicyclists, and runs like mad from the vacuum cleaner. Show your dog the world and all of its curiosities. Seek out new sights and sounds for your dog to experience so she can learn, with your help, that life is not that scary.

Depending on your household, your dog may be stimulated constantly with children playing and people coming and going; or she may lead a calm life with a single owner. Consider what your dog's daily environment lacks in stimulation and find ways to incorporate new and different things.

Here are some suggestions to get you started. Draft your own list as you learn what sights, sounds, and scenes make your puppy nervous.

- **On a walk:** cyclists, runners, baby strollers, school buses, children playing, passing cars, honking sounds, delivery trucks

- **At home:** vacuum cleaner, door bell, dish washer, television, radio, hair dryer, full grocery bags, and other items that trigger barking or running away scared

- **Surfaces:** walks on grass, the sidewalk, wet surfaces, gravel, tile. Your puppy is frightened when her paws sense different textures or extreme temperatures.

- **Animals:** other friendly, immunized dogs, squirrels, birds, cats, other household pets

- **Daily errands:** the bank, grocery store, post office, school grounds, drive-through, pet supply store, toll booth, gas station, etc.

- **Events:** a busy park, live music, a party, parades, street vendors

When you introduce your puppy to different (and scary!) social situations, comfort her and take these steps for socialization:

1. Introduce her from a distance. This applies to anything your dog will physically approach: trucks, busy streets, vacuum cleaners, street vendors, and so on. Gradually get closer to the subject, and allow your puppy to investigate at her own pace. Do not force her forward.

2. Reward her for bravery. Always provide your puppy a treat to reward her for trying something new or meeting a new person. Ask new people to feed her the treat. After confronting a significant social situation, reward her profusely with extra-tasty treats or play, and always lots of affection.

3. Expose her to children. If you don't have your own, invite over children of friends and relatives, or visit parks. Always instruct children how to pet a puppy before allowing physical interaction. Never leave your puppy unattended with a child.

Make Your Own Doggy Deodorant Powder

Some dogs have a natural body odor, even when they are bathed regularly. This basic deodorant powder recipe has been around for a long time, and it really works.

MATERIALS

2 bowls

1 cup (110 g) arrowroot flour, sifted

1 cup (110 g) cornstarch, sifted

¼ cup (18.4 g) baking soda

10 drops of tea tree oil

10 drops of sage, bergamot, grapefruit, lemongrass, or eucalyptus essential oil (from the natural foods store)

Empty shaker (such as a recycled Parmesan cheese shaker)

1. Mix the dry ingredients together in a bowl.

2. Add the oils and stir gently.

3. Sift the mixture into another bowl. Resift, if necessary, to distribute the oils well.

4. Put the mixture into a jar with a shaker top.

5. To use, shake over dog's fur, and brush.

Trick: Bow Down

Teach your dog a cheeky grand finale for tricks by training her to take a bow. The key is to differentiate the "bow" from "down." As always, train before mealtime so your dog will work hard for treat rewards. A clicker is helpful for teaching this trick. Or, you can use a verbal cue as the "click," such as "Good girl" or "That's right." Keep it consistent.

1. Start by catching her in the "let's play" position, where paws are down, rear is up, and tail is wagging. Dogs also make this pose when stretching after a nap. Click or say "Yes," and reward your dog for the incidental behavior. Repeat this a couple times when you notice her naturally bow and she will recognize that the position earns rewards.

2. Anytime she offers anything close to a bow, click, and give her a treat.

3. Coax the pose by holding the treat to her nose when she is standing. Lower your hand to the ground and mark the moment her front end drops (and hind is still raised) with a click, treat, and praise. If she goes into a full down, lure her back into a standing position and try again. Your goal is to click immediately when she bows and before her rear lowers into a "down."

4. When your dog consistently offers the bow, preface the action with command such as "Bow." She will begin to link the verbal cue with the trick.

5. As your dog builds stamina and stays in a bow for longer than a couple seconds, train a release cue, such as "Great show!" or "Show's over!"

How Does Your Dog Measure Up?

Underweight

Ideal

Overweight

Obese

Underweight: Her ribs are visible with minimal fat cover. Bony prominences (hips, shoulders) are easily felt with minimal overlying fat. There is marked abdominal tuck when she is viewed from the side and a marked hourglass shape when viewed from above.

Ideal: Her ribs are easily palpable with a slight fat cover. Bony prominences can be felt through a small amount of overlying fat. There is an abdominal tuck when she is viewed from the side and well-proportioned waist when viewed from above.

Overweight: Her ribs are difficult to feel because the fat cover is thicker, but the bony structure can still be felt. Bony prominences are covered by a moderate layer of fat. There is little or no abdominal tuck or waist when she is viewed from the side, and her back is slightly broadened when viewed from above. A slight pot belly, or rounding of the abdomen, is present.

Obese: Her ribs are difficult to feel because of the thick covering of fat. Bony prominences are also covered by a moderate to thick layer of fat. There is a pendulous bulge in her tummy and no waist when she is viewed from the side. Her back is markedly broadened when viewed from above. Fat deposits can also be found on her face and limbs.

Caring for Your Pet When You Are Ill

WHEN YOU ARE seriously ill, your dog is an especially important source of comfort and companionship. But caring for a pet can be difficult when you are sick. When you lose strength or mobility, simple tasks like walking a dog or cleaning up after him can become overwhelming. Whether you are suffering from a chronic disease, have a weekend spell of the flu, or have short-term physical limitations because of an injury, your dog still depends on you for care.

In the meantime, if you are sick from a contagious cold or other illness, be sure to protect your animal from sickness. This does not mean you need to separate from your dog while you get better. In fact, research indicates that companion animals enhance immune functioning by decreasing stress and increasing self-confidence and self-esteem. Dogs can be a source of affection and support, enable us to feel needed, and ease the pain, sorrow, and loneliness often experienced during illness. For people with serious medical conditions, the psychological and physical benefits of pet caregiving will usually outweigh the risk of acquiring an illness from the dog.

No dog will ever be guaranteed to remain disease-free, but the following precautions will help keep you both healthy:

- Wash your hands before and after handling your dog.

- Always wear rubber gloves when cleaning up after your dog and wash your hands afterward.

- Keep your dog's nails short to minimize scratches.

- Follow your vet's advice on keeping your dog flea- and tick-free.

- Keep your dog indoors as much as possible.

- If he must be kept outside, always use a leash to minimize scavenging, fighting, and other activities that can expose him to other animals and disease.

- Keep your dog's living and feeding areas clean.

- Keep your dog's vaccinations up-to-date.

- Always seek veterinary care immediately for a sick dog.

If day-to-day care of your dog becomes difficult, enlist the help of friends and family for feeding, walking, and cleaning up after him, or hire the services of a pet sitter. A dog walking service can be a great help in making sure your dog gets the exercise he needs if you are not able to take him out.

Opt for Natural Cleaners

THERE ARE A slew of products in the pet aisle designed to remove urine stains and deodorize the home. They are marketed as bottled miracles—your house will sparkle as it did before you brought in a dog. Be wary! The problem with store-bought cleaners is that they include fillers and unnecessary chemicals. You can quickly whip up these two cleaning recipes, bottle them at home, and rest assured that the ingredients are safe, concentrated, and effective. Chances are, you have most of the ingredients around your home already.

Baking Soda Carpet Cleaner

This cleaner is safe if the pup licks it up. Adding essential oils will leave behind a fresh odor when the carpet cleaner has been vacuumed up.

MATERIALS

1 (1-pound [454 g]) box baking soda

Flour sifter

100 percent organic essential oil, such as spearmint or lavender (optional)

Empty shaker (such as a recycled Parmesan cheese shaker)

1. Sift the baking soda to remove all lumps. Sift the essential oils along with baking soda, adding 30 drops of oil to 1 cup (225 g) of baking soda.

2. Pour the mixture into an empty shaker.

When cleaning a carpet stain, first fully absorb the stain (urine, vomit) with a cloth or paper towel (see Day 214). Do not rub the cloth over the stain. This will only cause it to further penetrate carpet fibers. Then, shake baking soda on the spot, covering it thoroughly. Let sit until the soda forms a crust. Vacuum up the baking soda.

Vinegar Surface Cleaner

This cleaner is safe for floors, inside a puppy's crate, and other hard surfaces.

MATERIALS

Distilled white vinegar

Water

Spray bottle

100 percent organic essential oil such as tea tree oil (optional)

Measure equal parts (fifty-fifty) white vinegar and water. Pour into a spray bottle and add just a few drops of essential oils for fragrance (optional). Tea tree oil works as a disinfectant.

Divorce and Our Dogs

DIVORCE IS A major life change for the people and pets involved. A dog that bonds with an owner who moves out of the home will wonder where his companion went. Furniture will move out and in, people will come and go, and the dog will lose his dependable, "normal" schedule. Through body language and voice, dogs easily pick up on the anxiety and tension and hostility that lead up to a divorce, and it can be traumatic for them to see their beloved owners at odds. The upheaval that is natural in a divorcing household will mean that things just aren't the way they used to be for your dog.

In the tense atmosphere leading up to a divorce, a dog may manifest signs of regression. He may become nervous and jumpy, and even retreat to another room during arguments. He may instinctively feel like he must protect himself with aggressive behaviors. Despite your disagreements, both partners must be firm and consistent in correcting his misbehavior.

If you have children, they may take out on your dog their hostility regarding the pending divorce: Instead of showing you how angry they are, children (especially small ones) may kick or hit the dog or otherwise treat him badly. It is up to you, as parents, to talk to your child and work on eliminating these actions: A bad relationship between dog and child will only add to the hostility already in the household.

The owner who gets custody of the dog may be tearful, lonely, and generally depressed. A person in this state may demand the dog's undivided attention, and not necessarily in a positive, healthful way. Dogs need privacy—just like us—and it is impossible for them to provide the sympathy and understanding that we may (unfairly) demand from them during this time. Your dog may react negatively by becoming clingy himself, losing some individuality, or picking up nervous characteristics.

Walks, feedings, and play periods can be thrown off when both owners aren't there to cover the schedule. If he's not getting his regular exercise, he may channel that extra energy into acting out, so do what you can to stick with his established routines.

If the departing spouse is attached to the dog, work out a visitation rights policy. Such an arrangement can be beneficial for both owners, giving the primary caregiver an occasional "break" from walking and playtime duties, if a schedule is agreed upon amicably.

Canine "Sense-abilities"

DOGS SEE, HEAR, touch, smell, and taste just like humans do. But their sensory awareness is more sensitive in many ways. Dogs rely on sound and smell as navigational tools. Your dog has an estimated 2 billion olfactory receptors, whereas humans have about 40 million. However, dogs' sense of touch is not as powerful as humans'. Understanding how your dog interprets the world will help you understand some of his quirks and behaviors.

Sight: Dogs do see in color—muted colors (see box at right). But they mainly rely on motion detection to "see." Dogs have sharp night vision, thanks to an additional reflective layer in the eye called the tapetum lucidum. If you ever think your dogs' eyes are glowing in the dark, that reflective layer is responsible.

Sound: Dogs' ears are their primary radar. Your dog may hear a squirrel from halfway down the street. Dogs hear through closed doors and secured windows. They detect acute frequencies that humans cannot hear. This is why some dogs make fantastic guard animals. Dogs can move one ear independently of another (the radar effect).

Smell: The nose knows. A dog's sense of smell may be 100,000 times more powerful than a human's. Smell is a way for dogs to communicate, "meet" other dogs and people, and identify their surroundings. When dogs smell each other's discreet areas, they're trading cards.

Touch: Dogs love to be rubbed and want always to be close to their human best friends. Touch is comfort.

Taste: When humans smell an unappealing food, they link that scent to the taste and will decline the item. Dogs love smelly food. Humans also are turned off by food that looks bad. Not dogs. Dogs smell, then taste—and they may eat so fast they don't taste the food at all.

Do Dogs See in Color?

It is commonly believed that dogs can only see in black and white, and shades of gray. Not so! Dogs can see colors ranging from yellows to blues and greens. However, what your pet sees is more muted than what humans do.

When to Hire an In-Home Trainer

PUPPY CLASSES ARE golden socialization opportunities for young pooches. It's never too early to begin training your puppy, and structured courses are often the push owners need to establish training regimens at home. But not all dogs respond to group classes. If your dog is a social animal who is more interested in making friends and "sniffing out" new pals, a private lesson at home may be more effective. Save the group class until after your puppy has learned some basics: sit, stay, down, heel. Then introduce her to a group class where she can get the double benefit of social time and training direction. By then, she will have mastered foundation commands and you will have more control over her in a class setting.

Your dog will benefit from private training if she . . .

- Is too distracted in a group to focus on commands

- Displays aggression toward other dogs or people; tackle this problem privately, then consider proceeding to group classes

- Has a shy owner who will not ask questions or request additional help in a group setting

- Needs to learn commands in her own environments: the backyard, living room, kitchen, neighborhood

What's more interesting to your dog: twenty other potential pals or a teacher's commands? Owners who enlist in a series of three private lessons—or even a single one-on-one to correct a problem behavior—generally see faster results. Also, the convenience of having a trainer come to your home is nice for owners with busy schedules.

Why Do Dogs Pounce on Toys?

YOUR DOG POUNCES on her stuffed squirrel as though the toy is the real deal. She leaps on top of her ball and covers it with her chin and paws, like a challenge in a game of keep-away. The toy-clobbering behavior is no need for concern as long as the action is playful. Pouncing is derived from your dog's innate instinct to capture prey.

Prevent pouncing from escalating into territorial growling or biting by teaching the "leave it" command. You should be able to disrupt pouncing without an aggressive reception from your dog. Integrate pouncing into play. Toss a toy and allow your dog to pounce on it and bat it around. Say "Leave it," and toss the toy for her to fetch. The game will exercise her natural desire to pounce while entertaining her, too.

Achoo! Are You Allergic to Your Pup?

YOU'RE SNEEZING, YOUR eyes are itchy and watery, and you can't blame the condition on hay fever: It's winter. Could it be that you are allergic to your dog? You never considered the possibility before. It's easy to misdiagnose allergies, especially if you tend to flare up in spring and fall, *and* if this is your first dog. On the other hand, you may have known full well you were allergic to dogs, explaining why you purchased a "hypoallergenic" pooch, such as a Poodle.

Bad news: Every dog is capable of triggering an allergic reaction in humans. Poodles and similar breeds with continuously growing coats that are frequently groomed get a reputation for being allergy safe because they shed less and are usually bathed more often. Certainly, one breed of dog may trigger allergies more than another breed. You'll scratch your eyes and sneeze when sharing the couch with a double-coated Golden Retriever, with its long, soft, and free-shedding hair. On the other hand, you may share a pillow with a Miniature Schnauzer without suffering a sniffle.

But never mind that Schnauzer. You own a dog, you sniffle and itch, and your physician (through allergy testing) has announced that your beloved is the cause. What do you do?

Following are tips to help the allergic enjoy pet ownership without needing to wear a protective mask in your own home:

Create a "clean" room: Reserve one room as a dog-free zone. Inside, place a HEPA air cleaner, which you will find at most home and garden or department stores. Having a room to breathe free will prevent your body from overdosing on "dog."

Cover pillows, sheets: Purchase impermeable covers for your mattress and pillows that prevent allergens from accumulating on sleeping surfaces.

Launder frequently: Wash articles such as couch covers, pillows, curtains, and pet beds on a regular basis; also wash and don't just brush off clothing that has attracted dog hair.

Vacuum: Invest in a good vacuum cleaner, and use it on floors, stairs, and (explore its attachments) upholstery. Look for a model that uses a revolving power brush, not just suction.

Bathe your dog weekly: This will dramatically reduce allergens in fur. No product marketed as an allergen reducer works as effectively as a good, old-fashioned bath. Consult your vet for recommended shampoos.

Is Your Community Dog-Friendly?

SOME CITIES ARE safer and more equipped for dogs than others. If you live in a community that embraces pets as members of the family, you'll find parks with cleanup bag dispensers, water bowls on the patios of restaurants, and store owners who keep jars of doggy biscuits by the cashier for pooches that patiently wait in the car for their owners.

Hospitality isn't the only factor in whether where you live is dog-friendly. Plenty of sidewalks and laws intended to protect dogs (leash laws) and neighbors (cleanup laws) are also signs of a city that cares about four-footed companions.

Answer these questions to find out how welcome your dog is there, and consider developing a task force to effect change if you think your community needs to be more open minded about pets.

- Do many households include dog family members?

- How far is the nearest fenced-in dog park?

- Will restaurants allow your pet to accompany you when you go there to dine? (Eating fast food in the car does not count.)

- How many hotels in your town accept pet guests?

- How many veterinarians practice in your city?

- Are there laws in your town that protect dogs?

- Are there events or festivals geared toward dogs in your town?

Pet Travel Documents

WHEN TRAVELING WITH your dog by plane, train, or other public transportation, you will be asked to show health papers for her (see Days 153–154 for how to make your pet's "passport"). If you are staying within your home country, you will probably need only a valid health certificate from your vet's office. A health certificate is valid for only thirty days, so if you're going to be traveling longer, be sure to locate a vet at your destination who will agree to see you and your dog and issue a new health certificate.

Other papers and regulations come into play if you are traveling outside your home country, and sometimes even to certain regions in your own country. The destination country may require a visa for your dog, and some countries require up to six months of quarantine.

It is essential to do your homework and learn the requirements and make arrangements before traveling with your dog, so you don't find yourself having to leave your four-footed travel companion at the gate.

The Internet can be very handy for finding preliminary information, but regulations can change. Always call the consulate of your destination country to confirm whether your pet requires a visa or other paperwork.

Why Do Dogs Tilt Their Heads?

YOU ARE TALKING to your dog (of course) and midsentence, he perks up an ear and tilts his head in a considered manner. How astute! He is listening carefully to your every word and he must understand what you are saying. This is yet another episode of emotional displacement. While your dog is hearing you, he is not actually listening and understanding.

Actually, your dog may have picked up on an entirely different noise that you can't hear. Dogs detect much higher frequencies than humans and tune in to sounds that originate from what seems miles away.

For instance, have you ever caught your dog barking in the living room only to look out the window and see your neighbor down the street slowly making his way toward your house? His tilting head may be an effort to adjust his radar, positioning himself to hear more clearly. The cocked head and alert ears are his way of saying, "Do you hear that? Is danger near?"

Dogs look out for fellow members of the pack. You *are* the pack.

Curbing Coprophagia

COPROPHAGIA, or the eating of feces, can be very embarrassing for the owner of a dog that is prone to this behavior. You are certainly not the only dog owner who's dealt with this issue, and you are not to blame for your dog's perverse cravings.

There are several different categories of coprophagia:

AUTOCOPROPHAGIA (when a dog eats his own feces)

INTRASPECIFIC COPROPHAGIA (when a dog eats another dog's feces)

INTERSPECIFIC COPROPHAGIA (when a dog eats feces from another species such as a cat or deer)

Coprophagia can be caused by physical problems such as exocrine pancreatic insufficiency, pancreatitis, intestinal infections, malabsorptive syndromes, and over-feeding. It can also be behavioral.

Behavioral reasons why a dog will eat feces include:

- **Attention-seeking behavior.** In times of stress or boredom, your dog may have learned that this (negative) behavior triggers a reaction from you.

- **Observance or allelomimetic behavior.** Your dog watches you clean up and sometimes "keep" poop (until you can find a trash can) so he copies the same behavior. Because you do it so often, it must please you!

- **Parental behavior.** A mother dog with pups may eat feces to clean the nursing area clean and to prevent the scent of the feces from attracting predators.

- **Learned behavior.** A dog may learn similar behavior from siblings or other dogs in public, such as at doggy daycare or the dog park.

- **Hunger.** A dog with hunger issues will seek out food in any form. This is common with dogs who are fed once a day and who remain hungry.

The best response: discipline your dog the moment he tries to eat waste by issuing a firm command to "Leave it!" while using a penny can (see Day 86). Your dog must develop a negative association with the behavior.

Ask your vet for a special powder, which when applied to your dog's food, creates an unpleasant flavor in the feces.

Sprinkle cayenne pepper or hot sauce on waste in the backyard. Do this every day and your dog could become discouraged very quickly. (This will also help form a negative association with all feces.)

Learning to Swim

NOT ALL DOGS are born to swim. Toy breeds, short-legged, and short-nosed dogs tend to be landlubbers. Swimming is not a healthy activity for puppies, elderly, or overweight dogs, or for those with medical conditions. Some dogs are perfectly fit to swim, but they're too afraid to take the plunge—and that is okay. A forced dunk in a pool could be so traumatic for your pet that he'll run away from large rain puddles. Certainly, there are other activities he can enjoy on solid ground.

When teaching your pooch to swim, enlist in a spotter who will stay outside the pool as you wade into the water to do the hands-on training. A water-experienced dog is also a good spotter and role model. He may teach your dog the basics by example.

- Use treats or toys to lure your dog to the top step of the pool entrance, where you are sitting. If necessary, guide him to the step on leash. Remove the leash before he enters the pool.

- Wrap both of your arms under his belly and slowly guide him into the water.

- Wade with your dog in arms a few feet from the steps. Position him facing the steps and allow him to paddle with your arms in place.

- Your helper can wait by the steps to guide your dog back to "land."

- Repeat this process a few times until your dog is comfortable. Increase the swimming distance once you are certain he is confident.

- Add fetch toys, treats, and plenty of praise to each swimming lesson to make the time a positive experience for your dog.

Before you teach your dog to swim, call your veterinarian and discuss whether the sport is suitable for your pooch.

Basic Grooming: Brushing

BRUSH YOUR DOG'S COAT DAILY, whether she has a long or short coat. This will remove loose hairs and flaky skin, and it will distribute natural oils throughout her coat. It will also give you quality time with your pooch. Dogs usually enjoy being brushed, because it feels like vigorous petting. Rub your moistened hands through her coat to lift loose hairs to the surface where your brush can reach them. This is also a great time to check your pet for hair mats, burrs (especially between the toes), sores, or lumps under her skin.

All dogs shed to some extent. Some breeds, such as the Poodle, Portuguese Water Dog, and Basenji, are light shedders. Others, such as the Golden Retriever, Samoyed, Collie, and German Shepherd, are heavy shedders. Bichons, Cocker Spaniels, and many Terriers require clipping or stripping (a process that removes loose hair from the coat) to look their best.

Many breeds can get by with just regular brushing, but some breeds need special coat care—such as stripping or clipping. Check with breeders and groomers and read books specific to your dog's breed to understand the best way to maintain her coat. You can learn to clip or shave your dog yourself, or you can pay to have it done professionally. If your dog sheds excessively, try gradually switching to a higher-quality dog food. A vitamin supplement that contains essential fatty acids might decrease some of the shedding and will add luster to her coat.

How to Clean Your Dog Brushes

Pull out all hair and gunk, and then soak nonwooden brushes for 30 minutes to an hour in a mixture of half white household vinegar and half water. Rinse very well, shake off extra water, then air-dry.

Creating Your Dog's Mudroom

A MUDROOM SERVES as a transition into your home, whether it's simply a space beside the door or a room of her own. Having a place to wipe your dog's feet after a tramp in the woods will help prevent mud and other messes from being tracked through the rest of the house. And a mudroom is a great site for a dog "pantry" (see Day 208).

If you have only a small bit of wall space to spare, you can hang a hook for your dog's leash, lay down a mat, and find a nearby drawer or shelf for a couple of towels. If you have a slightly larger space, consider adding a bench and a few storage pieces. If you're lucky enough to be building and can design your mudroom from scratch, your options are limited only by your imagination and your budget.

Here are a few ideas for a functional mudroom:

- Cubbies, peg racks, shelves, cabinets, and drawers are all good storage options.

- Open shelves with bins or baskets can be a more budget-friendly option than cabinets and drawers.

- Make use of space all the way to the ceiling to maximize storage space.

- Choose flooring that is waterproof and easy to clean—mudrooms are called mudrooms for a reason.

- A bench or chair gives you a place to sit to take off your own muddy shoes and to wipe down your dog's feet.

- Labeling shelves and containers will let all family members know where everything is and help them return things to the right places.

Dog Tails: Raiding the Fridge

My two pugs, Napoleon and Josie, are double trouble when they decide that "Mom" isn't paying enough attention to them. It's usually Napoleon, the instigator, who plots the household high jinks, but Josie is a quick conspirator. One evening, I came home and noticed a light on in the kitchen. I made my way to the room and found Napoleon sitting there peacefully amid a smorgasbord of groceries he had pawed out of the refrigerator and littered all over the floor. The place was a mess. Napoleon had torn open a bag of bread, leaving gnarled pieces in his wake. He dumped out a package of lettuce, making the scene look like a dysfunctional tossed salad. A few bottles of beer had rolled under the kitchen table, condiment containers were strewn about, and the kicker: Napoleon had scarfed raw chicken, leaving behind the licked-clean wrapping.

This wasn't a one-time ordeal. Napoleon raided the fridge four times—usually while I was talking on the phone. I finally decided to attach industrial-strength Velcro to the door in hopes of reinforcing the suction. I guess he just gets jealous when he's not the "main event." So far, the Velcro has worked like a charm.

213

If your fridge door(s) open easily, consider installing child latches made specially for this appliance.

Teaching Children about Strange Dogs

ALTHOUGH YOUR DOG is friendly to your children, it is important to teach them that not every dog is friendly and what to do when they meet a strange dog. Teach your children these rules:

- Never run up to a strange dog. Dogs can interpret this as a challenge and become defensive.

- Never approach a dog with the following: ears flattened against her head and laid back, or a tail between her legs; or any dog that is growling or snapping, or has raised hackles (hair standing up on the back of the neck).

- Always ask the owner before approaching and petting a strange dog. If the owner says yes, approach slowly, with your hand extended, palm up, so the dog can get your scent. If the dog looks interested or begins wagging her tail and "smiling" (yes, they smile), go over and say hello.

- Don't try to pet a dog on the head without first asking the owner if it is okay. Many dogs don't like to be petted on the head, and may bite if you try.

- Never try to pet a dog through a fence, or approach a dog that is tied up, without permission. Dogs in a yard can be territorial about their surroundings and try to protect them.

If you remember these suggestions and teach them to your children, you should never have a problem with a strange dog. It's a good idea to expose your dog to children—neighbors, relatives, your children's friends—in a supervised situation. This way, your dog will be less likely to respond territorially when a child approaches him to say hello. Remember, dogs are protective of their owners, and in their mind, other children pose a threat to their owners' safety. Teach your dog early on that children are friendly and do not present danger.

No More Drinking from the Toilet

DESPITE TRAINING PEOPLE in the household to put down the toilet lid, the dog always seems to find a wide-open water source in your bathroom. Assuming that training the open-lid offenders in the house is not effective, try these steps for teaching your dog to kick the toilet drinking habit.

- Train your dog to not enter the bathroom by using a penny can (see Day 86) propped behind the cracked-open door. When your dog noses through the can will tip over and make a ruckus that will send your dog flying in the other direction.

- Keep your dog's water bowl filled with fresh water at all times, and keep the water bowl cool. (Your dog likes that.)

- Place water bowls in various parts of the house so your dog doesn't have to go far— or into the bathroom—to get a drink.

Playing Flyball

IF YOUR DOG is a team player, flyball is a fast-paced sport he will enjoy. Flyball is a relay race with four dogs on a team. Four hurdles and spring-loaded boxes that shoot out tennis balls are spaced 10 feet (3 m) apart. Dog No. 1 jumps the hurdle, steps on the spring-loaded box, and runs to catch the flying tennis ball. The dog catches the ball and runs back over the hurdle course, jumping each obstacle. When the first dog crosses the start line, Dog No. 2 begins the course. The first team of four dogs to finish the course without errors wins.

Flyball tournaments are generally organized in double-elimination (best two out of three) or round-robin (best three out of five) formats. Each run of the course is called a "heat," and the first team to win two or three heats, depending on the format, earns a point toward their tournament standing.

Essentially, flyball involves teaching your dog this chain of events:

1. Release the dog

2. Jump over first hurdle

3. Jump over second hurdle

4. Jump over third hurdle

5. Jump over fourth hurdle

6. Approach box

7. Hit box to release tennis ball

8. Catch tennis ball

9. Turn

10. Return over fourth hurdle

11. Return over third hurdle

12. Return over second hurdle

13. Return over first hurdle

14. Cross finish line

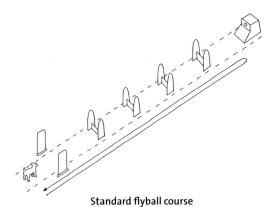

Standard flyball course

For more about flyball, see Resources, page 318.

Grooming a Squirming Pooch

IT IS IMPORTANT for dogs to stand calmly and relaxed for bathing, hair brushing, and cleaning ears, eyes, feet, and around the tail. Get your dog used to grooming when she is still a puppy or new to your household, so she will come to enjoy it rather than run from the water and the brush.

For two to three minutes, two or three times a day, run your hands over her entire body with a brush, practice opening her mouth, wipe over her eyes and in her ears, and even clean her rear end and tail. If in the beginning she doesn't like the brush on her fur, put the brush down, let her relax, and come back with a softer brush to try again.

When it's time to bathe her, start with warm, shallow water in the sink and give her lots of praise so she won't be afraid of bathtime. Choose a pet shampoo that is gentle on the skin and will not burn her eyes. Baby shampoo (for humans) that is tear-free does the job.

Hold and play with her toes often to get her ready for having her nails clipped.

Train her to stand still for brushing, especially if she's a breed that will need to go to the groomer. Getting her used to being handled will make it easy to groom her.

If you start early and use lots of positive reinforcement, grooming can become an enjoyable ritual for both of you.

If You Hire a Housekeeper

MANY CLEANING COMPANIES will ask you to provide cleansers, knowing that many people are conscientious about toxin-loaded products or may have allergies to certain substances. If your housekeeper does not inquire, be sure to give her a tour of your cleaning closet and request that she use the dog-friendly formulas you make or purchase (see Day 229 for easy household cleaner recipes). Write down any special instructions pertaining to the dog's play and sleeping areas.

If the same housekeeper regularly visits your home, your dog will soon get to know this person as a friend and not a stranger. But the first few visits, expect your dog to be on guard. Someone who does not belong in the home is inside—and cleaning. (Cleaning, alone, distracts many dogs, especially noisy vacuuming.) Make sure you are at home the first few cleaning visits.

Giver the professional a treat to feed to your dog, and introduce them properly. Assure your dog that this is a friend in a coaxing voice. Occupy your dog's attention while your housekeeper begins her work. The dog will eventually understand that you two will go about your business while the house is being cleaned.

A crate is a safe place for your dog, and you will likely want to secure him there while the housekeeper is busy. This is also a courtesy to the housekeeper. After you show the dog that this person is allowed to be in your home, lead him to his crate and give him a tasty treat. Stay nearby so your dog knows that you are safe. Ultimately, his barking and nervousness are because he is guarding you.

Service professionals who visit the home to fix plumbing, perform handiwork, or complete other projects in the house are strangers to your dog. Follow the same rules when these guests enter the home. Introduce your dog to this person, and be respectful of the professionals' duty: to get the job done. If your dog is in the way, contain him.

Dog Tails: A Dog's Trick-or-Treat

MY DOGLESS NEIGHBOR, Linda, treats our pooch, Alex, as only a favorite aunt knows how. She stocks the best treats near the front door of her home and doles them out generously. If Alex ever runs away, I know we'll find him waiting patiently on the neighbor's front porch for a snack and some attention. (For the record, he is, by no means, deprived at home.) He perches on her stoop, barks, and waits for her to answer her door and deliver the goods. His wildly wagging tail upon return is a sure sign of success.

Last Halloween, when the first group of trick-or-treaters rang our doorbell, our curious Alex ran to the door and watched me hand out candy to the costumed children. I shut the door, and he ran to the window and watched the group walk next door to Linda's house, where she, too, opened the door and distributed candy to the bunch. Alex saw a big problem: The kids were getting treats at Linda's house—his treats.

Sure enough, the doorbell rang again and more kids were handed treats. Alex butted through the door and joined the group to the next house, Linda's. He sat among the dressed-up kids, waiting patiently for his turn to get a treat. I waited nearby, watching the spectacle. What a scene! Linda knew what Alex was after, and she reached into her dog treat bowl and gave our dog a snack. Satisfied, he trotted off her porch and we walked home together. Every time the doorbell rang that night, Alex was off to Linda's like a shot to collect another treat. This year, she was sure to stock up on candy and on dog treats.

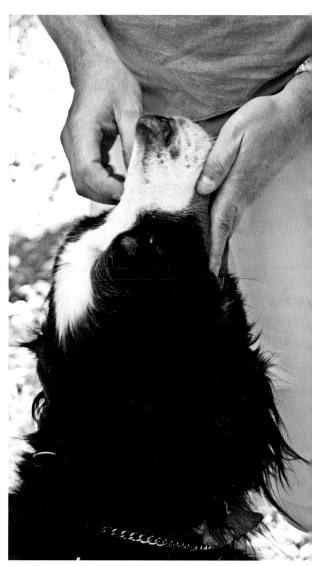

That Familiar Awkward Situation . . .

DOGS DO NOT conceal primal instincts when they discover another dog friend they want to get to know better. Their "humping" is a sort of get-to-know-you test where one establishes dominance. It's an activity where they decide, through this innate behavior, who is boss. When your dog attempts this action with you by embracing your leg, for instance, this is a sign of dominance that you want to stop immediately (you want to stop the action anyway because, frankly, it's disturbing). Your dog is telling you, "I'm the alpha. I'm in charge here." Break this habit before it translates to other disobedient activity, such as territorial growling or aggressive barking.

Keep spray bottles of clean water set to the "stream" setting around the house. When the dog starts, give him a blast of the water with the "no" command. If water doesn't work, try using a whistle, air horn, loud clap, or penny can (see Day 86).

Remember to have your dog neutered by the age of six months. After that time it will be difficult to drop this pattern, since he will have developed his full hormones and this behavior pattern will be ingrained, making it more difficult to unlearn.

Troubleshooting Leash-Pulling Problems

PULLING ON THE leash is one of the most common dog misbehaviors. Puppies and adult dogs alike can often be seen taking their owners for walks, instead of the other way around. Leash pulling can result from overexcitement or forgetting who the pack leader is, and it can be much more than an annoying habit. Leash pulling can lead to escape in the case of a break in the collar or leash, and an out-of-control, off-leash dog can be both destructive and dangerous to herself and to others.

If you are leash-training your new dog and all you have to show for it is a tug-of-war, there is hope. By implementing just a few corrections, you will find that she will respond well to leash training. Here are some pointers to curb an over-enthusiastic dog during leash training.

If the problem is one of control, however, some retraining may be in order. All dog training starts with the owner being established as the alpha dog or pack leader.

Without this basic respect and understanding, no effective training can occur. For dogs exhibiting control issues, a step back to basic obedience commands is in order:

1. Practice walking your dog indoors in a hallway during leash training. This will restrict her space and encourage her to stay by your side.

2. If your dog walks ahead of you, immediately call her name and turn around and walk the other way. This will teach her to follow your lead, rather than vice versa.

3. If your dog continues to tug at her leash, stop dead in your tracks each time she does so. Start walking only after waiting for a few moments. Each time she tugs, immediately stop walking. This will take a number of tries, but she will eventually get the message.

Proper leash training is critical to having a well-behaved dog, so be patient and keep working with her.

Dog Park Etiquette

TAKING YOUR DOG to the dog park can be the perfect way to spend a weekend morning. He'll get to play with his canine companions; you get to socialize with your neighbors and fellow dog lovers. The bonus: The energy he expends playing with his pals at the park means naptime and a break for you later on in the day. Before you high-tail it to the park, keep in mind certain canine etiquette rules:

• Observe the posted weight restrictions: Don't bring your full-grown Lab to a "small dog" park for pooches under 25 pounds (11 kg), even if you think he's the greatest dog on the block.

• Always pick up after your dog—it's your responsibility.

• Remember to close the gates. Most dog parks have double-gate systems: Lock both gates as you enter and exit so that no dogs can escape.

• Remove your dog if he becomes aggressive. Playful nipping is usually fine, but if your dog isn't playing nicely, you should take him out for a walk until he is ready to behave better.

• Be sure your dog is up-to-date with his shots and healthy. If he shows signs of fleas, ticks, or worms, or any contagious illness, keep him home to avoid infecting other dogs. Insects/parasites, viruses, and kennel cough can also be picked up at the dog park, so keep an eye out for signs of these in your dog's playmates.

Dog Park Safety

Dog parks can be great fun, but there are hazards to watch for, too. Keep your dog safe by following these guidelines:

• Keep an eye on your dog and his leash handy while you're talking with the other dog owners. You will need to get to him fast if a fight should break out, and he won't be so easy to control without his leash.

• Before you get to the dog park, have your dog jog on the lead for a moment to give him a little warm-up and confirm that he's in good shape. When he's done playing, if he seems to be limping or favoring a leg, call your vet.

• Remember that you are at a dog park, and dogs will play hard. Sometimes even the friendliest dogs can get into a mess and get scraped up. Keep an eye out for and promptly treat any deep scratches (see first-aid kit, Day 95).

• Wash your dog's feet and face and wipe him down when you get home from the park, just in case landscaping substances were used on lawn areas. This is also the perfect time to check his body for scratches and ticks.

• Be sure there is plenty of fresh drinking water, either at the park or brought from home. Some dog parks have hoses with running water to help keep your dog cool, and some even have man-made streams. Know the signs and treatment for overheating (see Day 305), and keep a small first-aid kit in the car.

Your Dog's Vital Stats

RECORD YOUR DOG's temperature and resting heart rate in normal conditions so you can refer to these baseline measurements when evaluating her health. When you suspect that your dog is ill, you can refer to these vital stats and determine whether your instincts are correct. If you are apprehensive about taking her temperature or pulse, ask your vet for a lesson.

TEMPERATURE

The average body temperature of a dog is 101.5° to 102.8°F (38.6° to 39.3°C). However, a dog's temperature can range from 98° to 102.8°F (36.7° to 39.3°C). If your dog's temperature exceeds 104°F (40°C) or is below 98°F (36.7°C), call your vet immediately.

Take your dog's temperature by using an oral, rectal, or ear thermometer. When using a rectal thermometer, dab water-based lubricant on the thermometer and insert 1 inch (2.5 cm) into the rectum, holding it there for about 1 minute. Ensure that it is clean when removed. Traces of blood, diarrhea, or black, tarry stool could be a red flag for an abnormality. Call your vet.

A dog's normal ear temperature is 100° to 103°F (37.8° to 39.4° C). An ear thermometer works by measuring infrared heat waves that are emitted from the dog's ear drum area. Be sure to place the thermometer deep into the horizontal ear canal for an accurate reading.

RESTING HEART RATE

Normal resting heart rate ranges from 60 beats per minute (bpm), a low rate for large dogs, to 120 beats per minute, a fast pulse for small dogs. Find your dog's pulse on her chest, near the elbow joint, or high on the inner side of the thigh where the leg joins the body. This is where the femoral artery is located. Always use two fingers when measuring a dog's pulse and count how many beats you feel in 15 seconds. Multiply that by four to get the dog's beats per minute.

The pulse will be faster on inspiration and slower on expiration. This is normal and is called sinus arrhythmia.

Following are normal resting heart rates for dogs based on size:

Small: 90 to 120 bpm

Medium: 70 to 110 bpm

Large: 60 to 90 bpm

Record this information and store with your dog's medical records.

GUM CHECK

Heart rate and temperature are key indicators of your dog's health. But you should also check your dog's gums, which give clues about blood flow, oxygenation, and circulation.

Gum color: Normal gum color is pink; pale, white, blue, or yellow gums are cause for concern

Circulation test: Apply brief pressure to the gums, then release. The area should pale rapidly, and then return quickly to a normal pink color. This is a basic way to gauge capillary refill time and, in effect, test circulation. Gums should return to normal color in a couple of seconds. Otherwise, call your veterinarian.

223

Not sure if your dog is breathing? Place a mirror in front of your dog's mouth and nose. You'll know he is breathing if the mirror "steams up" with condensation.

Make a Home Grooming Tool Pouch

THIS SIMPLE-TO-MAKE pouch is a great place to store your dog's grooming tools. You can hang it on the back of a door, the inside of a cupboard, or on the wall.

MATERIALS

Sturdy fabric, such as denim or upholstery material, approximately 16 x 24 inches (40.5 x 61 cm)

Sewing machine, or hand needle and thread

Fabric chalk or washable fabric marker

Eyelet kit (available at craft and fabric stores)

Scissors

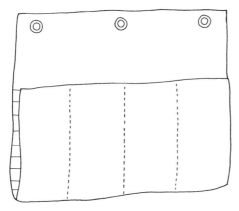

Assembly diagram for pouch

1. Fold the fabric, right sides together, so one end is about 6 inches (15 cm) shorter than the other end (see diagram).

2. Sew the sides together, then turn right side out.

3. Decide how many pockets you want and where you would like them to be. Mark the seam locations with the chalk or fabric marker.

4. Sew the seams to make the pockets.

5. Mark locations for three eyelets across the top of the pouch: one in each corner and one in the center.

6. Carefully snip a small hole at each mark.

7. Follow the eyelet kit manufacturer's instructions to attach an eyelet at each hole.

8. Hang the pouch and fill it with your dog's grooming tools.

VARIATIONS

- Use fabric that coordinates with your décor, or a dish towel.

- If you can't sew, use fabric glue instead, following the manufacturer's instructions. Allow it to dry thoroughly before using the pouch.

- Add ribbon, rickrack, or other trim to decorate.

Pouches make great gifts when filled with grooming tools or treats. Personalize it with the dog's name for an extra-special touch.

How to Throw a Dog Party

DOGS LOVE A good party: It's a chance to play with other dogs and humans and have some treats. Any occasion is a good excuse to throw a party: a dog's birthday, a new puppy, a fundraiser for an animal shelter. A successful party is the result of good planning. Here's a checklist to get your party off to a good start:

- Pick a theme, such as a costume party (a great way to reuse those Halloween digs), a garden tea in the backyard, or a bring-your-favorite-toy party (guests can leave with a new toy).

- Decide on your guest list and determine how much you will budget per dog/owner pair.

- Create a guest list. Choose six to eight dogs who are well socialized and get along with each other.

- Make sure the chosen location is secure, fenced in, and safe for dogs.

- Obtain the proper permission—from your town, neighbors, and so on.

- Create or buy invitations. Think cute, clever, unique, and fun.

- Mail the invitations three to four weeks before the party. Or, take advantage of free invitation websites where you can create custom e-mails and easily manage responses online.

- Decide on what you will serve to eat—remember the human guests, too! Prepare a snack, not a meal.

- On the day of the party, set up a shade canopy if your location is sunny. Ready-made canopies are available at most sporting goods and discount stores, or make your own (see Day 290).

- Put down a waterproof indoor/outdoor rug inside the shade canopy.

- Gather bowls and rope toys—at least one per dog.

- Fill several stainless-steel water bowls.

- Set individual treats at each dog's place setting.

- Put disposable cameras at each table for people to take puppy shots.

225

Here's a cute way to make little cakes for your dog's birthday or any occasion. For each cake, spread a dog biscuit with liver pâté. Stack another dog biscuit on top. Frost with whipped cottage cheese, and decorate with dog treats.

Preventing Escape from Fenced Yards

IT IS USUALLY better for your dog to spend outdoor time in a fenced yard than tied out on a chain. However, fences aren't always foolproof: Some dogs actually view their yards as "prison break" challenges. A loose dog is against the law in most communities. But worse than that, it is asking for trouble, in the shape of larger dogs, cruel humans, and fast cars. Keep your dog safe by giving him many ways to stay occupied in your yard and by shutting off all possible escape routes.

Dogs who escape often are lonely or lack adequate outlets to spend their energy. Make sure that your dog gets long walks, lots of playtime, and regular human interaction. Teach him commands and tricks to keep his mind occupied; try to hold a practice session every day. Be sure that your dog has plenty of interesting toys. Consider getting a dog walker or using a dog daycare center to provide him with extra stimulation. (Some employers are even letting employees bring their dogs to work. See Day 334.)

If your dog consistently escapes by climbing or jumping over the fence, add an extension to the top of your fence that leans in at a 45-degree angle (be sure to check with your city's building department first).

If your dog is a digger, bury chicken wire horizontally at the base of the fence or lay heavy rocks along its bottom. If you have a persistent digger, you can also use the chicken wire vertically, overlapping the existing fence and burying about a foot of the chicken wire below the ground level of the existing fence. This will help keep your dog from digging down farther than the chicken wire might go if it is just laid and buried at the base of the fence.

Regularly check all the fence panels to make sure there are no gaps between or under the fence that the dog might be able to wiggle through. Even if it is only a 6-inch (15 cm) gap, your dog could still get through it if he is determined to go wandering.

By making sure that your fences are secure, you are ensuring that your dog, your family, and you will have years to play together. After all, your dog is a member of the family, too, and you want his playpen to be safe for him.

How to Let Your Dog Go Off-Leash

YOUR DOG IS ready to go off-leash once he has passed obedience training and you trust his instincts. If you know your dog is likely to bolt after a rabbit and forget your calls and promise of treats, then going off-leash is probably not an option for your pooch, unless he goes off-leash in a fenced-in area. Regardless, you'll begin training your dog to go off-leash in a fenced area so you can carefully judge his response to freedom and begin teaching him how to walk when he is "free."

When you take the leash off, your dog should not run off, while you chase frantically behind, yelling for him to come back. To get him to heel without the leash, you must train him to heel on the leash first. When he can do that reliably, then you can train him to free heel.

Here's how to teach your dog how to heel:

1. Take your dog off his leash.

2. Walk in a straight line. (Angling into your dog will cause him to heel wide.)

3. Walk briskly. Don't walk at the pace of your dog.

4. Don't wave your hands about—hold your left hand close to your body.

5. Make sure you always give the first command in a happy tone of voice. (Your dog needs to know that you are happy; don't try to teach him anything if you're in a bad mood.)

6. Change your voice to a commanding tone or call his name sharply if he doesn't keep up to your walking pace or if he ambles away.

7. After the second command, gently pat your side and give praise. (Give praise at every appropriate opportunity)

8. If forging (trying to get ahead of you) is a problem, or if he attempts to dart off, you must stand still! Signal back with your left hand and repeat the heel command forcefully, then pat your side coaxingly.

9. If your dog is large, carry his leash folded twice, with the snap end in your right hand. If he fails to pay attention, call his name loudly or reach out and spank him playfully on the hindquarters with the end of the leash. You should then coax your dog close by patting your side. (Never hit hard or in such a way that you cause the dog pain. A light spank is all that's needed.)

10. If all attempts to keep your dog at heel position fail, it's time to put the leash back on, give it one good jerk to bring him in close, and try again. The change in voice, followed by flattery, with the occasional use of the leash, should eventually teach your dog to stay at your side at all times.

Remember, training your dog is not unlike training your child to behave in a way society expects. Provide rules and boundaries. Be firm about what is right and what is not. Praise whenever you have an opportunity, whenever your dog performs as asked. When your dog is doing a good job of learning, give him the commendation he deserves! Praise him while he is actually learning and performing well.

A DIY Designer Collar

YOU CAN UPGRADE your pet's plain, nylon collar into a flattering neckpiece. All you need is patterned ribbon and a sewing machine. You've seen the price tags on the decorative collars. Many are little more than fortified ribbon. An abundance of inexpensive ribbon is available at fabric outlets and craft stores that can be used for this project. Upgrading your pooch's collar is so easy you'll want to create collars for every holiday. These also make great puppy gifts for owners welcoming a new "baby" home.

MATERIALS

Ribbon of choice

Needle and colored thread (to match ribbon color)

Scissors

Nylon collar, sized appropriately for your dog

1. *Select ribbon for the collar.* Take the collar with you to the craft store to be sure you select ribbon of the appropriate width. You do not want to cut the ribbon horizontally, so avoid ribbon thicknesses that exceed the width of your collar.

2. *Cut the ribbon to fit.* Unbuckle/unsnap the collar and lay it flat. Measure the ribbon against the collar and cut to the appropriate length.

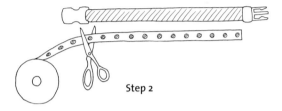

Step 2

3. *Fasten the ribbon to the collar.* Choosing thread to match the ribbon colors, then sew alongside either edge of the ribbon. For thicker collars, you may sew a center stitch for reinforcement. Create a small stitch on either end to polish the look.

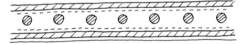

Step 3

Choosing a Professional Groomer

A PROFESSIONAL GROOMER is another key member of your dog care team. Even if your dog is not of a breed that requires regular grooming, a professional groomer can make your dog extra beautiful for special occasions, such as getting holiday photos taken.

When looking for a groomer, ask for recommendations from family, friends, and your vet—even strangers who have well-groomed dogs. Once you have a candidate, consider the following:

• Is the person a licensed groomer? (This is required in most places.)

• Is the facility clean?

• Is the facility safe?

• Is the groomer kind and considerate?

• Does the groomer have access to a vet?

• Are all cages humane?

• Is the room cool in temperature?

• Does the facility have the proper tables?

• Are all tools clean?

• Are the scissors sharp?

• Does the facility have a good reputation in the community?

• Are its personnel easy to communicate with?

• How does the groomer handle the dogs? Avoid groomers who use tranquilizers.

• Does the groomer provide anal gland expression, for dogs who need it?

If Disaster Strikes–Will You and Your Dog Be Ready?

WOULD YOU BE READY in case of an emergency? What happens if Mother Nature strikes and you have to leave? Or if there is a gas leak or an extended power outage—do you have a plan? No matter where you live, you should have an emergency plan that covers both evacuation and staying put.

If you keep all your dog's things together in the dog pantry (see Day 208), it will be easy to gather what you need if you have to evacuate quickly. Make a checklist of the essentials and post it in a prominent place for easy reference. Your checklist should include food, water, his leash, a blanket, and his essential papers. Remember, though, in the event of a fire or other immediate danger, just get out. Don't stop for anything.

Authorities recommend that you have at least seven days' worth of supplies, food, and water on hand at all times. Make sure that your emergency stash includes food, water, and medication (if necessary) for your dog, too. Rotate your stock every so often so you don't end up with expired food, and if you change the type or amount of food you feed your dog, make sure your emergency supplies reflect those changes.

Make sure your dog's ID tag is always current, legible, and in good shape. Consider having him permanently identified with a tattoo or microchip.

How to Get Your Dog to Sit Pretty for the Camera

HAVE YOU EVER gone to someone's house or out to dinner, when—all of sudden—out come the family photos? Have you received an avalanche of family photo cards in the mail at holiday time? Well, dog lovers can show off the four-legged members of the family, too. But how do you get that great shot? Here are a few tips to get a picture that will make your friends and family say "oh, how cute!"

• **Photograph in natural, indirect sunlight.** You'll get the best colors and avoid harsh shadows, and you won't have to use a flash. Try to avoid open fields, busy roads, and dog parks—unless you want your dog in action, of course. High grassy areas and sand dunes make nice locations. If you're in a situation where you have to use a flash, try desensitizing your dog to it first. Practice flashing the camera and rewarding him with a "good boy" and a treat, so he becomes used to it.

• **Apply peanut butter.** Make sure it is at room temperature and put some in his mouth, on the tip of his nose, or the side of his mouth. As your dog licks at the peanut butter, you'll get all kinds of happy facial expressions. (If you're in the mood for a sour photo, try a little bit of lemon or lime juice. You just need a little bit to get him to mug for the camera.)

• **Hold his attention with toys, bells, and balls.** Bring to the session his favorite toy or ball, or anything that makes a noise. While he's in "stay" position, dangle it or throw it up in the air, or squeak or rattle it to draw his attention. This will draw out great action and head-turning poses from your pooch. Having a helper to handle the toy, retrieve those that have been thrown, and wrangle the dog into place is a great asset.

No matter the method, be sure to reward your dog for a modeling job well done. You should end up with some great photos for your brag book and holiday cards.

Choosing the Right Outdoor Shelter for Your Dog

IF YOU KEEP your dog outside for even part of the day, you will want to provide your pooch with adequate shelter. This means you will need a shady place for her in the spring and summer months and a warm place in the winter. Here are some tips for keeping your dog safe and comfortable while outdoors.

- **If you have a dog run** (see Day 185), make sure that at least part of it is shaded, so your dog can get out of the sun. If you have a fenced yard, make sure that there is a spot that is naturally shaded by trees, or put up a tarp on stakes that she can get under to be out of the sun. Remember that dogs can get heatstroke and sunburn just as we can, and they need to be protected from it (see Day 290).

- **If you are in an area that has colder temperatures** and wish to purchase a doghouse, get one that is sturdily built and the correct size for your dog. It should include a floor raised off the ground, so that the air can circulate around and under the house. This will also keep the wood of the floor from getting wet in the rain, which could lead to rotting. If you can find one with a removable roof for cleaning, that is a bonus. You also want it to be heavy enough that it won't blow away or move in a strong wind. You wouldn't want to traumatize your dog or see him go flying across the yard if the house is not staked down.

- **If you have a puppy,** choose a doghouse that is suitable for the size she will become as an adult—you don't want to have to make this purchase more than once. (See Days 118–119 to learn how to make a doghouse.) Make sure that there is enough room for her to get in, turn around, and lie down. She doesn't have to be able to hold her head up when entering, but you don't want her to slouch, either.

If possible, try to get one with a door that is offset; this will keep the wind, rain, and snow from getting into the house. If your dog will be outdoors on hot or cold days, consider an insulated doghouse.

The right shelter or doghouse will keep your dog comfortable and happy in all kinds of weather.

Rub Dry Your Wet Dog

To help prevent winter chills and illness, your dog should be dried with a towel immediately after coming in from the rain. Likewise, if the temperature drops and snow is falling, those melting snowflakes, if not properly dried, can severely chill your dog.

Sweetening Bad Breath

PUPPIES CAN DEVELOP terrible breath because of blood in their mouths from cutting new teeth. Dogs that nosh on smelly foods without frequent teeth cleanings can also exhale a nasty stench. Brushing your dog's teeth is the best way to sweeten his breath. By doing so, you reduce plaque and tartar, help prevent gum disease, and remove bacteria—the source of bad breath.

Sometimes you need a quick fix, such as if guests are about to arrive and your pooch's breath is unbearable. Aside from brushing your dog's teeth, you have a few options for improving foul breath:

Switch food. Especially if your dog dines on soft food, switch to less-smelly kibble.

Provide hard, clean bones. Chewing on special dental bones can clean teeth between brushings. Pressed rawhide also cleans teeth because of the friction between the teeth and hard bone that helps remove plaque and bacteria buildup.

Mints and breath strips. There are breath mints for dogs, and even breath strips that dissolve on your dog's tongue. These products work fine as cover-ups until you can brush your dog's teeth.

Visit the vet. If bad breath persists, discuss the situation with your vet.

Regularly brushing your dog's teeth is still the top choice (see Day 68 for how to do this).

Agility Training

AN AGILITY COURSE is an oversize playground for dogs filled with colorful tunnels, jumps, chutes, suspended tires, and weave poles. Dog agility is a fast-growing sport that is mentally and physically stimulating for dogs, and just as fun for owners who train their pets to run the courses. Agility provides valuable bonding time; it improves attention, off-leash control, and confidence.

Agility courses contain obstacles that challenge dogs to jump, climb, weave through poles, and crawl through tunnels. Before dogs can participate in agility training, they should have completed basic training and shown temperance in social situations with dogs and people. Because agility requires close people–dog contact, aggressive and unruly dogs are not ideal agility students. To the other extreme, dogs that are overly social and rush up to other dogs should be taught restraint. There are pre-agility classes and obedience training that help dogs learn social skills and necessary commands to participate on the agility course.

In competition, dog and handler (you) teams are timed as they run the course in a set pattern. The handler guides the dog through jumps and helps him negotiate obstacles. Agility-trained dogs are quick movers and sharp thinkers. The dog that finishes with the fewest course faults and fastest time wins. There are organized trials where teams participate. You'll find local agility clubs and training courses. Contact your vet or ask dog-owner friends for references.

Some common obstacles that agility dogs learn to conquer include:

Jumps: These include winged or wingless hurdles, panels, and jump walls. There are also specialized jumps, such as water, brush, and wishing well jumps.

Contact obstacles: These are climbing obstacles, generally made from wood. They include the dog walk, A-frame, and teeter, which looks like a seesaw.

Weave poles: Dogs weave in and out of a series of upright poles.

Tunnels: Pipe tunnels are formed to make various shapes. Chutes are collapsed tunnels with a rigid entry barrel. Once dogs go through the barrel entry, they must snake through the collapsed material before reaching the open end.

The pause table: This 3-foot (91.5 cm) square provides a break from the action. (A break is a bummer for energetic dogs that may protest to get back on the course.)

You can purchase dog agility equipment from catalogs and set up your own backyard obstacle course where your pet can practice or just play around. Many dog owners say they have met great people friends through agility courses and trials. Events are exciting, and training is fun for dogs. (See the Resources, pages 318, for more on agility training.)

Preventing Doggy Dandruff

IF YOUR DOG'S sleek, black coat is speckled with what look like minuscule snowflakes, your pup has dandruff. (Yes, dogs get it, too.) Dandruff is a result of dry and/or flaky skin underneath fur. Many dogs have this condition, but owners might not notice dandruff if a dog's coat is fuzzy and golden. A black coat doesn't hide conspicuous white flakes.

You may need to adjust your dog's bathing ritual to help restore moisture to the skin beneath the coat, and take measure to prevent skin dryness in especially arid climates or during winter weather, when home heaters tend to dry out skin. Consider your own skin when the weather is cold. You probably apply lip balm and body lotion more frequently and lavishly than during summer months.

These bathing and conditioning tips will clean up a flaky coat, and alleviate itching and scratching.

- Always bathe your dog in lukewarm water. Test the water temperature on the back of your arm. Hot water dries out skin and prompts flaking.

- Try baby shampoo or pet dandruff shampoo that contains sulfur or salicylic acid. You can also use moisturizing colloidal oatmeal soap. When using medicated shampoos, leave lather on your dog for five minutes so active ingredients will work. Avoid using medicated dandruff shampoos for people; the chemicals contained in them may be harmful to your dog. Never use shampoos containing insecticide, such as flea formulas. These strip the skin of natural oils.

- Groom (brush) your dog regularly to redistribute skin oils and prevent dandruff. Choose a soft brush that will not aggravate sensitive skin.

- Oil sprays designed for dog dandruff can restore moisture. Or, after rubbing lotion on your own hands, rub and massage the excess onto your dog's coat so it penetrates deeply.

- Ensure that your dog's diet contains enough fat (approximately 10 to 15 percent; consult your vet). Serve your dog premium food, and consider adding a pet fish-oil supplement to improve metabolism of fats in skin tissue.

- Watch for scabs, crusting, and itching, and consult your vet if dandruff persists despite treatment. Skin issues can indicate more serious internal problems.

Odor Controller: Natural Air Freshener

THIS ALL-NATURAL air freshener features a simmering potpourri crock with a blend of pet-safe ingredients to address pet odors (avoid store-bought blends, which can be toxic if ingested), and its scent won't overwhelm you like some commercial air fresheners. You can simmer the pot in your kitchen, and its scent will travel throughout your home—it's similar to cooking a tasty roast all day that fills the home with comfort-food smells. Look for potpourri crocks manufactured for the express purpose of slow-cooking herbs and essential oils. If you do not own one, you can improvise by using a slow cooker or small saucepan on the stove, the latter of which you should be in the home to monitor. Regardless of your heating method, watch the water level, adding more water as needed so the crock or pan doesn't boil dry.

MATERIALS

1½ cups (355 ml) warm water, or follow the crock manufacturer's instruction

4 cinnamon sticks, broken into pieces

A few drops of all-natural essential oil, such as lavender, lemon, or orange (from the natural foods store)

4 teaspoons (9 g) nutmeg

4 teaspoons (9 g) ginger or one medium-size piece of crystallized ginger

1 tablespoon (7 g) whole cloves

1 teaspoon (5 ml) almond extract

4 teaspoons (9 g) allspice

1½ teaspoons (21 g) vegetable oil (helps with binding the scents and rapid water absorption)

Other Ideas for Air Fresheners

Mix ¼ cup (115 g) baking soda with 1 quart (946 ml) water in a spray bottle. Shake well and spray. The baking soda absorbs the odor. You can also add a couple drops of 100 percent organic essential oil from a natural foods market.

Another option is to spray undiluted white vinegar in the air. The vinegar smell evaporates very quickly, taking odors with it. Or place a bowl of vinegar on a surface above your dog's reach, and let it sit for a few hours to absorb odors.

Combine all ingredients in the potpourri crock. Plug the crock in and enjoy the fresh scent.

Preparing Your Home for an Aging Dog

HAVE YOU NOTICED your dog missing the dog door altogether and bumping his head into the kitchen cabinet instead? Is your nearsighted dog presenting you with rumpled socks instead of his favorite toys? Is it hard for him to jump up onto his favorite chair? Just like humans, pets age, go blind, and get aches and pains.

When you notice daily activities getting difficult for your aging dog, take time to go through your house and look for things that might be dangerous or difficult to navigate, just as you did when he was a puppy. Is there furniture with sharp corners in the normal path of travel that a dog with failing vision might run into? Is his food kept in a room that requires him to go up or down steps to get to it?

Think about purchasing (or making, Day 184) an elevated feeding station, which will make it easier for your pet to eat and drink. It positions food and water in such a way as to improve posture. In human terms, it is the difference between our bending down to eat off the floor or being seated at a table.

When his ability to jump decreases, he may need a step stool to help him up onto the couch or the bed. He may eventually get to the point where he needs a ramp to help him up the stairs and in and out of the car.

Heating pads in the winter and foam padding in the bottom of his bed will make sleeping a little more comfortable.

Your dog depends on you to be his No. 1 caregiver, from puppy stage to the golden years. With the help of adjustments you make at home to improve his comfort level, he will age with dignity and enjoy these slower times.

236

Suddenly Scared: Adolescent Insecurity

YOUR PUPPY GROWS at warp speed her first year. Packing approximately seven human years into twelve months, she evolves from toddler to teenager, and eventually matures by her first birthday (see Day 1). During her development, she will experience two periods of time where she may act shy or apprehensive when confronted with new people or situations. The two "fear factor" periods are generally between eight and eleven weeks, and later on between five and twelve months of age. Both fear impact periods last about three weeks, and your patience, training guidance, and careful observance of the dog's behavior is critical to help her adjust and feel safe.

During these vulnerable times when puppies tend to be on guard and timid, avoid overwhelming circumstances and concentrate on building your puppy's confidence through training and rewards for positive behavior. Beware of using negative vocal intonations or other reactions to the puppy's behavior. Puppies learn from their bad experiences, and they remember these incidents as they mature. For instance, a child pulls a puppy's ears and causes the puppy to whimper and become scared. The puppy now avoids children, or acts uncharacteristically aggressive when children try to pet or play with her. She recalls her bad experience and associates all children with ear-pulling, which agitated and scared her.

Be especially careful of the people and situations you expose your dog to during these fear impact periods, and socialize your dog, using plenty of positive feedback. Your dog will rely on you more than ever as a security blanket—a trusted parent. Do not breach that trust.

Following are some pointers to help your puppy ease through adolescent insecurity:

- Avoid confrontation if your puppy is especially apprehensive or timid.

- Train using positive reinforcement so learning is a fun experience for your puppy.

- Your puppy will rely on you for guidance and security. She may need your reassurance more now than during other times in life. Do not put her in situations where she must be all alone in a scary place. Now is not the time to travel by plane or train.

- Make fun visits to the vet that do not involve a medical exam. Simply stop in, say hello, and give your dog a treat. This way, your dog will associate the vet's office with safety and friendliness.

Stop a Mouthing Puppy

YOUR FURRY CHILD means no harm. Her bites don't puncture, they aren't accompanied by snarling or aggression. Her wagging tail and playful jig indicate that the gentle "mouthing" is an affectionate game. But this behavior is a bad habit, and by allowing your puppy to mouth—softly biting down on your hand, finger, leg, name the appendage—your message to her is: "Using teeth is just fine with me."

Biting and mouthing, in fact, are two different problems. Mouthing is generally playful, not a full-out bite but a gentle gumming action. If your puppy is teething, you can safely assume that the urge to chew is associated with dental discomfort and a dire need to exercise those pin-sharp pearly whites. Still, you must refer to Day 156 and teach your young pup to prefer sinking into bones and safe dog toys.

If mouthing persists after your puppy gets adult teeth, even if the behavior is purely innocent, you must work to stop it immediately. Mouthing can quickly spiral out of control if your puppy gets too excited, and if she is not trained otherwise, no one is at fault when the game finishes with broken skin and bad feelings.

By now, you're probably convinced that your puppy has an oral fixation—all puppies do, really. Aside from eating and being loved, chewing ranks high as a top dog activity. Still, you can train your puppy to stop "mouthing" with these tricks:

Pressure-point stop. When the puppy opens her mouth, place your thumb under her tongue and middle finger under her jawline. Apply pressure, squeezing together your thumb and finger. This is an uncomfortable feeling for dogs. Your puppy will get the message. Follow this action by saying in a flat tone, "No biting."

Get a yuck reaction. Keep 100 percent clove oil on hand. Dogs detest the taste. Rub some oil on your fingers, shoes, and other areas that fall victim to mouthing. While some dog owners use hot sauce for this purpose, the clove oil is less messy and more effective because not all dogs have adverse reactions to hot sauce.

Kiss instead. A final trick is to teach your dog to kiss rather than bite down. When your puppy gets her mouth going, look her in the eye and say, "Give me a kiss!" This is a risky correction for children to use, but if you're the alpha dog in the house—the main caregiver and the one your dog views as "in charge"— this command can be effective. Teach it like this. You say: "Give me a kiss!" Then give her a peck on the nose and say, "Good girl!" Reward her with a treat. Its shaping the behavior. If you kiss her and give her a treat, she will learn to kiss back. Repetition will teach her that if she gives you kisses, she gets yummies. You can eventually wean her off the treats. This method is not effective for all dogs and really depends on your pet's disposition.

Places to Look When Your Dog Is Hiding

EVERY ONCE IN a while, your dog finds a hiding place so good that you can't find him. Here's a quick checklist of places to look if your dog goes missing in your home.

- Inside closets

- Inside shoe boxes

- Behind the washer or dryer

- Behind the refrigerator or stove

- Inside the dryer (be sure to always check your dryer before turning it on)

- Inside the washer (check before loading and starting up)

- Inside the refrigerator (believe it or not, they can get caught inside when the door is open and you do not see Mr. Curiosity jump inside for a look around)

- Inside the dishwasher

- Behind any standing semi-built-in furniture, such as a bookcase or dresser

- Under beds

- Under or behind furniture

- Inside a reclining chair

- In open dresser or desk drawers, including behind the drawer

- Under the bedcovers or behind pillows

- Behind radiators

- In any cubbyholes there may be in your furnace

- Inside woodstoves or fireplaces

- In open luggage, backpacks, tote or duffel bags, or shopping bags

- In the bathtub

- Behind large potted plants

- In a closed-off room or garage you opened just for a moment

Treating Carsickness

TRAVELING WITH YOUR best friend should be fun for both of you. A car ride provides dogs a change of scenery and bonding time with their owners. There are opportunities to see and experience new things, and to possibly earn treats if the destination is a pet supply store that welcomes animal customers. (Most of them do, so long as your pet is immunized.)

Carsickness can spoil the mood.

If your dog is prone to getting a sick stomach during car rides, first be sure that the reason is motion sickness and not stress or fear. Behavior caused by these underlying problems—vomiting, shaking, clinging to the owner for safety—can surface when a dog is in an uncomfortable situation. Also, talk to your vet and investigate whether medical issues are triggering carsickness. For instance, inner-ear disturbances can cause dizziness and nausea.

For many dogs, learning about the car by riding in it often eases stress and accompanying sickness. Start taking your puppy on short car rides early on—drive him to the bank, grocery store, or park. Take him to destinations where he will get out of the car and play or go for a walk. Your dog will associate the car with fun and relate the trip with a reward. Also keep your dog in the car during errands for short periods of time, then return home. This will teach him that not every car ride results in a trip to the doggy toy store.

Here are some tips to prevent your dog from getting a sick stomach during a car ride:

- Be sure water is readily available. Bring a water dish and bottled water in case your dog needs a drink.

- Position your dog so he sits facing forward while the vehicle is moving. Be sure he can see out a window and crack a window for fresh air.

- Do not feed your dog prior to traveling by car if vomiting is a problem.

- To prevent motion sickness, consider giving your dog ginger capsules, bulk dried ginger torn into small pieces and fed as a treat, or ginger extract. Read the label carefully, and consult with a vet prior to administering any remedy.

Always Crack the Windows Open

Even if you will leave your dog in the car alone for 5 minutes—and even if the temperature is cool by human standards—always be sure to crack windows to allow fresh air to circulate in the car. There are far too many tragic stories in which owners have left their dogs in hot cars for very little time, only to return and find an overheated pup. If the condition worsens, your dog may actually die from heat exhaustion. It doesn't take long for a dog to perish in a hot car. Err on the side of caution and crack windows no matter the temperature. If the weather is too hot or humid, do your dog a favor and leave him at home.

Cleaning Up Garage Dangers

SOME OWNERS USE their garages as dog safe zones, treating the space like an extra-large crate that allows plenty of room to move around and "take care of business" without soiling the house. This solution is appropriate if the garage is heated and stays cool enough in the summer to be comfortable for your pet. Garages used as "pet suites" should be cleaned out thoroughly, and all equipment and tools should be stored in secure cabinets and on shelves the dog(s) cannot reach.

Even if your garage is not a "doghouse," you should be aware of common dangers that can cause harm to your pet. When you puppy-proof your home (see Day 106), the garage is often overlooked, and yet our dogs can easily bolt into this space from a mudroom door. You need to apply puppy-proofing practices to your garage, too. Here's what to do:

Secure chemicals, paints, and automotive supplies. Scan the garage to see what products are within a dog's reach, and store anything dangerous, such as paints, motor oil, turpentine, insecticides, ice-melting products, and swimming pool treatment supplies, on high shelves or behind closed cabinet doors.

Conduct a ground inspection. Sweep up nuts, bolts, screws, nails, and other sharp objects that can be harmful if stepped on or swallowed. Check the area under your car for any puddles—only a few licks of dripped motor oil, radiator fluid, or antifreeze can be disastrous (as little as 2 tablespoons [28 ml] of sweet-tasting antifreeze can kill a 20-pound [9 kg] dog!) Store sporting equipment such as golf balls and racquetballs out of reach. In particular, these smaller, slippery balls are choking hazards, and golf balls and paintball pellets are toxic if swallowed. Finally, make sure large, heavy items such as bicycles, skis, and kayaks are secured so they can't fall over on cavorting canines.

Remove rodent traps and baits. Rodent baits are designed to attract their victims with a sweet taste and smell, which can attract unlucky dogs as well. Check under your house, in garden sheds, and in the corners of your garage for old traps or baits that may have been left by a previous occupant.

Use caution when working with dangerous equipment or products. It's great fun to have your dog keep you company while doing home improvement and maintenance projects. But there are certain times when it's best to work solo, like when you're using power tools, lawn mowers, and caustic chemicals—on these occasions, keep her inside so she can't get underfoot and injure you or herself.

Dog Tails: Tank, the Protective Parent

WHEN I WAS growing up, we had a Golden Retriever named Tank. He earned his moniker because of his eating and drinking habits. His actual breeder name was One Ash Tallis Canon, but few people knew that. He moved in with us when I was two years old, and he clearly thought that my sister and I were his puppies. In fact, as far as he was concerned, our whole family was his responsibility. Every night, he made rounds to each bedroom and peeked in to be sure we were safe. Then, he would lie at the top of the stairs all night.

Tank went nuts when I learned how to ride a bike beyond our driveway. He would spot me from inside the house and run around to all the windows to get a better view of me as I rode past. If I ever went out of sight, he barked frantically.

When I was in fifth grade and a junior Girl Scout, I was working on my "learning to take care of your pet" badge. I learned how to feed Tank and brush him, and my mother showed me how to take him for a walk. We lived on the corner of a pretty quiet residential street and a busy thoroughfare.

My instructions were to walk Tank around the block—his usual route. Our walk started out with great success. Tank followed every command and he even "heeled" on cue. But as we approached the corner, he just sat down.

Tank would not allow me to walk down the busy street. I called him, tugged the leash, and coaxed him to continue the walk. He wouldn't budge, and Tank was a lot stronger than me. Eventually, I gave up and turned toward our house. Tank perked up and trotted easily back home while I guided him by leash.

The next night, he repeated the same behavior—stopping before the corner, putting on his brakes, and not giving up until we traced our steps back home. The third night, I altered the route because I knew Tank was not going to walk near that busy street. He walked there with my parents without hesitation, but he thought I was too young. I was, after all, his "puppy."

Small Dog Syndrome

SMALL DOGS GET a bad rap for being yippy, yappy, snappy, and high strung. They're tiny in stature but big in attitude. With people, we call it a Napoleon complex. But dogs don't care about size. Small dogs think they're big, and so they act like it. Have you ever seen a Bernese Mountain Dog sheepishly back away from a feisty Chihuahua? There's the big dog and the *big* dog. (The Chihuahua is the latter, of course. He figures that other guy is no competition.)

If dogs don't care about size, then why do small dogs fight so hard to act big?

Actually, the behavior they are reflecting is domination, and because we accept that yipping and snipping is "small dog stuff," we allow them to get away with it. Discouraging dominating pack behavior, such as jumping and growling, can prevent small dog syndrome.

Now, let's rewind and consider why small dogs have a reputation for big attitude—and remember, we are speaking in generalizations.

Growling: aggressive or no worry? When a German Shepherd growls, the immediate response is to correct the dog. This is a definite problem. If a Yorkshire Terrier goes into a yapping fit, well, that's normal, right? Wrong. Your dog's growl is an attempt to dominate a situation. The large dog is trained not to growl while the small dog gets away with making noise—and developing up a nasty attitude.

Barking: bad or cute? A large dog that barks is more likely to be reprimanded than a small dog that yips. Barking is bad, yipping is kinda cute—or at least that's what we teach our small dogs to believe by not correcting the behavior. In fact, barking is a dominant behavior. As the alpha and pack leader, your job is to say, "No."

"My couch!" Unacceptable or implied? Your Great Dane eases on to the couch (he doesn't have to jump) and cozies up next to you while you watch television. Your response: "Get down!" A West Highland Terrier pup paws at your leg because she wants to sit in your lap while you finish a favorite movie. "How cute!" you think. "She wants to watch the movie, too!" It's okay for your lap dog to enjoy couch time, but you must initiate the invitation. When your dog paws at your lap and you comply, guess who is in charge?

Essentially, small dog syndrome is rooted in people's willingness to overlook bad behavior. Because small dogs can be picked up and won't knock you over when they jump, we tend to slack on obedience training. Stick to a training plan and teach your small dog foundation commands and she will start *really* acting like a big dog: docile, respectful, and well tempered.

Is Your Puppy Ready for "Big Dog" Food?

PUPPY FOOD IS calorie dense and fortified with important fats and vitamins to aid development and give young dogs a healthy start. For these reasons, puppy food is served to dogs their first year of life. But if an adult dog noshed on puppy food for a week, his belly would tell the story. Mature dogs do not require the level of fat that playful, growing pups do.

When should you help your dog transition to mature food?

Your vet will offer the best advice, based on your dog's health and development progress, but the general rule is to switch from puppy to adult food after one year. Some practitioners say that a dog's metabolism slows after being spayed and that postsurgery is a good time to begin feeding mature dog food to your pet. This recommendation is arguable.

Your puppy's physical size and breed are determining factors of when to switch to adult food. Small-breed dogs tend to mature much sooner than larger breeds. A Scottish Terrier will peak in size at about nine months. A Basset Hound will continue to grow well into its first year. When your puppy approaches its adult height, consult your vet about making the transition.

FOOD TRANSITION TIPS

A dog's stomach is highly sensitive to changes in food and drink. Gradual transition to new food—whether you switch puppy food brands or your dog graduates to "maintenance" food for mature dogs—will prevent gastrointestinal upset. Ultimately, you'll be a much happier pet owner (think: cleanup) if you spend a week or two helping your dog transition. Some dogs with tougher stomachs can handle the switch in a few days.

Day 1–4: Mix together 3 parts puppy food, 1 part adult food

Day 5–8: 1 part puppy food, 1 part adult food

Day 9–12: 1 part puppy food, 3 parts adult food

Day 13–14: All adult food; watch out for health issues

If your dog is prone to stomach upset, transition more slowly, mixing food for three or four weeks until you completely switch the dog's diet to adult food.

Build Your Own Wooden
Dog Toy Storage Box

A TOY STORAGE box is handy for keeping your dog's toys up off the floor when he's not playing with them. Custom decoration and a padded top make it a nice addition to any room.

MATERIALS

Large drop cloth

Unfinished wood storage box—this can be any size that will fit in the space you have

Fine-grit sanding sponge or sanding paper

Tack cloth or clean, lint-free rag

Disposable sponge brushes

Primer

Nontoxic semigloss paint, any colors you want (for base coat and decoration)

Stencils

Painter's masking tape

Staple gun

Staples (be sure they are shorter than the thickness of your box top)

Measuring tape

Sturdy fabric to cover the top of the box with at least 6 inches (15 cm) allowance on all sides, prewashed, preshrunk, and ironed

High-loft quilt batting, cut to the size of the top of the box plus 1 inch (2.5 cm) on all sides.

1. Choose a protected work area with plenty of air circulation where you can leave the box for at least 24 hours to dry. Cover your work surface with the drop cloth.

2. Sand the whole box once, then wipe clean with a tack cloth.

3. Apply one coat of primer and allow to dry according to the manufacturer's directions (usually about 30 minutes).

4. Apply two coats of semigloss paint, according to the manufacturer's directions. Let the paint dry completely before proceeding.

5. Decorate the outside walls of the box with stencils. Tape the stencils into position, then apply the paint with a sponge brush. Allow the paint to dry completely.

6. Position the batting on the box lid with a 1-inch (2.5 cm) overlap all around. Fold the edges under and tack into place with a few staples.

7. Position the fabric over the batting with an even overlap all around. Starting with the center back, fold the fabric over the edge of the box and tack into place with a staple. Now, fold over the opposite edge, pull it taut (but not too tight), and staple that. Whatever tension you have established between those two staples, aim to continue it as you staple the rest. Leave the sides unstapled for now.

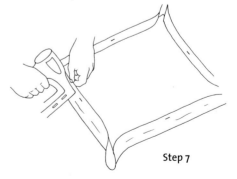

Step 7

8. Staple the opposite edges of the sides, as you did for the back and front.

246

9. To finish the corners, pull the point of each corner of the fabric tightly over its respective corner of the box, under the edge, and staple that into place. Tuck the excess fabric of each point neatly under the side fabric extending from it, and staple those edges. Keep the tension even.

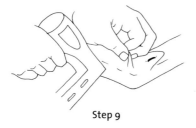

Step 9

10. Work your way around the lid, stapling every 2 inches (5 cm) or so and watching carefully to avoid wrinkles.

11. Fill the box and enjoy!

You can decorate your box any way you like. Instead of stenciling, use large sponge stamps dipped in paint, rubber stamps with ink, or paint designs freehand. Cut out shapes from wallpaper and attach those. Decoupage pretty paper or photographs and seal with a clear sealer. Or try rub-on transfers or vinyl wall clings, which come in a wide variety of patterns.

Stock an At-Home Grooming Kit

GROOMING AT HOME can be a good bonding exercise for you and your dog—and it saves money, too. Simply gather your tools and supplies; choose a portable, reclosable container; and you're ready to go.

Anything will do for a grooming box. Try a plastic tub with compartments, but you can even use a bucket or baskets—anything that will hold all of your grooming supplies and keep them upright and organized. If you're using a container that isn't waterproof, you may want to line it with plastic to protect against spills. If you clip or scissor cut your dog's coat, you may choose to keep these sharp implements in a separate box.

Choose the correct tools and supplies for your particular needs. The list below will stock a basic kit; add or subtract items as appropriate for your situation.

- Rubber mat
- Towels (3)
- Blow dryer
- Hemostats for removing ear hairs
- Bristle brush
- Dematting brush
- Wire brush
- Nail trimmer or clipper
- Tweezers
- Wipes
- Blunt-tip scissors
- Clipper, large
- Flea comb
- Regular comb
- Shampoo
- Conditioner
- Bluing (for white dogs)
- Ear wash
- Eye wash
- Flea drops or spray
- Toothbrush
- Dog toothpaste
- Treats

Top Ten Indoor and Outdoor Hygiene Tips

TIPS FOR GOOD HOUSE HYGIENE

- Buy a good-looking toy box where you can stash your pet's extra playthings.

- Cover sofas, dog beds, and bedspreads with washable flat bedsheets.

- Vacuum twice a week or as needed.

- Keep the water bowl on a tiled or linoleum floor or place on a large, waterproof tray to prevent floor damage, and avoid using a combination food-and-water bowl that allows the kibble to fall into and spoil the water.

- Run an air filter in the room you and your dog use the most.

- When the weather is nice, feed your dog outside to reduce mess from runaway kibble.

- Brush your dog at least weekly outdoors.

- Wash your dog every three months, or more often if smelly.

- Housebreak your dog. Keeping a house clean from habitual accidents is an uphill battle that you will lose.

- Use a hypoallergenic, unscented detergent to launder linens, towels, and clothes.

TIPS FOR GOOD OUTDOOR HYGIENE

- Generously spread lime pellets over the grass to neutralize urine odors.

- Pick up your dog's eliminations often.

- Try to lead your dog to smooth, easy-to-pick-up-from surfaces, such as a bed of pine needles, grass, concrete, or firm ground. Dogs relieve themselves where you teach them to go, so make a point of leading your dog, not being led, at the onset of potty training.

- Remove toy parts, broken glass, and trash from the lawn.

- Keep doggy areas pesticide-free. Release predatory live ladybugs and praying mantis cocoons instead.

- Choose dog-friendly, hardy, nonpoisonous plants that can withstand abuse and trampling.

- Keep a bowl of fresh water outside. Watch out for decorative ponds that support mosquitoes and parasites.

- Secure fences; look for any holes or loose boards or wires.

- Make sure your dog has an outdoor safe haven, a covered house away from sun, wind, and rain.

- Correct your dog for destroying tree bark, roots, and bushes, and provide enough toy distractions to keep him playing.

Air Travel with Your Pooch

SOME DOGS HANDLE air travel well, others don't. Unfortunately, there is no test to determine if your dog is a friendly flier. But if he tends to get carsick, or is timid and anxious when faced with new experiences, you may consider boarding your dog.

If you must fly with your pet, never sedate him. Make sure the outside temperatures at your origin and your destination will not be too hot or too cold at the time of day you will be traveling if your dog must travel in cargo, as extreme temperatures can make the stress of travel much worse for your pet. Many airlines will not ship dogs if the temperature will rise above or fall below certain extreme temperatures.

If your dog is traveling in the cabin with you, you will have greater control over his safety and care, but you will also have greater responsibility in making sure he does not disturb other passengers.

Discuss in-cabin pet travel with your airline prior to your trip. Be sure to ask what kind and size of carrier must be used. Find out how the airline will accommodate doggy bathroom trips. Prepare a travel bag with food, treats, and toys your dog can chew quietly. (In other words, leave Mr. Squeaky at home.) Plush toys and chew bones are appropriate. Bring extra bottled water for your dog, and a dish or water feeder. You can purchase mechanisms that fasten on to the top of a squeeze-top water bottle (as opposed to a cap top). They work by turning the water bottle upside down, and the feeder clips on and forms a ladlelike bowl. By squeezing water into the ladle, the dog can have a mess-free drink of water on the go.

Once you have booked your flight, other transportation, and hotels, remember to confirm and reconfirm the reservations for you and your pet. Confirm thirty days ahead, then two weeks before your arrival, and one last time two to three days before you leave. It may seem redundant, but it's better to take the time to ensure a smooth trip than be surprised by a change in flight time or cancellation that you could have prepared for.

Bon voyage!

To My Dog I Pledge . . .

- I WILL ASSUME responsibility for the well-being of my dog.

- I will endeavor to provide clean water and wholesome food to my dog.

- I will provide my dog with daily aerobic exercise.

- I will engage my dog with the community, participating in play groups, sports, or social activities.

- I will develop my dog's intellectual capabilities.

- I will open up my heart to my dog.

Dog Tails: Bread-Loving Basset Hound

OUR BASSET HOUND, Betsy, was a foodie at heart. She didn't discriminate. She would launch her 90-pound (40.8 kg) body up on the countertop, her front paws perched on the edge. From this vantage point, she could get a good look at her dinner prospects. Hanging on to the counter edge, she would crane her neck and let her nose guide her to the goods. Anyone who ever thought Basset Hounds were squat and lazy thought differently after watching Betsy grow to the size of a child when she balanced on two hind legs to snag a treat. She was often successful.

Betsy's appetite stoked newfound agility. She learned to open drawers, which is where she found her best prize: a full loaf of soft, wheat bread. The kitchen drawer was shut, but a tiny corner of the plastic bread bag was left exposed. Mom had made our packed-lunch sandwiches and tucked the bread back in its hiding spot. We could not keep it on the counter because Betsy was a carb-loving hound with refined olfactory capabilities. She could smell bread, smell it strong.

Betsy knew opportunity when she saw it. There was barely enough bag to grip between a person's thumb and first finger, but she was stubborn and determined and, for a very short time, left alone in the kitchen.

My brother and I left for school and Mom was upstairs—not for long, but just long enough for Betsy to begin her kitchen acrobatics. She jumped up to the drawer (or at least, this is how we imagine it since no one was there to witness it). She pressed her jowls against the drawer and clamped onto the bag with her teeth. She jerked back and pulled the drawer out along with her. Down came the bread bag—the prize. She raced off, loaf in mouth, to the living room where she scarfed down every slice and the package in minutes. Mom found Betsy on her side with a belly full of yeasty bread.

Betsy drank water for the next three days, didn't eat a bite of kibble. As she tanked up, the bread loaf inside of her soaked in water like a sponge. Betsy expanded like a blimp. She was a motionless, exhausted, stuffed hound. Mom called the vet. Since Betsy wasn't actually sick, we let the bread hangover run its course. She eventually came around, and unlike humans who would probably avoid the substance that sickened them after overindulging, Betsy was still every bit as interested in bread. However, our family did move the loaf to a shelf—still within smelling distance, but far from her reach.

Creating a Freestanding Shade Canopy for Your Dog Run

This homemade shade canopy is a quick and easy way to keep your dog out of the sun. Choose the size and style of the fabric to customize it for your needs. Use water-resistant fabric if you want to make it weatherproof.

MATERIALS

Four pieces of 2 x 4–inch (5 x 10 cm) wood, 6 feet (1.8 m) long

Handsaw

Sandpaper

Tack cloth or clean, lint-free rag

Wood stain and sealer, or paint

Paintbrush

Fabric, your choice of size and type

Pinking shears

Staple gun

1. To make the stakes, using the handsaw, cut one edge of each wood piece at a 45-degree angle (to make a sharp point for staking—some lumberyards will do this for you).

2. Sand the wood to remove splinters and prepare it for finishing. Wipe the dust with the tack cloth or rag.

3. Stain and seal, or paint, each stake, following the manufacturer's instructions. Allow to dry thoroughly.

4. Cut the unfinished edges of your fabric with pinking shears to keep them from unraveling (or you can hem them with a sewing machine if you want a more finished look).

5. Mark four spots on the ground that correspond to the corners of the fabric.

6. Drive the stakes into the ground at these spots (see variation below if you don't have soft ground).

7. Staple the fabric to the tops of the stakes.

8. When the fabric gets worn or faded, pull out the staples and replace it with new fabric.

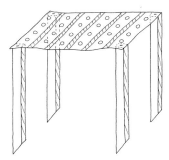

Assembly diagram for canopy

Variation

If you don't have soft ground, or want to set up the canopy on your patio, purchase four large planters, a large bag or two of gravel, and enough soil to fill the pots. Rather than driving the stakes into the ground, center each stake in its own pot. Fill each pot with gravel 6 to 8 inches (15 to 20 cm) deep, holding the stake centered and vertical as you do so. Firmly pack soil on top of the gravel. If desired, put a few nontoxic plants in the soil. Place the planters at the corners of the fabric, and staple the fabric to the top of the stakes.

How to Clean Your Dog's Ears

REGULAR WEEKLY EAR CLEANING is important for all dogs, but especially for dogs who do a lot of swimming, or dogs with ears that flap over. Moisture can build up in the ears and start an infection. Ear mites can be a nuisance also, and dogs' ears need to be checked regularly so these pests don't take up residence.

MATERIALS

Veterinarian-approved ear wash (look for one with presoaked cotton pads)

Cotton balls or cotton pads

Veterinarian-approved ear-drying powder

1. Relax your dog by talking to her in a low voice and praising her. Gently pull open the ear so you can see the top and the inside of the ear canal.

2. Soak a clean cotton ball or pad with ear wash. Swab the inside of the ear thoroughly, removing the brown residue. Sweep your index finger into the ear canal, using a circular motion, for deeper access. Never use cotton swabs, which can puncture your dog's eardrum. Repeat with fresh cotton balls or pads until all brown residue has been removed. (Don't forget to give praise!)

3. Squeeze drying powder onto a fresh cotton ball or towelette and apply to the inside of the ear. Fold down the ear and massage at the base of the ear in a circular motion to help the powder dry. Ear-drying powder is really a liquid that dries as powder. It creates a moisture barrier in your dog's ear that helps prevent odor-causing yeast or bacteria from taking up residence in the ear canal.

If your dog has trouble with ear cleaning, start slowly and do it daily—and incorporate treats as rewards! Starting when your dog is a puppy will make this routine easier for both of you.

254

Cleaning Ears

1. **Pull back the ear so you can see into the ear canal.**

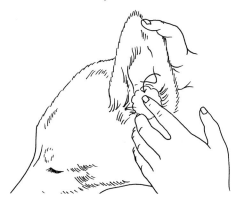

2. **Swab the ear canal with a cotton ball or pad and cleaning solution, using your index finger for deeper access.**

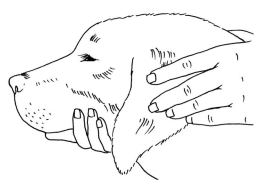

3. **Apply the drying powder to the ear with a cotton ball. Fold down the ear, and rub at the base of the ear in a circular motion to help the powder dry.**

Making a New-Dog Welcome Basket

NEW DOG PARENTS are usually showered with toys for their new pet, but puppies need more than toys. If you have an occasion to welcome a new puppy into a friend's life, a gift basket of care items and other essentials will be much appreciated.

Find out what kind of puppy or dog she is so you can buy appropriately sized things. Choose a basket to put everything in; a basket that can be reused later for toy storage is a good idea. Use a cloth liner or shredded paper in the bottom of the basket if you like, and arrange your gifts attractively in the basket. Finished baskets can be wrapped in cellophane, if desired, or left open and simply adorned with a big bow.

Items to consider include:

- Grooming items: brush, comb, shampoo, conditioner

- Cleaning and deodorizing products for puppy messes

- Treats suitable for puppies

- Rawhides: cow ear, pig ear, spirals (be sure these are not too small so they are not a choking hazard)

- A dog blanket (see Day 38)

- A photo album or blank book for a dog journal (see Day 31)

- A cute collar or leash

- A book on dog first aid

- And, of course, a few toys (who can resist?)

You're in Love–Is Your Dog?

YOU ARE IN a new relationship and want to introduce your special someone to your canine companion. Breaking the news to your one-and-only that there's another person in the picture can be tricky. However, if you go about it the right way, you can strengthen the relationship with your new interest, and your loyal companion—that's your dog. Before you get too nervous, remember that your dog sees you as the pack leader and will take her cue from you.

Allow your new interest and your dog to meet each other for the first time in neutral territory, before inviting the person into your home for the first time. You can meet in a park or at the beach—somewhere away from home. If the dog shows signs of jealousy, have your significant other do a bonding activity with him, such as a walk or a game of catch. Another great tip for the first-time introduction: Make sure that your friend has a pocket full of treats.

Invite him or her to feed the dog occasionally. Have your guest play with your dog and give her treats.

If your relationship progresses and a new companion moves in, be patient with your dog as she gets used to sharing your time and attention. Have your partner take over some of the fun activities to become "part of the pack." Before he or she moves in, consider leaving some of your companion's clothing around the house, so the dog gets used to the scent.

Be confident and deliberate in your introductions and blending your households, if it leads to that, and your dog will accept this new pack member, and be happy for another human to play with, no doubt.

When Your Puppy Hits Adolescence: What You Need to Know

ADOLESCENCE IN DOGS can start anywhere from four to six months of age, depending on the breed. At this stage, your puppy starts to develop his adult teeth, confidence, and more bulk in muscle. Some breeders and trainers refer to adolescence as the "fight period"— just like a human teenager, an adolescent puppy is feeling confident and testing his boundaries. Adolescence is also an investigation stage, where puppies want to go off and explore.

Adolescence is often when destructive behavior occurs, such as chewing on furniture, not coming when called, and general disobedience.

During this period, your puppy's brain and body are flooded by hormones and under stress from growth and muscle development and the general trials of going from puppy to adult.

Fortunately, unlike the human version of adolescence, the dog version usually will not last more than four to twelve months. It's important during this time is to continue daily training, recall training, and positive behavior rewards. If you remain positive and consistent in your training, your dog will come out of adolescence well adjusted and ready to start the next phase of his life: adulthood.

Microchipping: High-Tech Identification

PET IDENTIFICATION IS crucial to your being able to get your dog back should he wander off and get lost. ID tags are important, of course, but what if his tags get lost, too? New microchip technology provides us with a permanent way to identify your dog to strangers so he can be returned to you.

Before microchipping came along, many people tattooed their show dogs on their belly and their thigh. When microchipping became available, many owners went to this system because it is less painful and much faster. As it grew in popularity, the costs came down and it became more widely available. Today, microchipping is offered just about everywhere, and it is relatively inexpensive.

The microchip is the size of a small grain of rice, and is encoded with a number that can be read by a handheld scanner. The vet uses a special injector to place it under the dog's skin. Some dogs will yelp or cry during this process, others may not notice the process happening. Be sure to use a lot of rewards and praise while the process is taking place. If your dog is picked up and brought to the pound, they can read the chip with a scanner, call the number in, and contact you. You must keep your contact information up to date with the database administrator, however.

There is one potential problem with microchipping: Competing microchip technologies have recently come to the marketplace, and not all scanners can read all the microchips that are out there. You may want to check to see which scanners your local shelters have before choosing which type of microchip to implant.

GPS collars for dogs have recently become available. The collar contains a GPS transmitter that will let you know where your dog is and help you find him if he gets out.

Safety Tips for Night Walking

SOMETIMES YOU HAVE no choice but to walk your dog in the dark. Follow these safety precautions when walking at night.

- Walk with a flashlight.

- Use reflective tape on your dog's collar and leash for added visibility—or purchase a collar and leash that have reflectors or that light up.

- Wear shoes that have reflectors on them, or add reflective tape to them.

- Wear light-colored clothing. Consider a jacket made for joggers that has reflective material built in.

- If you have to walk alongside a road and there is no sidewalk, make sure you walk against the traffic. This increases your visibility to drivers and allows you to see what's coming toward you.

- Keep your dog on her leash and make sure her leash is secure.

Mix Your Own Natural Bug Repellent

As YOU SEEK out all-natural cleaning solutions that are safe for you and your pets, you'll find that essential oils are commonly used in cleansers and disinfectants. Not only do they smell nice, they repel undesirable bugs that can carry disease and they keep flies away.

You can find organic essential oils at natural foods stores. The oils generally share an aisle with vitamins and supplements. Reach for such essential oils as lavender, wintergreen, and citronella, which all help keep the flies away from you and your dog. Choose the one you like best and saturate a clean makeup sponge with it. Place the saturated sponge in a glass dish and set it out in the area you want to protect. A few drops of essential oils go a long way. Use these precious ingredients sparingly.

To deodorize garbage cans and dog waste containers, dab essential oil on a cotton ball and place the saturated cotton in the container with the lid shut.

What I Have Learned from My Dog

We humans could learn a lesson or two from our dogs, who are perfectly content with a day of napping, eating, walking, and begging . . . for naps, food, and walks. The balance they add to a household is good medicine. If our dogs were to set the "house rules," these would be their commandments:

Ask, and then chew.

The best way to get to know someone is to play with them.

Fresh air is the best medicine.

If you are ill, lie down until you feel better.

If you find something smelly in the yard, do not roll around in it.

If you snatch someone else's food from the table, be sure to lick up the crumbs.

If you get caught doing something wrong, try to look as cute as possible.

Hugs are a healthy way to start the day.

If you don't get what you want, never stop trying.

There is such a thing as unconditional love.

Appreciate life's simple pleasures.

Be patient.

Good companions improve and extend life.

The world is an endlessly thrilling place, full of excitement and surprises around every corner.

Smell out every situation.

It's O.K. to sleep in and lick yourself.

Treats are no reason to feel guilty. The more treats the better. (Can I have a treat?)

Never pass up the opportunity to go for a joyride.

Always greet loved ones at the door with unabashed enthusiasm.

Practice obedience, when it's in your best interest.

260

Dog Tails: The Cost of Dog Ownership

OUR ENGLISH BULLDOG, Murphy, has expensive taste. He has a habit of devouring things that he shouldn't, and the vet bills are a bonus. So far, here is the tally:

Prescription glasses

Sunscreen

Emergency visit to the vet to ensure that Murphy hadn't eaten a lethal amount of sunscreen

Oakley sunglasses

Ball of twine

Chocolate bar

Emergency call to poison control to ensure that Murphy didn't' eat too much chocolate: free (thank goodness!)

Tennis ball

Tennis ball removal from stomach

A happy, healthy bulldog who will probably continue to eat off-limits items: priceless

Although all of this health care costs could have bought us a weeklong Caribbean cruise!

Doggy Fashion: Coats and Sweaters

DURING THE WINTER months in cold climates, dogs need protection from extreme weather, too. Coats and sweaters can protect them from snow, ice, damp, and cold.

You don't want a dog coat or sweater to be too long or too short. If it's too long, he may soil it when doing his business. If it's too short, it won't keep his entire body warm. It's best to take your dog with you to the pet store, if you can, but if not, you'll at least need to get his measurements and take them with you so you can select the right size.

When measuring for a dog coat or sweater, get your dog to stand, not sit. Sitting changes the line of the back and may give you a false measurement. Use a tape measure to measure from the base of your dog's neck where the collar normally lies to the base of your dog's tail. This is just above where the tail extends from the body. That's the size of coat or sweater you want.

Usually coats and sweaters come in even sizes, so if you have a measurement of 19 inches (48.5 cm), try an 18-inch (45.5 cm) coat. The inch won't make much of a difference, and it's usually better to be a little shorter than a little too long. You don't want the coat or sweater you choose to bind or bunch up on your dog.

Get your dog used to wearing a sweater or coat by letting him "try on" the clothing indoors and wear it for a short time; then remove it and praise him with a treat. Gradually introduce clothing, and be gentle when putting on sweaters and coats.

261

Enticing a Finicky Eater

DOGS CAN BE finicky eaters when they're feeling lethargic or a little sick. It can be frustrating when your dog won't eat, but you should try to get him to do it so he stays healthy and keeps his strength up. Here are a few techniques you can use to try to entice him.

You don't want to change your dog's diet altogether unless the vet has told you to do so, but you can add gravy to his regular food to make it more attractive.

First start with making your own homemade gravy by using beef or chicken broth, making sure you use a special flour, which is milled extra thin for easy thickening or even use cornstarch; both will help to thicken the liquid.

Put ½ cup (120 ml) of low- or no-salt beef or chicken broth in a pan and bring to a simmer. Slowly whisk in 1 teaspoon of flour or arrowroot powder and continue to whisk until thickened. Add finely chopped bits of meat. Allow to cool, then pour over your dog's food.

If gravy alone doesn't work, try to add chopped hot dogs or liverwurst mixed well into the kibble.

There will occasionally be days when a dog may not want to eat at all. This is normal. As long as he is drinking water don't worry, but if he has stopped drinking, or if he doesn't resume eating after a day or two, call your vet.

Hiking with Your Dog

ONE OF THE most fun, time-honored activities that you and your dog can do together is hiking. Hiking is more challenging and stimulating than walking because you experience a new environment other than your around-the-block route, and you negotiate nature's obstacles as you move along paths or blaze your own trail. Imagine all the new smells your dog will discover! A change in setting is beneficial for both of you, and neither dog nor owner need be in excellent physical shape to hike. Essentially, the sport involves walking on ground other than sidewalk with a backdrop other than neighbors' houses. If you can walk, you can hike. Your dog will thank you for the new sights and sounds by taking a big nap when you return home.

Before you pack up the dog treats and get on the road to a nearby hiking trail, do some investigating online or by calling your local park system to find out what trails are appropriate for your and your dog's fitness level. Many areas have published guides available that show and rate different trails: beginner, intermediate, or advanced. Stick to the right level, and don't push yourself or your pet too hard. Also, be sure to have enough water and food for both you and your dog.

Keep your dog on a leash on the way to and from the trail, and be sure you know the leash rules on the trail you intend to hike. Even if your dog is allowed off leash during the hike, you must be able to control her in public places, just like when you are in a dog park. You don't want to be rude or overwhelm other hikers. You must know how your dog will react when meeting another dog or hiker on the trail. Keep her leash tied to your waist or belt loop so it's accessible at all times.

Before hiking, be sure your dog is up to date on her rabies vaccinations. Know the natural hazards in your location, such as rattlesnakes, predators, or dangerous terrain. Consider bringing along a first-aid kit (see Day 95) to deal with common hazards.

Don't forget to bring along your camera! Hiking with your dog can offer many opportunities for great shots: streams, fallen branches, harmless wild animals. A priceless picture of your dog encountering something new will be a cherished memento of your hike.

The Dog Days of Summer

HOT SUMMER DAYS can lead to overheating, dehydration, or sunburn for your dog if you don't take precautions. During hot weather make sure your pet is in an area that is well-ventilated with good airflow. You can simply aim a fan at her crate, for a sure fix. If she's outside, make sure she has access to adequate shade. Supply her with plenty of fresh water. Most important, never leave your dog unattended in a car, even if it doesn't seem that warm. Temperatures in a closed car can climb quickly, and dogs are more susceptible to overheating and dehydration than humans. And, in many places, leaving your dog alone in the car is against the law.

OVERHEATING

Some signs of overheating include a swollen tongue, cloudy eyes, excessive panting, and white gums. If left untreated, the dog could die.

Treatment: Get the dog into a shaded area and ventilate with a fan. Run cool—not cold—water over her. Apply water to the abdomen and the area where the legs connect to the body. This will help cool her faster, similar to how humans can put cool water on pulse points to feel more immediate relief from heat.

DEHYDRATION

If left untreated, dehydration can cause organ failure and, eventually, death. Signs of dehydration are a dry nose and mouth, eyes that are sunken and dry, and lost skin elasticity.

Treatment: Get the dog rehydrated as soon as possible. Water can be used, but must be offered in small amounts in short intervals. If a severely dehydrated dog is offered too much water, she could begin to vomit, which can cause further dehydration. Electrolyte drinks can be used for rehydration. If you suspect severe dehydration, get her to your vet immediately.

SUNBURN

Signs of sunburn include redness and hair loss from the ear tips, abdomen, and the bridge of the nose. Although most pet sunburns may be minor and heal with time, repeated exposure can lead to skin cancer in pets, just like in people. Lighter-haired pets are more likely to get sunburned than darker-haired pets.

Prevention: Avoid going outside between the hours of 11 a.m. and 3 p.m. Certain breeds that are susceptible to cancer (check with your vet) should be protected from the sun more. Spray-on sunblock made specifically for dogs is now available, but the ones made for babies work, too. Just be careful to keep it out of your dog's eyes. Or you can use a bodysuit made of UV-blocking fabric.

Treatment: Spray the area with cool water at 30-minute intervals, or use a cold compress held over the burn. Witch hazel applied every few hours will take away the heat of the burn, and skin conditioners can be used as well. You can also give your pet a bath in lukewarm water with colloidal oatmeal mixed in the water. Aloe gel can also be added; this will help cool the sunburn and help it heal faster.

Check the color of your dog's gums. If they are pink and look hydrated, she's in good shape. However, if they are white, blue, brown, yellow, very red, very pale, or white call the vet right away—this can be a sign of a serious medical condition.

264

Create a Pet Portrait

NOTHING BEAMS, "I love my dog," more than a pet portrait on a mantel or side table. There are many ways you can create a pet portrait, even if you don't consider yourself artistically inclined. Make a photograph of your dog into a slide and project the image onto a canvas to trace. Fill in with color. You can also, using computer graphics, alter a scanned pet picture into a cartoon or black-and-white image.

Simply print onto the paper size of your choice and paint. Finally, you can send a favorite picture to a commercial company to have it transformed into a paint-by-numbers canvas. Pretty neat, and you don't have to let on to your amazed friends that you had some help. Lastly, if you have the funds, hire a professional artist or photographer to create a portrait of your pet. Pick an artist who specializes in animal portraiture and has an artistic style you prefer.

Dog Tails: The Singing Dog

JUSTICE IS HIS NAME. He's become quite the "golden" crooner. I guess music runs in the family.

It started when he was young. I'm not quite sure how. He came to it naturally with no real prompting on my part. I was singing and playing my guitar one day, and then I hear this gentle howling off in the corner. Justice the Golden Retriever was looking at me, wagging his tail, very interested in the music.

I almost fell off my chair.

I stopped, Justice stopped. I started singing again, and he started again with a perfectly pitched doggy howl that nearly matched my tone. He pointed his muzzle in the air, just like a wolf, and belted it out.

But never by himself. No, he has to have a singing partner. Me. He's quite shy about it. He's never felt comfortable singing in front of others. Just when he's with me. It's a dad and dog thing.

Justice likes to sing late at night. When I'm on the couch and Justice is a little bored, looking for some attention, I ask, "You want to sing?" He starts pacing anxiously, happily. He waits.

Then I start doing my best Pavarotti imitation (which isn't very good), and the next thing I know it's a high-pitched dog-man duet. And it goes on and on. As long as I keep it up, he's right there with me, nose in the air, howling.

I say "You're a good singin' dog, Justice, a very good singin' dog." Justice smiles. It makes his day.

Once, Justice really took me by surprise. I was playing a recording of my band's recent session with the volume up loud. While I stood focused on listening to the recording, from behind me came Justice's barreling dog howl—almost as if he's singing a third-part harmony.

I said "Justice, have you been taking singing lessons from someone? You're getting awfully good at this."

Lately, he's taken to just chiming in when I'm playing my guitar. I think it's in his blood now.

What Kind of Sleeper Is Your Dog?

HOW MANY TIMES have you just laughed at how your dog is sleeping? Is he dreaming, or is he just taking a nap? Is he curled up, stretched out on his back with his legs wide open, or on his tummy, all bundled up? Most dogs fall into one of these four categories of sleepers.

SIDE AND BELLY SLEEPER

Most of the time when the dog is sleeping on his side, or sleeping on his belly with all four paws laid out, he is dozing. Less often, he may fall into a deep sleep from this position.

BACK SLEEPER

To many dog owners, this is the funniest of all positions: four paws in the air. A dog gets dream sleep and is the most relaxed in this position, because his stomach is exposed to the air, so he is able to keep cool, and none of his muscles are tense, so he is able completely relax. In this position—and the side positions to a lesser extent—is where you will witness a lot of the funny dream states happening, including kicking, wagging tails, nose and whiskers twitching, muffled barks and cries, mouths moving like they are eating, feet running, snoring, and, sometimes, flat-out bliss.

CURLED-UP-IN-A-BALL SLEEPER

This is a common resting or napping position. Dogs wake up very quickly from this position.

LYING BACK-TO-BACK

When a dog sleeps back-to-back next to another dog, they are bonding: They feel safe protecting each other. When they lie on their backs next to you, they are taking time to bond with you. When there is a pack of dogs, they tend to sleep all together, although sometime the alpha dog will sleep apart or in a higher position.

Your Dog's Sleeping Habits

It's important to understand your dogs sleeping habits: even a gentle dog can get grouchy if it doesn't get enough sleep. Dogs sleep almost half their lives—about twelve hours per day. Sometimes you may be playing with your puppy and he just passes out: He just can't help it, he needs his sleep. The temperature in a room will influence how your dog sleeps, so be sure the temperature is comfortable for him. Like us, dogs have different stages of sleep. The deepest sleep is called REM, when they are completely relaxed. The phrase "let sleeping dogs lie" is not just a saying: Consider that 60 percent of dog bites happen to children when they wake a dog who is in a deep REM sleep. If you need to wake your dog, call his name softly without touching him.

Why Buy Premium Pet Food?

SHOP ANY GROCERY or pet store's dog food aisle, and you'll be faced with what seems like an endless array of choices, some brands costing twice as much as others, if not more. Why the difference?

The biggest difference is usually the protein source. Premium brands may use chicken, lamb, fish, bison, or duck as their primary protein. Most bargain brands use grains, such as corn, wheat, or soy. Some bargain brands do use meat, but as meat by-products or meat by-product meal, which are usually not high-quality sources of protein.

Dogs are carnivores, and grains are hard for them to digest. More of the food passes through their digestive systems unprocessed, meaning that you have to feed your dog more bargain food than premium food to get the same nutrition. More of it just ends up undigested in the backyard in your dog's feces. (The exception to this is rice, which is mostly digestible by dogs.) Your dog may be eating a lot but not eating well. She may even be eating herself ill. Research has linked grain consumption with increasing rates of diabetes in dogs.

Most fat in dog food is stabilized with a preservative so that it will not go rancid in the bag. Some bargain brands use artificial preservatives, whereas premium brands use mixed tocopherols or vitamin E as a preservative.

Also watch for indigestible fillers such as cellulose, which is wood fiber. Even premium brands will slip this ingredient into "diet" food to fill up your dog's tummy. It has no nutritional value.

Although the premium food may look like it costs more, it can actually be more economical in the longrun. Your dog can digest it better, you don't need to feed her as much to get the same nutrition, and you'll have less poop to scoop.

(See Day 316 for more on dog food.)

Friendly Tug-of-War

DOES TUG-OF-WAR teach aggression and possessiveness? Or does the game satisfy certain breeds' oral fixations and prevent them from exerting "mouth" energy on furniture instead? Tug-of-war has gotten a bad rap, and if you don't set ground rules, the game can get out of hand and teach bad habits. Mainly, your dog will think he's the alpha in charge. However, when played correctly, tug-of-war is a natural energy outlet that helps dogs release excitement and play drive. Some breeds naturally want to burrow and use their mouths, such as Terriers and Dachshunds. Tug-of-war is a healthy way to bond with your dog, and a great time to teach such commands as "drop it."

First, set ground rules for tug-of-war. Here are some tips to guide your play:

Start young. Begin playing tug-of-war when your dog is a puppy and during early training.

Teach "drop it." Similar commands are "trade you" and "mine." Essentially, you teach your dog to give up the desired tugging item by offering him a treat and saying "Drop it" (or another command). Be consistent. Play the tugging game, then allow your arm to go slack. This indicates you are no longer competing or playing. Have a treat ready in your free hand and hold it next to your puppy's clenched mouth. Say "Drop it." Your dog will learn to eat the treat, then eventually to just drop the toy on command. "Drop it" is essentially for healthy tug-of-war play.

Be the alpha. You should initiate the game, not your dog. You also decide when the game is over by saying the command "drop it."

Homemade Flea Collars

THIS EASY PROJECT makes a great-smelling collar that naturally repels fleas. You can store the leftover oil to refresh the collar or to make flea wipes (see Day 319).

MATERIALS

Plain cotton strapping (from the fabric store)

Side-release buckles to fit the strapping

1 tablespoon (14 ml) 100 percent organic citronella oil

1 tablespoon (14 ml) 100 percent organic tea tree oil

1½ teaspoons (7 ml) 100 percent organic rosemary essential oil

1 tablespoon (14 ml) 100 percent organic lemongrass essential oil

1 tablespoon (14 ml) 100 percent organic tangerine essential oil

1. Measure your dog's neck. Add 4 inches (10 cm) to this measurement and cut the strapping to that length.

2. Mix the oils together in a glass bowl.

3. Soak the strapping in the oils for 20 minutes.

4. Remove the strapping from the bowl. Air-dry for about 5 hours.

5. Store any remaining oil in a dark glass container in the refrigerator.

6. Attach the buckles to the ends of the strapping, following the manufacturer's instructions.

Fixing Scratches on Your Wood Furniture

YOUR DOG WILL inevitably scratch a piece of furniture at some point. Chair legs, table bases, bookshelves within reach—these are chewing temptations for dogs, and we usually find this out the hard way, despite puppy-proofing efforts. The good news: You can hide or repair scratches with basic household products you already have in the pantry.

- Shoe polish that matches the wood color

- The meat of a walnut or pecan

- Colored markers

- Commercially prepared, boiled linseed oil

- Wax crayons designed for wood, available in wood-stain colors

For surface scratches, you can puff up the wood to the surface (or close enough to it) by squeezing water from a wet paper towel onto the wood. Lay the wet paper towel over the wood, and iron the wood on a low setting as you would a shirt.

For deep scratches or to fill in missing chunks of wood, first determine the wood type, and then visit a local lumberyard and ask for wood shavings or discarded wood scrap in that variety. (You'll make your own shavings if a scrap is provided.) Mix the shavings with carpenter's glue until you achieve a paste consistency. Rebuild the furniture by applying the mixture to the damaged area. Once dry, smooth the area by sanding and staining the wood. You may also need to supplement this technique with wax crayons or wood-stain pens to match the original wood color.

Meet Mayzie

AFTER LIVING IN our home for about a year, my husband and I barely knew the neighbors. We were childless, dogless newlyweds who had moved from our high-rise apartment to a corner house in a lakeside bedroom community where biker gangs are bands of bicycle riders, and loiterers are mothers and fathers who stall on street corners to talk. Parents run with baby strollers and couples walk side by side, tugging behind them wagons of tots, and maybe a dog.

And oh, there are lots of dog walkers on our street: about a half-dozen Labradors, a feisty Puggle (Beagle-Pug mix), an athletic Weimaraner, a talkative Schnauzer, a yippy Poodle, and a burly black Mastiff, among others. The dog parade passes our house every day, their owners making morning and evening treks around the block— rush hour for working dog walkers. With children, it's easy to meet the neighbors. They pop over into adjoining backyards to check out the really cool swing set. Eventually, a parental meeting ensues (around dinnertime). With dogs, owners have exposure on their side. Because of daily circles around the block with their dogs on leash, owners learn every human (by face) and dog (by name). And if a puppy is involved, introductions—"How adorable!" "What's her name?"—fly faster than any welcome wagon could.

We're social people, we thought. We sit on our front porch. We wave to passersby. Still, how easy is it to strike up random conversation without a prompt (dog or kid)?

Things changed the first week Mayzie, our Scottish Terrier, came home. She was so tiny she could be cupped in our hands. Her black fur was a puffy cloud, and her tail wagged in circles at the sight of anything new—especially potential friends. To anyone who gave her an admiring look (and even those who tried not to), she scurried right up to their feet and rolled on her side, submissively (tail still wagging). This was her invitation for a belly rub. We met lots of people, and mostly their dogs. (We admit, we remember the dogs' names and sometimes not the owners'.)

We joked about the fact that everyone seemed to come out of the woodwork all at once. Mayzie was our social ambassador. "It shows we're responsible—not hooligans," affirmed my husband, straightening his tie to confirm his reasoning.

When we first introduced Mayzie to a leash, she didn't want any part of it until she realized she could travel up and down the street, which meant more attention. The sidewalk became her red carpet. Rather than gracefully making her way up the road, she sprinted to the nearest visible person, then stopped for some loving attention. Before long, neighbors were greeting her by name at the first sign of her trolling down the sidewalk.

We feel quite at home in our neighborhood now, thanks to Mayzie. We're a family, and Mayzie as the doted-over child—and the star— at least in our eyes.

Reading a Dog Food Label

WHAT'S IN A bag of dog food? Increased focus on healthy living and recent problems with pet food contamination have made us all more conscious of what our dogs are eating.

Food labeling is strictly regulated, and that goes for dog food, too. Ingredients must be listed in order by the amount within, so a food with more chicken in it than anything else must list chicken as the first ingredient, then the next most abundant ingredient, and so on.

But be careful! Sometimes manufacturers will list different forms of the same ingredient to make it appear that they contain more of something desirable and less of something not so desirable. For example, you could see ground whole corn, and a bit further down the list you could see cornmeal, and even further down the list you could see corn middlings (a by-product of corn-processing).

All these different forms of the same thing could add up to more than the first ingredient listed. Just because you see chicken listed first doesn't mean you should stop reading the label.

Conversely, make sure that protein foods, not grains, appear in the first several ingredients in the list. Chunky canned foods should be real protein sources cut into chunks, not ground meat felted into chunks with the addition of such grains as wheat.

(See Day 310 for more on dog food.)

Starting Training on the Right Foot

It is never too early to begin training your puppy. As soon as you introduce a pooch to your home, she will explore her surroundings and, eventually, test the limits. She will learn your schedule and, over time, adapt to the environment. During this discovery period, you should begin training basic commands (see Day 80). The same energy your dog spends learning a bad habit could be directed toward adopting good behavior.

Training is a never-ending process. You will exercise your dog's mental muscles daily, reminding her on walks to heel and wait, or asking her to sit and "drop it" if she runs off with a favorite shoe. Your dog will learn to enjoy training time, and the learning will keep her stimulated.

Here are some pointers to remember during training time to make the experience positive for both of you:

- Keep training sessions short and end on a positive note.

- If your dog does not catch on to new commands, or you feel she is falling behind, set her up for success by backtracking that day and practicing commands she knows, so she can earn rewards.

- Introduce distractions gradually as you and your dog gain confidence.

- Practice training sessions at different times during the day, and in different locations to prevent boredom.

- If you become frustrated, stop and take a break.

- Remember, you are not perfect—and neither is your dog.

Does My Dog Really Need Boots?

IN SOME PLACES, winter can be brutal, with deep snow, cold temperatures, and ice. You suit up in winter gear before heading out into the cold and ice, and your dog may require similar protection for safety and comfort. Dog boots do the same thing your boots do for you: protect feet from winter weather and foot injuries.

Dog boots are good in climates where sand is used for traction in icy conditions and salt and other chemicals are used to melt snow and ice. Sand can get in your dog's feet and cause an irritation, like a grain of sand in a pearl, and salt and chemical ice melters can irritate or even burn his paws.

Many mushers use boots to protect their dog's feet and keep them warm and dry when racing. Many hunters use leather boots to protect their dog's feet when they are tracking game in the woods or a field.

Boots are also used to protect your dog's feet after foot surgery. They provide a barrier between your dog's foot and the ground, where he may encounter feces, urine, and lawn chemicals that could irritate or cause an infection in a suture. They work much better than plastic bags that easily puncture or wear away.

(See Resources, page 318.)

Fit Your Dog for Boots

The best way to fit your dog for boots is to take him to the store with you, so he can try on various footwear. (Yes, there are many options.) Otherwise, trace your dog's foot, including the nails, while he is standing and take this sketch to the store.

Dog boots are sold in sets of four and are made of many different materials, such as nylon, fleece, leather, and plastic. There is even a version with a suede bottom and a knitted leg that is held up with adjustable suspenders. As with introducing any clothing, let your dog get used to the boots indoors. Slip them on his feet and fasten them, then praise him and give him a treat. A few minutes later, take them off. Let him sniff the boots (so he knows they are his), and always reward him when you put them on.

275

Homemade Flea Wipes

THESE TRAVEL-READY flea wipes will help keep fleas naturally at bay.

MATERIALS

1 tablespoon (14 ml) 100 percent organic citronella oil

1 tablespoon (14 ml) 100 percent organic tea tree oil

1½ teaspoons (7 ml) 100 percent organic rosemary essential oil

1 tablespoon (14 ml) 100 percent organic lemongrass essential oil

1 tablespoon (14 ml) 100 percent organic tangerine essential oil

4 ounces (120 ml) 99 percent pure aloe vera gel

1 package plain, unscented disposable wipes

1. Mix the oils in a shallow glass bowl or baking dish (or reuse the oils mixed for Day 312).

2. Add the aloe and blend very well.

3. Remove the wipes from their packaging and place them in the oil mixture. Soak the wipes for 2 to 3 hours.

4. When the wipes are saturated, transfer them to an airtight plastic bag. Store in a cool, dark place.

5. To use, rub a disposable wipe over your dog's body once a day.

How to Make a Dog Bed

THIS DOG BED is quick and easy to make. If you don't sew, use nontoxic fabric glue instead of sewing the seams. You can splurge on pricey fabric, or keep it simple with plain cotton. Make a couple of covers in different fabrics if you want to be able to change the look.

MATERIALS

Sewing machine

A premade square pillow, down- or poly-filled, with a good muslin cover

Fabric (enough to cover your pillow; make sure it's machine washable for easy cleaning)

Pinking shears

Hook-and-loop tape (a strip 1 inch [2.5 cm] longer than the pillow measurement)

Thread to match your fabric, and a sewing needle

When selecting the size of pillow for your type of dog, just remember that you want her to be able to stand up and turn around a few times. This way she can nest, and find her sweet spot to lie down on. As a guideline, use 25 inches (63.5 cm) for a small dog, 36 inches (91.5 cm) for a medium-size dog, and 40 inches (101.5 cm) for a large dog.

1. Prewash your fabric in hot water. Dry and iron it.

2. Lay your fabric out on your work surface.

3. Measure your pillow from seam to seam. Add 2 inches (4 cm) to this measurement to get the width of the fabric you need, and double the measurement and add 2 inches (2 cm) to get the length. For example, a 24-inch (61 cm) square pillow will need a piece of fabric that is 26 x 50 inches (66 x 127 cm).

4. Cut your fabric.

5. Hem both of the short ends.

6. Fold the fabric so the two short ends meet, right side together.

7. Stitch the two sides together up each side with a ⅝-inch (1.5 cm) seam allowance, leaving the hemmed side open.

8. Sew the hook-and-loop tape to the open ends.

9. Turn the cover right side out, and insert the pillow. Close the hook-and-loop tape, and introduce your dog to his new bed.

277

Dog Tails: The Pack Mentality

WE'VE ALWAYS HAD at least three dogs at our house—some people think we were crazy for having a farmful of Bassets at one point. But the dogs are our entertainment. They're comics, complete clowns. We loved nothing more than watching them romp outdoors and then barrel into the kitchen during dinner to sniff and sample what was being served. Each dog brought a unique talent to the pack: Wiggle loved salad (and preferred carrots). Maudie liked to be dressed up in our son's surfer shorts and sunglasses—and she did not want to be laughed at. However, one dog, Sister Phred, was the undisputed queen bee.

Sister Phred was the head of the pack for her fourteen years. She raised the pups and called the shots on our farm, which had as many as fifteen dogs in its heyday. Sister Phred was a Samoyed/Shepherd mix, and her cohorts were Stout the mutt and Cootie, a Poodle/Schnauzer/ Terrier mix with a kinky double coat that made her look like a Yeti when it snowed. Once we began to breed Basset puppies, Sister Phred adopted the babies as if they were her own.

Over time, the pack expanded and broke into two denominations: the inside group and the outside crew. The insiders lazed on the screened-in back porch, and the outsiders rabble-roused in the backyard. There was a pecking order, and Sister Phred was in charge of both troops.

Her power was body language: No one disobeyed Sister Phred. We knew when she was delivering orders because she would approach one of the Bassets and nose the Basset in the direction she wanted him to go. She appointed her "court," including a vice president who was in charge of feeding. Chow master was a critical job—ensuring mealtime harmony—and she took assigning it very seriously. Sister Phred approached a very solid Basset and steered him toward the feeding area. Then, Sister Phred promptly left the Basset there at his new post. Every dog had his own dish, and no one stole kibble from neighboring bowls as long as Sister Phred's assistant was on guard.

In the pack system, the dogs teach each other—even housetraining and socializing puppies—so forget about training, and be careful when interfering. Every once in a while, our backyard crew broke into a brawl over something trivial, such as a stick coveted by dueling Bassets. I would wrangle the troublemaker onto a leash, and one by one lasso leashes around the other members of the clan, tying them to separate posts in the backyard until they settled down. Once they did, they happily returned to their business, no grudges.

Toxic Foods

Do you have a counter surfer or a dog who loves to tip over the garbage and check out the offerings? Although many of the foods we eat are harmless to dogs, some aren't.

FOOD	SYMPTOMS & HEALTH ISSUES
Chocolate	Excessive stimulation of the central nervous system, heart muscle, and skeletal muscle. Can result in restlessness, stiffness, hyperthermia, seizures, and death.
Caffeine and coffee	Same effects as chocolate.
Grapes and raisins	Can cause acute kidney failure, vomiting, lack of appetite, diarrhea, lethargy, abdominal pain, and failure to produce urine.
Onions or onion powder	In many processed foods (baby food, ketchup, soup, lunch meat and hot dogs). Increased risk for fever, vomiting, weakness, and collapse. Can cause hemolytic anemia in Japanese breeds (Akita, Shiba Inu, and Tosa).
Garlic (in high doses)	Same effects as onions.
Macadamia nuts	Can cause weakness, depression, ataxia, rear leg paralysis, and abdominal pain.
Black walnuts	Can cause depression and difficulty breathing.
Moldy walnuts or dairy products	Can cause mycotoxin, or poisoning of the nervous system, that yields tremors, seizures, or even death.
Licorice	Muscle damage and alteration in adrenal hormones. Can cause weakness, collapse, and death.
Xylitol (an artificial sweetener in sugar-free candy and gum)	Can cause a sudden drop in blood sugar. Signs can develop quite rapidly, sometimes less than thirty minutes after eating. Can result in depression, loss of coordination, and seizures.

Deafness in Dogs

LOSS OF HEARING is a common health issue in dogs, particularly as they age. However, there are many ways to help your dog compensate for poor hearing or complete hearing loss. Deaf dogs can be trained to respond to hand signals in addition to spoken commands. (It's actually not a bad idea to train your dog to understand these signals even if she hears perfectly well.)

Deafness will not diminish any of your dog's other basic instincts and needs. For example, high-energy breeds still need lots of exercise; dogs with herding or hunting instincts need appropriate outlets.

The owner of a deaf dog has a greater responsibility to provide a safe environment for the dog's exercise and playtime. Avoid letting a deaf dog off-leash, unless she is in a fenced yard or other protected space.

Remember that dogs use body language as their chief communication method, so deafness does not affect much about dog-to-dog relationships. (For example, a submissive or dominant pose is the same with or without the accompanying whine or bark.)

It is important that all of your family members use the same hand signals, so your dog doesn't get confused. (You can help pet sitters or long-term guests by writing up a sheet with the basic signals.) And don't be surprised if your hearing dogs also learn these signals—especially the one that means, "I have a treat." If you interact regularly with deaf humans, consider training your dog with American Sign Language commands in addition to hand signals. This will open up a new world of communication between your dog and deaf humans.

Remember that deaf dogs can react badly if startled out of sleep. If you must wake your dog, put your hand in front of his nose and let your scent awaken the dog. You can also very gently touch the same place (such as a shoulder) each time you wake your deaf dog. By the same token, don't grab or pet your dog from behind, even if she is awake, as she may not realize you are there and start. Always make sure you are visible first.

Doga: Yoga for Dogs

DOG LOVERS HAVE a knack for figuring out ways to involve their dogs in every aspect of their lives. They certainly have with yoga for dogs—or doga. Doga means simply practicing yoga with your dog. Doga can be beneficial to your pooch because it increases muscle flexibility, decreases stiffness, and helps strengthen social bonds between your dog and you.

Some maneuvers common in yoga actually come naturally to dogs, so doga isn't entirely foreign to them. For example, the downward-facing dog pose in yoga was actually borrowed from dogs.

TYPICAL DOGA POSES

Adho Mukha Svanasana: Downward-Facing Dog

Urdhva Mukha Svanasana: Upward-Facing Dog

Bhujangasana: Cobra Pose

Sivasana: Corpse Pose

Ask your dog to "stay," to hold poses. Then, ask him to assume his normal, relaxed position by saying "Okay" or your preferred release word. You may find that your dog has a shorter attention span and will be more apt to be distracted. Until your pup is four months old, limit his exercise to play and hold off on doga. Some doga classes even teach massage and acupuncture (see Days 340 and 347 for more on acupuncture and massage).

Giving Your Dog a Haircut at Home

ALTHOUGH SOMETIMES IT'S best to save large-scale makeovers for the professional groomer, you are perfectly capable of trimming your dog's hair at home. You won't even need an electric clipper, which requires an experienced hand. However, a good pair of scissors made for cutting hair (available at many pharmacies) will help you turn your dog from a scraggly mess into Prince Charming.

Trim away any hair hanging in front of your dog's eyes. Be careful that the point of the scissors is directed away from his eyes. Always leave a 1- or 2-inch (2.5 to 5 cm) ridge of hair above his eyes; this will act as an "awning" to provide a little protection from direct sunlight.

You can free his ears from long hair fringes by trimming around the outline of each ear, leaving a 1-inch (2.5 cm) border.

To trim away any extra beard hair (which can become discolored and encrusted with food scraps), just follow the outline of your dog's mouth and chin area.

Uneven hair under his tummy can be cleaned up with a good pair of scissors, as can excessive tail hair.

Check the bottoms of his feet and trim any excess hair between his pads. Grit, gravel, and dirt can become entangled here, creating sores between the pads. While you're examining his feet, check the length of your dog's nails. If you can hear a noticeable clicking sound as he walks across a wood or tile floor, his nails are too long. Long nails can cause lameness and aggravate arthritis or hip dysplasia, because your dog's weight is not properly distributed when he has to walk funny to avoid putting uncomfortable pressure on his nails. Clip nails using a pet tool for this purpose, avoiding cutting into the quick (the dark vein).

Recipe: Sweet Potato
(Please Don't Call it "Pound") Cake

HERE'S A RECIPE for a perfect treat to serve at a party for all your pup's closest pals.

INGREDIENTS

2 cups (450 g) cooked, cooled, and mashed sweet potato

1 teaspoon (5 ml) vanilla extract

½ cup (100 ml) honey

4 eggs

½ cup (100 g) vegetable shortening

3 cups (380 g) unbleached all-purpose flour

2 teaspoons (9.2 g) baking powder

½ teaspoon (2.3 g) baking soda

2 teaspoons (5 g) ground cinnamon

½ teaspoon (1.2 g) ground nutmeg

1. Preheat the oven to 350°F (180°C). Grease a 10-inch (25-cm) tube pan.

2. In a large bowl, beat together the sweet potatoes, vanilla, and honey until well blended. Add the eggs, one at a time, beating 1 minute for each egg. Add the shortening and beat until well combined.

3. In another bowl, mix together the flour, baking powder, baking soda, cinnamon, and nutmeg.

4. Slowly add the flour mixture to the sweet potato mixture. Beat on slow speed until combined.

5. Pour the batter into the prepared pan. Bake for 60 to 70 minutes.

6. Cool the cake on a wire rack.

7. Serve in thin slices.

8. Store in a sealed container in refrigerator.

YIELD: 20 servings (depending on size of guests)

Note: To cook sweet potatoes, wash, peel, and cut the potatoes into quarters. Cook, covered, in boiling water for 25 minutes. Drain and rinse until smooth.

283

Winter Workers

WHAT DO YOU DO with a dog that is really strong and full of energy? Slow him down by letting him drag you cross-country for miles. The formal name for this activity is skijoring. The sport is like dog sledding without Alaska and the sled, and with only one dog. Purchase a skijoring harness for your dog, strap on your cross-country skis, and head for the snow. Bring a friend to encourage your dog to run toward across a snowy field while you ski behind. If you have never mushed with your dog before, you may spend a lot of time standing still or going fast only sporadically. Run, run, run, STOP, sniff. Unless you jog with your dog, he may not understand, initially, the idea of maintaining a consistent pace. Give lots of praise and work with him to hold a speed. Most likely, if you lose your balance and fall down, your dog will stop and wait for you to get up. Isn't that nice? Wear gloves and be prepared to take a fall. Recover by a warm fire, with a cup of cocoa. Not up for the snow and skis? Strap on a pair of Rollerblades and attach a leash to your dog's body harness. Let him pull you along a paved bike path. You may be pulling him by the end of your excursion, but that's what friends are for. If skijoring or in-line skating are not your style, try sledding with your dog—it's fun for both of you!

Why Do Dogs Stick Their Heads Out of Car Windows?

HAVE YOU EVER wondered why your dog sticks his head out the window or puts it close to the vents blowing fresh air into the car?

Dogs like to smell what's going on around them. A dog can smell the whole area in minutes with his head out the car window: everything from food to other dogs and maybe a female dog in heat. There is a smorgasbord of scent out there for him.

As cute as this may be, hanging out of car windows is dangerous to our dogs, for a couple of reasons. If your male dogs gets a whiff of a female dog in heat, he could jump out of your car to go after her, even if the window isn't all the way open. Also, all that rushing air is not good for his ears, and it can dry out his eyes. Most of all, it can be very dangerous if another car passes too closely or you have to swerve and end up close to a mailbox or pole.

Be safe and do not let your dog hang his head out the car window.

What to Do If You Find a Stray Dog

IF YOU FIND A stray dog, the best thing to do is to call your local animal control officer, who knows how to handle a stray dog and may already have a report of a missing dog that matches the one you found.

Be careful when approaching a strange dog. If she seems friendly, restrain or secure her with a carrier, leash, or rope so she will be ready when the animal control officer arrives. If your local animal officer is unable to respond, you may need to drive the animal to a shelter yourself.

If the stray dog is injured or needs medical attention, be aware that you may be charged for her care if you take her to a vet's office. You might want to call your local animal hospital first and see if they have a "Samaritan" fund that helps pay for the care of stray dogs.

Coping with Hip Dysplasia

HIP DYSPLASIA IS the thickening of the bone at the hip joint when the femoral head angles outward. In moderate cases, a gap in the joint occurs, creating unstable motion for a dog. In severe instances, the pain becomes uncomfortable, leading to crippling. Unfortunately, hip dysplasia is common among a number of breeds. However, certain exercises can help.

You don't want to run or jog with a dog with hip dysplasia, as that only exacerbates the problem, and depending on the seriousness of the dysplasia, this may cause your dog pain or make the condition worse.

In general, any low-impact exercise is great, allowing muscle and strength to gradually return. The ideal exercises are swimming or walking on a lead on grass. Swimming is a great exercise because it takes the weight off the hip joint and enables your dog to exercise with less pain. Walking on grass is better than walking on hard surfaces because the spring of the soil and grass eases the pressure on the joints.

Always check with your veterinarian for the appropriate level and type of exercise.

Emergency Tip: Restraining a Dog for Treating an Injury

IF YOUR DOG gets injured, you'll need to restrain her so she will not flee as you treat her. The friendliest dogs can bite back when scared or in pain. Do not hesitate to use a muzzle as long as your dog is conscious. The device is designed to protect you and the dog.

If you are by yourself, follow these steps to restrain your dog so you can safely treat her:

Approach calmly. Speak in a low voice and do not make sudden movements. If the dog does not know you, allow her to sniff the back of your hand. Do not stare directly into the dog's eyes. This can be intimidating.

Prevent fleeing. Use a 6-foot (1.8 m) leash to prevent the dog's running away. Never use a leash if the dog has a neck or throat injury.

Muzzle the dog. Put on a commercial dog muzzle according to instructions. (See Resources, page 318.) Or, use a makeshift muzzle, such as a necktie, gauze, panty hose, or fabric strip that is approximately 18 inches (46 cm) long. Use a belt or leash as a last resort. Wear heavy leather or work gloves before trying to muzzle or leash your dog. These will protect your hands in case your dog resists the muzzle by biting. (Even nice dogs will bite when forced into a muzzle.)

Safety at Home: Practice a Fire Drill

YOU PREPARED A first-aid kit (Day 95) and you organized your dog's vital information so you can easily access registration papers, medications, and vet contacts (Day 25). You are acutely aware of Mother Nature's whims in your region—the likelihood of tornadoes, hurricanes, flooding.

Regardless of where you live, a house fire is a universal threat. You can mentally draw a plan for safe escape, but if you do not practice your strategy, how will you know that it is efficient and logical?

Children practice fire drills at school. Hotels post "in case of fire" instructions on the insides of guest room doors. You should lead your dog(s) through a fire drill by simulating an event at home. Here's how to do it:

1. *Decide how you and your dogs will escape.*
What if the fire starts in the kitchen? What if the living room is blocked and you cannot pass through it? How will you exit if the front door is not accessible? Map out several routes based on what-if scenarios. Practice each escape route once a year, but not during the same day. (That would be far too much drama for your dogs.)

2. *Set a timer to 20 minutes.* This will serve as your signal to evacuate. Go about your business until the timer sounds. (In other words, don't wait in front of the door until the timer buzzes and rush out—the point is to simulate a real-life situation.)

3. *At the buzz, gather your dog(s).* Do so in a quiet manner, putting each dog on his leash and collecting your pet's first-aid kit and vital papers. Keep in mind, in a real fire, you may not be able to access these extras.

4. *This is not a walk.* If your dog expresses excitement, calm him down in a reassuring tone. Allow the timer to continue buzzing. This exercise is good practice in maintaining composure (you and the dog) despite the noise and unannounced exit.

5. *Sit and stay.* After exiting the house, instruct your dog to sit and stay. Wait outdoors for five minutes, not allowing your dogs to lead you on a walk or root around the yard. The point is to practice staying calm and obedient despite the unexpected "buzz" and exit.

Note: All pet owners should have window decals for their home that inform firemen and other first responders that there are pets inside. See Resources, page 318.

Common Dog Phrases and English Translation

EARS PULLED AGAINST head. Tail between the legs, one front foot pulled off of the floor. Rolled over on back, whimpering. Lips pulled back. Licking other dog's muzzle or your face. *"I'm shy and will let you be in charge."*

Frozen body. Cowering or lowered head. Growling or baring teeth. *"I'm fearful and will bite, because I am scared."*

Dog bows and possibly yaps or barks and growls. Tail wagging. Face relaxed with eyes open. Ears out to sides or relaxed. Jumps or runs near other dogs to encourage play. *"Will you play with me?"*

Dog stands tall, stares, and does not avert gaze. Approaches in a straight trajectory and, with or without further warning, attacks. Growling may not begin until attack ensues. *"I am a bully."*

Dog stands tall with hackles raised and throws head over the neck of other dog. Ears pulled close to head. Bumps or forcefully rolls other dog with body. Pushes in front of other dog through doorways and on stairs. Blocks path of other dog. Gives forceful corrections. Eats first and enforces food privileges. *"I'm top dog."*

Dog stands tall. Ears fanned out. Eyes wide. Tail up. Silence or muffled barks followed by loud barking. *"What's that noise?"*

Apartment Living with a Dog

MANY APARTMENT BUILDINGS and rental homes these days are pet friendly. Expect to pay a little extra rent and/or be asked for a special pet deposit to keep a pet, and there may be some restrictions about size and where you can exercise your dog. If you are looking for a new place, be sure to ask about the rules before signing a lease, and if you are already in an apartment, be sure you are being a responsible pet owner by abiding by them.

Low- to medium-energy dogs are best for apartment living. You need to find a breed that can be enclosed daily and can run off energy on daily walks and trips to the park (see Day 255). There are a few big breeds that will do fine in an apartment. Once you've done your homework and have settled on a breed, talk to as many people as you can who have that breed and live in an apartment.

Dog walking can be a concern when you live in an apartment and are gone for long stretches of time. You don't have the option of letting your dog out into a yard while you're off at work. The good news is that many cities have a number of dog-walking services to choose from that will come and take your dog out during the day when you are off at work. Also, there are dog "litter boxes" available these days, only with grass instead of litter, that you can train your dog to use and that will come in handy in an apartment.

Small breeds that tend to do well in apartments:

Affenpinscher

American Bulldog

American Hairless Terrier

Basset Hound

Bichon Frise

Cocker Spaniel

Clumber Spaniel

Beagle

Basenji

Dachshund

Some terriers, including Yorkshire Terrier and Jack Russell Terrier

Petit Basset Griffon

French Bulldog

Lhasa Apso

Larger breeds that can do well in apartments with enough exercise:

Brittany

Springer Spaniel

Akita

Mastiff

Bullmastiff

Doberman Pinscher

Great Dane

Bernese Mountain Dog

Before you move in, take a photo of any existing damage and have the landlord acknowledge it by signing a condition report. If your dog causes any damage once you are living there, fix it promptly. This will show the landlord that you are a responsible tenant and make her more likely to rent to dog owners in the future.

How to (Neatly) Collect a Stool Sample

YOUR VETERINARIAN WILL ask you to bring a fresh stool sample to checkups to test for parasites and proper digestion. Stool says a lot about a dog's health, such as whether she is digesting properly, has worms or infections, and whether her nutritional needs are being met by her diet. Be sure to collect a sample within 15 minutes of a meal. Ahead of time, label the bag in permanent marker with your name, the dog's name, and the date and time of collection. Always scoop the sample into a clean, zippered plastic bag.

Picking up "doo" is not a fun job, but it's one we do daily as dog owners. For a no-mess pickup, use latex-free, nonsterile gloves. Use a piece of scrap cardboard or a poop scoop (spatula) to transfer the stool into the bag. Seal the bag tightly. (That is one instruction we surely do not have to tell you.) Place in a second, opaque bag that can be recycled after you reach the vet.

Companion Dogs

MOST PEOPLE KNOW about service dogs, such as Seeing Eye dogs, but many don't know about companion dogs and the valuable function they serve. The term *companion dogs* has two meanings. Aside from dogs inherently being our companions, some dogs are known as *companion dogs or therapy dogs* and are used in nursing homes, children's hospitals, schools, and other places to help people get well (as well as to learn about dogs).

Proper "vocational" training is the key to success for companion dogs. Basic puppy classes are often not enough for this; your pooch may need another set of classes or private training to learn advanced obedience and dog therapy techniques.

Valuable skills for companion dogs include:

- Allowing strangers to pet or groom them

- Leaving food that is not theirs alone

- Calm acceptance of loud noises or other distractions

Most companion dogs must wear a special vest marking them as such when in a hospital or school setting, much like a service dog's vest. Talk to your trainer to find out more about volunteer companion dog opportunities for you and your dog.

Dog Acupuncture

ACUPUNCTURE IS THE use of fine needles inserted into specific points on the body for therapeutic purposes. This ancient technique originated in the Far East. It is based on the principle that there are specific energetic pathways (meridians) throughout the body, which connect all the internal organs and structures. When the flow of chi energy along one or more of these meridians is obstructed, the result may be an imbalance in the energy or disease. By stimulating key acupuncture points in the body with needles, an acupuncturist seeks to restore balance to the normal energy flow along the meridians and consequently, to holistically balance the body. Acupuncturists believe that imbalances in chi are the root of disease.

Acupuncture in animals works the same way it does in humans and can be used to support any disease or health condition. Acupuncture can be used for any pet and is most appropriate for pets that are sensitive to drugs, pets that are not a good candidate for surgery or other invasive techniques, and senior pets to help restore their life force energy to help prevent degenerative diseases.

See Resources on page 318 for more information on finding a veterinarian licensed in acupuncture.

If Your Dog is Lost

WHAT HAPPENS IF your pet gets out and runs away? First, check with your neighbors. Often, a good neighbor will recognize a local dog roaming unescorted and hold her until you come calling. Enlist the support of your neighbors by asking them to help you do a foot search, calling out your pet's name, or squeezing her favorite noisy toy. Send the kids on the block out on their bikes. Post fliers with a photo and a reward, and put an ad in the daily or weekly newspaper your community reads for local interest.

The next step is to call the local animal control office or shelter. Some people call a private rescue service if they find a strange animal on their property. They come, retrieve a hiding animal, and bring them somewhere safe until the owner finds them. These services may list "found" dogs on their website or make other efforts to find the owner. If you have one or more of these services in your area, be sure to call them, too.

It is important to actually go to the local shelter. Your pet's description may not be enough to make a positive ID on the phone, so bring a photo with you. Animal shelters hold their charges for a limited time and get new animals all the time, so check on a regular basis. If all else fails, it's time to call in an expert. Pet detectives can be located through a Web search or your yellow pages. They will post fliers for you, place ads on the Internet and local papers, and deal with the reward (or ransom), as needed.

Once your pet is located, if he's been gone for a long time, take him to the vet to make sure he is healthy and hydrated. Be sure to get new name tags and collars, if his are missing, and consider a microchip (see Day 296). To prevent future escapes, make sure your fences and gates are secure at all times (see Day 260).

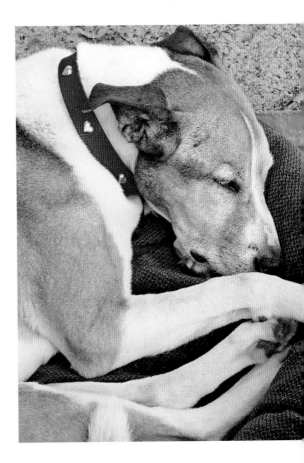

Dog Tails: Tomato Vine Bandits

OUR TWO YORKIES love tomatoes. They run into the garden and pull ripe tomatoes right off the vine, no matter the red fruit's size. (They don't go after the green ones.) Baby reds, plump juicy ones, and the grand-daddies of the vine—they are all at risk of being detached by our dogs, who scarf them up like the best treats on earth. We eventually installed a fence around our garden to keep out the dogs. Otherwise, our bounty would have disappeared before we could say the word "sauce!" Even when we slice tomatoes for salads or sandwiches, the dogs smell their favorite snack and run to the kitchen in hopes of getting a scrap.

Are tomatoes a dangerous food for dogs?

Although this fruit isn't an abundantly popular favorite flavor among dogs, tomatoes are not toxic and will do no harm to your dogs. It's a good idea to keep your dogs away from the actual plant—the green part—as there is some controversy over the toxicity of the vine, which is in the nightshade family.

If your dogs paw-pick their own ripe red ones from the counter or serving dishes, you should not be concerned about the stems. But by treating your dogs to a thin slice in their bowls, you can monitor how much tomato they eat and be sure none of the greenery is included.

In small doses, carrots are a healthy, low-calorie treat for happy snacking dogs. (In enormous quantities vitamin A poisoning could become an issue.) Carrots are crunchable and appealing to many dogs' palates. You can purchase "baby carrots" (precut, prewashed carrot nubs that come in a handy bag) for your dog for no-prep snacking. Bite-size carrots are also easily packed to-go for snacks away from home.

Is Your Dog Ready for the Office?

IF YOU OWN A business and set the rules, or work for a company with progressive HR policies (Bring Your Dog to Work Day!), your four-footed companion may be a welcome character in the office. Any dog would prefer to punch the clock with his owner rather than stay at home alone. In the workplace, research has shown that pets reduce stress. Dogs can improve worker morale, employees are more likely to work later because the environment feels like home, and companies can attract and retain better employees.

Some companies have a single "office dog" that employees help walk, feed, and care for during the day. In return, the dog lifts workers' moods, provides them an exercise outlet, and offers the comfort of a soft coat to pet. Every furry rub seems to absorb stress and convert bad vibes into warm fuzzies.

Other businesses allow owners to bring their dogs to work. They must adhere to certain guidelines, and everyone in the office should agree on the policy. Managers find that advertising a dog-friendly environment eases potential employees' concerns about leaving their pooches at home. Today, with so many people telecommuting and enjoying the flexibility of home offices, luring a fantastic worker to an office job requires creative policies like this.

Finally, if you work alone, an office dog is your main man: your head administrator, social director, and VP of PR (puppy relations). There's no better company than a dog burrowed under your desk for a long snooze. Dogs also force you to take much-needed breaks during the day for walks and play.

Is your dog ready for the office?

Consult with coworkers. Find out if anyone is allergic to or afraid of dogs, or otherwise objects.

Puppy-proof your cube. Remove poisonous plants, hide electrical cords and wires, secure toxic substances such as correction fluid and permanent markers, and place any questionable items out of your dog's reach.

Bathe and groom. Don't take a dirty pooch to the office. You wouldn't forgo a shower before work, so why should your dog?

Prepare a doggy bag. Pack a tote with food, toys, a leash, paper towels, cleanup bags, disinfectant, and a portable kennel (optional).

Avoid forced interaction. Not all coworkers will think your dog is the cutest, best animal in the world. Keep treats at your desk for colleagues who want to charm your dog. (A biscuit offering is a sure pleaser.) But do not insist that everyone pet and dote over your dog as you do.

Design an exit strategy. Where will your dog do his business? Identify the nearest door to outside and decide where he can safely eliminate.

Office Rules

Be sure your manager enforces these policies if every employee can bring a dog to work.

- Dogs must be immunized; a file should be kept containing shot records.

- Flea control is a must.

- No barking

- Put in place a three-strikes rule so unruly, disruptive dogs aren't invited back into the workplace.

Training: Coming and Going

AT HOME, YOUR dog is obedient and responds to the command "come" by correctly walking toward you and sitting down in front of you so you can reach out your hand and reward him with a treat or chin rub. But at the dog park, you say "Come," and he keeps an arm's distance. Why the hesitation?

In playtime situations such as dog parks or agility courses, your dog knows that "come" has a double meaning: come, and time to go home. He knows you want him to come closer so you can snap on his leash. The command introduces a conflict in meaning in social situations because "come" is associated with an unhappy ending. (At home, the ending is quite tasty if a meaty treat is involved.) Your dog follows your command, but is punished by restraint and a swift exit from the park.

You need to offset the negative association. At home and the park, reinforce "come" with a game of tug-of-war, treats, or a "trade" toy. Here's how the situation would play out at the park:

EXERCISE ONE

Owner: "Come!"

Dog: Follows the command, but will not come close enough for physical contact.

Owner: Offers a "trade" toy. Holds out the toy (or treat) as an appealing offering. When the dog accepts the reward, praises him and allows him to keep the toy.

EXERCISE TWO

Owner: "Come!"

Dog: Follows the command but keeps a distance.

Owner: Lures the dog with a treat. Praises him. Snaps on the leash. Then releases the leash and allows the dog to play for a while longer. (Repeat this exercise to show your dog that the leash doesn't necessarily mean playtime is over.)

Construct Your Own Jingle Toy

THE PLUSH TOYS for sale in pet stores carry hefty price tags, especially if your dog wears them out within weeks. You want to spoil your pet with a collection of engaging, adorable toys—without emptying your wallet. You can easily make your own jingle toy: a plush, stuffed shape of your choice with jingle bells imbedded inside that are less grating on the nerves than high-pitched squeaky mechanisms. Your dog will love the noisy, squishy character. You can make hand and feet shapes, farm animals, geometric cut-outs, or even a silhouette of your dog's breed.

MATERIALS

Fabric of choice (fleece, faux sheepskin, an old tube sock)

Polyfill stuffing

Jingle bells

Natural-fiber thread (not nylon)

Pins

Sewing machine (or sewing needle to hand-sew)

Pinking shears

Small stitching scissors

Tracing paper and a pencil

1. Choose and trace a shape. Trace your hands or feet, borrow ideas from a coloring book. Mimic the shape of a favorite dog toy so you have a backup on hand should it become overloved (and destroyed in the process).

2. Pin and cut. Double up fabric by folding it so you only have to cut the shape one time. Pin tracing paper with pencil-drawn shape on to fabric. Use pinking shears to cut along the lines. Remove pins and tracing paper. Your shapes are complete.

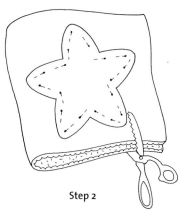

Step 2

3. Rev up the sewing machine. You can also hand-sew these toys, but a sewing machine makes a nice, tight stitch quickly. Place the fabric shapes so the exteriors face in (fuzzy sides together). Sew along the perimeter of the shape, leaving a ¾-inch (2 cm) seam allowance. Leave an opening to insert stuffing. You may want to make a double stitch (back over your stitches) to improve strength.

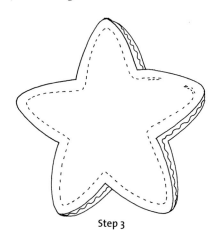

Step 3

4. Stuff the shape. Fill the shape with stuffing until half full, then insert a few jingle bells. Continue filling until the shape reaches desired puffiness.

5. Hand-sew the opening. Using organic thread, because nylon thread can slice and injure dogs' mouths, stitch together the opening, reinforcing the area by double-stitching if necessary.

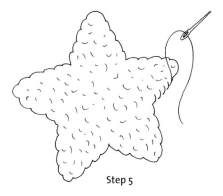

Step 5

The Benefits of Dog Massage

THERE'S NOTHING MORE relaxing than a professional massage—it's a mental escape and time for physical rejuvenation. Your dog will feel the same way if you schedule an appointment for him with a canine massage therapist. These trained masseuses can address specific pain issues, or simply give your dog a soothing rub-down. Dog massage focuses on the whole body. The dog lies on a bed on his side at first, and gradually the masseuse will rotate him onto his back and other side, working the body in circular motions, and rub to release tension and stress. If you are skeptical, you should watch the process and how a dog looks after the massage: blissed out as if he woke up from the best nap of his life.

Because of our centuries of breeding dogs, they no longer have optimal structure for good movement. This means their muscles get sore over time and their joints can break down over the years. Massage can help prevent this soreness and damage, or alleviate pain if this process has already begun. (You may not know that your dog is experiencing pain since pack animals instinctively hide their pain to avoid being thrown out of the pack.)

Older dogs with arthritis and stiffness may have difficulty exercising, leading to further pain and stiffness, which leads to even more inactivity. Massage can diminish pain levels in arthritic dogs as well as improve flexibility and range of motion. This helps these dogs feel and move better, allowing them to be more active. Ask the masseuse to teach you some techniques to practice at home so you can provide therapy to your dog in between appointments. Massage is a great bonding activity and health benefit.

Conditions improved by massage include:

- Inactivity due to injury, illness, old age, or obesity
- Poor circulation in muscles
- Sluggish lymphatic system
- Recovery after surgery or injuries
- Arthritis

Recipe: Walnut-Carob Bonbons

CONSIDER THIS RECIPE a sweet excuse for treating our pooches to "dessert"! (Remember, always use treats as rewards for good behavior, and treat in moderation.)

1 cup (200 g) vegetable shortening

1 teaspoon (5 ml) vanilla extract

¾ cup (115 g) walnuts (not black walnuts, which are toxic to dogs), finely chopped

2 ¾ cups (345 g) unbleached all-purpose flour

1/2 teaspoon (2.3 g) baking powder

1 cup (180 g) carob chips, unsweetened

1 tablespoon (15 ml) canola or other mild vegetable old

1. Preheat the oven to 325°F (170°C).

2. In a large mixing bowl, cream the shortening with a mixing spoon or hand mixer. Stir in the vanilla, mixing well. Fold in the walnuts.

3. In a medium-size bowl, combine the flour and baking powder.

4. Add the flour mixture to the shortening mixture and beat until well blended.

5. Roll pieces of dough into 1-inch (2.5 cm) balls. Place the balls on an ungreased baking sheet.

6. Bake for 15 minutes. Transfer to wire racks to cool.

7. Place the carob in a microwavable dish and stir in the oil.

8. Microwave the carob at 50 percent power for 1 to 2 minutes, until softened, then stir until smooth; or melt in a saucepan on low heat.

9. Gently dip the baked bonbons into the melted carob and sprinkle with the chopped walnuts.

10. Store layered between sheets of waxed paper in an airtight container.

YIELD: 30 bonbons

Note: This recipe can also be made with finely chopped, unsalted peanuts. Remember that variety is the spice of life.

Does Your Dog Have a Godparent?

CONSIDER DESIGNATING a godparent for your dog so he will have a "second-in-command" master and you will rest assured that if your health declines, your dog will be in good care. A pet trust is a binding legal document to make sure that your dog receives proper care in the case of your death or disability. This document will ensure that funds will be available to take care of your dog while your will goes through probate or if it is contested. If your situation is not complicated, and you don't want to hire an estate lawyer, these documents are available online and can be downloaded and filed for a very reasonable price.

Be sure to discuss arrangements with your pet's godparent beforehand. You want to make sure it is someone who is not only capable of taking care of your dog, but wants to. Create a written list of instructions, including contact information for your dog's vet, where your dog's health and other records are kept, and vital personality information about your pet that the person might not otherwise know, such as that she dislikes being among small children.

Is Your Dog Dreaming?

DOGS DREAM ABOUT running, eating, sniffing, and chasing. Like people, dogs enter light sleep and intense REM cycles, when dreaming occurs. If you notice your dog flinch and twitch at sleep onset, that signals light sleep and you can easily wake him. Once dogs enter a deep, REM cycle, the brain is active and their body responds accordingly. Their eyes may move back and forth, you'll see their paws shifting, scratching, and they may wag their tails. During REM, dogs can pant, sniff, and murmur. Despite activity taking place in the room, a dog in REM is not easily awakened.

Dreaming is vital to a dog's health. It's a time for data processing and memory storage—for mental replenishment and brain development. For this reason, puppies require a significant amount of sleep. Excited owners that keep their puppies awake for too many hours a day to play are, in essence, robbing their pups of critical development time.

Older dogs also need a great deal of sleep to repair from daily activities and restore energy for basic functions: eating, walking, socializing, and so on. Dogs may spend up to fourteen hours a day in REM sleep.

Should you wake up your dog if he is dreaming? There are two schools of thought. One says, do not wake your dog, even if he is whimpering and pawing in his sleep. If startled, he may unintentionally respond with aggression. The other camp says to gently wake up your dog by petting him softly and speaking in a calm, reassuring voice.

Will your dog remember that heated chase or great big steak when he wakes? Perhaps that sad look he gave you when you put out yet another boring bowl of kibble is a sign your dog is remembering his dream.

Just Say "No"

"NO, MAYZIE! NO!"

What's wrong with this command?

Mayzie loves the sound of her name. When she hears it, she gets treats, hugs, and special attention. Mayzie is like music to her ears. The problem is, you want to reprimand Mayzie for bad behavior. The command you want her to hear is a firm, serious "No!" But your dog, on the other hand, only hears her name. The "no" part of the command disappears—but "Mayzie" is understood, loud and clear. This is a classic example of negative reinforcement.

Never say your dog's name when using a disciplinary term such as "no." Save her name for "Good, Mayzie," and "Here, Mayzie." Emphasize her name when she displays positive behavior, and restrain from using her name when your tone drops.

To you, "No, Mayzie" means plain old "No."

To your dog, hearing her name is the equivalent of "Hey, cutie! Let's play!"

Common Behavior Problems and Solutions

Is YOUR DOG underutilized and without a job? Left to her own devices, she may just take up a job around the house. Most dogs choose to pursue instinctual work, using such natural talents as barking, eating, chewing, begging, and fighting. Having goals, careers, and challenges is as healthy for dogs as for humans. Keeping mentally and physically challenged and feeling needed are important to health and longevity. Give your dog a job that uses her skills: fetching the newspaper, picking laundry or toys up off the floor and putting them into a basket, finding your lost keys in the house.

Here are some self-appointed jobs you may wish to retrain your dog from continuing:

Security guard (barking): Squirt gun, Hush command with reward treat (keeps the mouth too busy eating to bark).

Professional greeter (jumping on people): Practice four-on-the-floor for all petting. Warn guests ahead of time to be firm with your dog if she jumps. Raise your knee up as she starts to jump to dissuade her. Practice having your dog sit at the front door while you ring the doorbell. Increase the level of difficulty by having visitors enter while she remains seated. Reward good behavior.

Panhandler (begging): Never give table scraps at the table. After you have finished eating, put a morsel of food in the dog food bowl. If your dog begs while you are eating, growl at her; remember, you are the alpha dog.

Wood refinisher/demolition man (chewing on the furniture): Spray bitter apple on tasty-looking furniture corners. Place plenty of toys on the floor to distract her. Note: Bitter apple contains alcohol and may damage some wood surfaces.

Debate champion (talking back): Seek professional help because asserting yourself suddenly with an aggressive dog may result in injury (to you). Talk to an expert about ways to regain control.

Bully (biting): Same as above. Work with a professional dog behaviorist.

Professional wrestler (roughhousing): Send your dog outside to burn off the excess energy. Play a game of fetch or give her a toy to play with. For inappropriate racing indoors, block the running dog with a quick "Slow" command.

Shoplifter (stealing food): Make a habit of keeping paws off the counters and tables. Keep the kitchen off-limits to your pet. Use correction or a squirt gun. Only feed the dog from her bowl. Set up the repeat offender by sprinkling hot sauce over an abandoned plate of food.

Garbage man (trash looter): Use a trash can with a lid. Employ correction or a squirt gun. Throw a loud rattle near the trash can as your dog approaches it.

Couch potato (furniture lounger): Place a comfortable mattresslike cushion on the floor for your dog. Praise your dog for resting on her designated mat. When your dog is sitting on her cushion, go over to her and pet her. Keep a squirt gun near off-limits furniture, as a visual deterrent.

Globe-trotter (runs away from home): Do not leave the dog unattended outside. Inspect the yard for barrier defects. Consider perimeter training. Make sure your dog has proper identification. Keep her busy with a dog sport, excursions, and plenty of playtime. Find fun ways to practice "come" to entice her to respond to your call.

Winter Weather Caution

Do you remember your dog's first experience with snow? Like a curious, boundless child, your dog discovered a whole, new winter wonderland filled with fresh smells. Bouncing into snow piles, rolling around in a yard newly dusted with white powder—what a thrill! For dogs, snow ranks right up there with fallen leaves.

Enjoy the change of seasons with your dog. But beware of winter hazards that can harm his health. First, don't allow your dog to eat snow. He'll be tempted to stick his licker into a snow pile for a taste. Sure, it looks clean and pure. But snow is frozen rain, and you wouldn't put a bucket outdoors before a storm and collect drinking water for your dog. (Plants, maybe—but animals, absolutely not.) Snow can cause spasms in the gastrointestinal tract, which can cause diarrhea, stomachache, and colds.

As you clear walkways, choose sidewalk de-icer that is safe for dogs. Or, avoid using salts in areas where you will walk your dog. After using ice, sweep and collect excess pebbles. If you must sprinkle a dose of salt on your porch for safety purposes, lead your dog out the back door. Salt will irritate paws and cause sickness if your dog ingests it.

Prepare your dog for outdoor play by ensuring he will keep warm and dry. Heavy-coated dogs do not need extra insulation, but smaller dogs and those with short hair (or a fresh haircut) may need a sweater to stay toasty during walks. You may also consider protective dog boots if ice between paw pads is a concern (see Day 318).

Hiring a Dog Walker

IF YOUR JOB demands that you leave your dog home for eight hours or longer, you may consider hiring a dog walker to exercise and socialize with your dog during the day. This arrangement is appropriate if your dog accepts "strangers" entering the home. (Of course, you should introduce your dog to his walker before hiring the service.) Your dog cannot be overly possessive of you. Beyond preferring you as his No. 1 companion, he must be willing to take commands from a dog walker. If you have worked through the basic training steps, your dog will be prepared to let a dog walker take the lead.

A dog walker can visit your home once or twice a day. The first walk may be with another appropriate, approved group of dogs that are relatively the same size. A walker may take the clan to a park, on a hike, or to a beach.

This activity may be 1½ hours long, not including pick up or drop-off. The second walk is for owners who work late and will not return home for five to six hours following the first walk.

Before you select a dog walker, be sure this person is licensed and bonded, to ensure your dog's safety. Find out about the walker's experience, and ask for references. (*Call* those references.) Know in advance whether your dog will share a walk with others or get one-on-one time. Ask whether pickup and drop-off are included in the fee. Interview the dog walker in person, and invite him or her to your home to meet your dog, who will surely have an opinion. Watch how the walker and your dog interact before signing up for the service.

Dog Blogging

A DOG BLOG is a fun way to share photos and stories of your dog with your friends and family. There are a number of options for creating your own free dog blog that are easy to use, even if you don't have a lot of computer experience.

First, decide on which blogging service you want to use. There are several high-profile, well-known services, and an Internet search on "dog blog" will turn up other options that are more specifically focused on dogs. Some services will place a small ad on your blog page in exchange for providing the page free.

Once you have chosen a service, follow the instructions at the site for setting up an account. You'll need to have a valid e-mail address; this can be your own—you don't need to set up a special one for your dog unless you want to.

Once you have your account, you can start to set up your page. There are many different layouts and backgrounds and fonts to choose from, and you can upload your dog's photo and write a short bio for her.

Blogging is like writing a diary; each entry is dated. When you post a new entry, it appears at the top of the page and older entries are pushed down. You can usually control the number of posts the page shows at a time. Once posts are pushed off the page, they go into an archive, and visitors to your dog's blog can go back in time by selecting articles out of the archive.

Your posts can be stories, poems, tips, ideas, projects, photos—whatever you like. You can even upload videos and include links to other information on the Internet. You can present the blog from your point of view, or you can write it as if your dog were writing it herself. If you enable the comments feature of your blog, people all over the world can respond to your posts.

Blog Ideas

Posts can be stories, poems, tips, ideas, projects, photos—whatever you like.

- You can upload videos and link to other information on the Internet.

- Present the blog from your point of view, or you can write it as if your dog is writing it herself.

- Enable the comments feature of your blog so people all over the world can respond to your posts.

Ideal Farm Dogs

IF YOU LIVE in a farming community or enjoy a property with several acres, you may want a farm dog to keep you company and potentially help out on the land. Your farm dog may be a lazy Basset Hound that is more interested in guarding the refrigerator than your sheep, or an ambitious Border Collie that will herd livestock in from the pasture each night. Some dogs work on farms. All dogs see the land as an amusement park. There's room to roam, sniff, root around, chase furry animals, and paw around in a mess of outdoor treats, including the kind from your pasture that you don't want tracked into your home. Dogs are naturals on the farm. Choose a pet to be your right-hand helper, and train him so he stays safe on your land.

Certain breeds are skilled at herding sheep, protecting cattle, and working as canine security guards. Herding breeds are obedient, and can be trained to perform herding tasks on your farm. They are gentle workers, but show gumption and strength in their ability to face up to stubborn animals. Herding dogs cooperate with their handlers, while using their own initiative to get the job done.

There are herding organizations and training classes for dogs, and these groups will also be a valuable resource as you decide what dog is a best fit for your farm.

Some common herd breeds include German and Australian Shepherds, Shetland Sheepdogs, Collies, Pembroke Welsh Corgies, Australian Cattledogs, and Old English Sheepdogs.

Clicker Training

CLICKER TRAINING IS an extremely fast way of training your dog. The marker-based system was developed by Karen Pryor, a scientist known for using this *positive reinforcement* technique for dogs, cats, horses, birds, and other small animals. Clicker training is motivating for owners and dogs because of the quick results. The method is based on operant conditioning: reinforcing positive behavior on contact. Eventually, dogs kick bad habits in favor of earning rewards and owner approval by performing good deeds. Those deeds may be basic commands like sit, stay, down, come. Clickers are also great for teaching tricks, and for discouraging such annoying traits as barking or ankle-biting.

In clicker training, owners use a clicker tool to praise the dog on contact so he knows exactly what behavior elicited the response. A treat or play session is immediately rewarded.

The sequence goes like this:

1. Give command.

2. Dog performs command.

3. Give clicker an immediate click.

4. Treat and praise.

The clicker takes humans' delayed reaction time and command inconsistency out of the equation. For instance, you might say, "Come, Jack." Then you repeat, "Jack, here, come on." Next you say "Jack, come here now." Jack has no idea what to do.

When he does finally walk to you, you say, "Good job!" But last time you said, "That's my boy!" and before that your praise remark was "You're the best dog ever!"

With the clicker, you say the command *one time*. Using a treat to lead the action (sit, come, down), click as soon as your dog obeys, then reward with the treat and praise. Clickers are effective because they eliminate human error from training. The clicker tells the dog exactly what he is doing to earn the treat. When his rear end hits the ground and you click, he knows that sitting yields reward. Next time he considers jumping up on you or a guest, he may decide to sit in hopes of getting a treat. Dogs aim to please us.

With two five-minute sessions a day, you can quickly teach your dog the basics. (See Resources, page 318, for more about clicker training.)

Collar Wisdom

CHOOSING THE RIGHT neckwear for your pooch is confusing, with so many styles and materials available. There are pinch collars, buckle and snap collars, choke chains, and harnesses. You'll find collars made from nylon and leather, and designer neck gear with embroidered designs (see Day 262 to make your own). We discussed how to choose a proper leash on Day 44. A collar is part of the outfit. It must be comfortable, durable, and effective for training and walking your dog. Here are some guidelines to help you narrow down the robust market and choose a safe collar that suits your dog's needs.

Consider what use you expect to make of the collar. You may choose different collars for training and downtime. Pinch and choke collars are fine when the dog is supervised. They are never to be left on a dog unattended. A simple nylon buckle collar is comfortable for a dog during downtime.

Go for easy cleaning. Leather collars are attractive and durable, but more difficult to clean than basic nylon. The choice is yours, but nylon is more cost effective and you can dunk it into your dog's soapy bath and the collar will clean up nicely.

Lead with a harness. Harnesses, also called halters, restrain the dog's whole body. Rather than pulling on her neck, you lead her by her torso. Harnesses are sized for every type of dog—they're not for big breeds only. Small dogs benefit from a harness because their neck is fragile and cannot tolerate leash pulling. Any dog wearing a harness is easier to manage on a walk.

You may allow your dog to go collarless in the house. When you want to take her outside, she needs her neckwear. Buckling a collar onto a squirming pup is no easy feat. Avoid the frustration by training your dog to "sit" when you put on her collar.

Recipe: Doggy Smoothie

BE A CREATIVE bark-tender and design your own doggy smoothie. Instead of pumpkin, try using 2 tablespoons (30 g) peanut butter, 2 tablespoons (30 g) mashed banana, or half a jar of any flavor baby food (check that it doesn't contain onion) that appeals to your dog.

2 cups (450 g) plain low-fat yogurt

1 tablespoon (15 ml) water

2 tablespoons (30 g) pureed pumpkin

1. Using a hand mixer, beat all ingredients in small bowl until well blended.

2. Freeze for 1 hour, stirring every 15 minutes, then serve.

Note: This treat must be frozen or refrigerated until served.

Installing a Safe Doggy Door

DOGGY DOORS PROVIDE freedom to trained pooches, and convenience to owners who won't have to stop everything to take their dogs outside. Also, if your dog is a door-scratcher, a doggy entrance could deter the behavior. After all, his real desire is to open the door, and a doggy door will allow him to do just that.

Pet doors should exit to a fenced-in area with a gate that locks from the inside. Your dog should not be able to dig under or jump over the fence. Pet doors are convenient, but they are no excuse to leave your dog alone to roam the backyard for hours on end. You should be in the vicinity in case of emergency.

For your personal safety, look for a pet door that can be closed and locked. Doggy doors are easy access for burglars, but there's no cause for concern if the pet door can be secured. You can find rubber-flap pet doors with self-locking mechanisms. Higher-end doggy doors are made of aluminum with better insulation to minimize drafts. There are doors suitable for glass doors and even for walls.

There are now even electromagnetic doors that open when a "key" attached to your dog's collar sends a signal to unlatch the door.

Doggy doors are a great solution for some dogs and owners. But before you install one, consider some common issues:

- Other animals may enter the home through your doggy door.

- Burglars can squeeze through larger dog doors or find a way to unlock the main door. (This is why you must invest in a pet door that locks.)

- A fenced-in backyard is not 100 percent safe. Your dog may find an opening, and a stranger can still trespass and take your dog.

The solution to all of these potential problems is to always be home when the pet door is unlocked and in use. Never leave your dog outdoors in a fenced-in area for long periods of time, and be sure you can see the area from a window.

Celebrating Your Dog's Birthday

EVERY DAY IS A "personal day" for your dog. She wakes up, lazily stretching before easing herself out of (your) bed. She saunters to the kitchen for a bite to eat, enjoys a long walk in the sun, then plays, naps, eats, and is loved all day long. That's a dog's life. Her birthday, however, is a perfect excuse to splurge on a new toy or just spend time at the park. Here are some ways to commemorate her special day:

- Pack a picnic and head to the nearest park. Don't forget a Frisbee or her favorite fetching toy. Spend some time enjoying each other's company.

- Bake your dog homemade cookies, and deliver goody baskets to other doggy friends in the neighborhood. (See Days 83–84 for a lip-smackin' recipe.)

- Take the day off. If you normally spend the day in an office, plan a personal day on your dog's birthday and give her the best present ever: your company. Take a long, leisurely walk, explore a hiking trail, or visit a pet store.

- Teach her a trick. Dogs like to learn, and training your dog is valuable bonding time for both of you. Besides, she'll feel smarter and, perhaps, more loved as you praise her for clever obedience.

Top Dogs: The American Kennel Club

The American Kennel Club (AKC) was founded in 1884 and maintains the world's largest registry of purebred dogs. The AKC joins other international organizations that recognize purebred dogs and organize dog shows and events for fanciers and their pets. If you are searching for a purebred dog, these organizations are a great resource for finding breeders and understanding breed characteristics so you can choose a pet that best suits your lifestyle (see Day 101).

Over the years, the range of dog breeds has diversified and expanded exponentially. In 1884, there were just nine registered AKC breeds. Today there are 161, and the list is growing. There are oodles of options for future dog owners today, especially with the introduction of popular mixed breeds—"designer dogs" like the Labradoodle (Labrador Retriever + Poodle) and Puggle (Pug + Beagle).

So what's the "top dog?" The Labrador Retriever is a longtime favorite family pet, but dog lover's have befriended many breeds over the years. Throughout the twentieth century, the German Shepherd, Boston Terrier, Cocker Spaniel, Beagles, and Poodles all enjoyed long runs as the most popular dog.

The most popular AKC breeds, 1884 and 2008

MOST POPULAR BREEDS: 1884

Pointer

Chesapeake Bay Retriever

English Setter

Gordon Setter

Irish Setter

Clumber Spaniel

Cocker Spaniel

Irish Water Spaniel

Sussex Spaniel

MOST POPULAR BREEDS: 2008

Labrador Retriever

Yorkshire Terrier

German Shepherd

Golden Retriever

Beagle

Boxer

Dachshund

Bulldog

Poodle

Shih Tzu

Index

Resources

ALTERNATIVE PET THERAPY ASSOCIATIONS

DOG ACUPUNCTURE

International Veterinary Acupuncture Association (IVAS)
www.ivas.org

American Academy of Veterinary Acupuncture (AAVA)
www.aava.org

DOG MASSAGE

International Association of Animal Massage and Bodywork
www.iaamb.org

Pet Massage, Ltd.
www.petmassage.com

PET REIKI

Optimum Choices, LLC
www.optimumchoices.com

Wild Reiki and Shamanic Healing, LLC
www.reikishamanic.com

ANIMAL WELFARE ORGANIZATIONS

American Society for the Prevention of Cruelty to Animals
www.aspca.org

Humane Society of the United States
www.hsus.org

PetSmart Charities
www.petsmartcharities.org

Royal Society for the Prevention of Cruelty to Animals
www.rspca.org.uk

ASSISTANCE DOG PROGRAMS

Assistance Dogs International
www.assistancedogsinternationa.org
International database of sources

Canine Companions for Independence
www.cci.org
Provides highly trained assistance dogs to people with disabilities

AVAILABLE FROM QUARRY BOOKS

The Home Spa Book for Dogs by Dr. Jennifer Cermak, Quarry Books, 2005

The Safe Dog Handbook by Melanie Monteiro, Quarry Books, 2009

BREED INFORMATION

American Kennel Club
www.akc.org

Australian Kennel Club
www.ankc.org.au

Canadian Kennel Club
www.ckc.ca

The Kennel Club of England
www.thekennelclub.org.uk

CAMPING, HIKING, AND SNOW GEAR

Fido Fleece Coats and Booties
www.premier.com

Outdoor Dog Supplies: Midwestern Mountaineering
www.midwestmtn.com

Musher's Secret Paw Balm
www.jefferspet.com

CAR SAFETY PRODUCTS

Kennel Aire
www.kennel-aire.com

Pet Ego
www.petego.com

Orvis
www.orvis.com

GENERAL PET SUPPLIES

Drs. Foster and Smith
www.drsfostersmith.com

Petco
www.petco.com

PetSmart
www.petsmart.com

Zoo Plus
www.zooplus.co.uk

DIET AND NUTRITION BOOKS

8 Weeks to a Healthy Dog by Shawn Messionier, DVM, Rodale Press 2003

The Good Treats Cookbook for Dogs by Barbara Burg, Quarry Books, 2007

Dr. Pitcairn's New Complete Guide to Natural Health for Dogs and Cats by Richard H. Pitcairn and Susan Hubble Pitcairn, Rodale Books 2005

Home-Prepared Dog & Cat Diets by Donald Strombeck, DVM, Wiley-Blackwell, 1999

The Natural Pet Food Cookbook: Healthful Recipes for Dogs and Cats by Wendy Nan Rees, Howell Book House, Wiley Publishing Inc. 2007

DOG TOYS

Boomer Ball
www.boomerball.com

Herding ball
www.boomerball.com

Kong Dog Toys
www.kongcompany.com

Nylabone Healthy Edibles
www.petsmart.com

Sterilized Natural Bones
www.petedge.com

DRINKING FOUNTAINS

Drinkwell fountains
www.petfountain.com

EMERGENCY PREPAREDNESS PRODUCTS

Evacuation Harness
Rock-n-Rescue dog harness
www.rocknrescue.com/acatalog/Dog-Harness.html

Rescue Alert Stickers
Window Decals
www.aspca.org/site/PageServer?pagename=pets_emergency

FIRST AID SUPPLIES AND INSTRUCTION

DOG FIRST AID BOOKS

Be Red Cross Ready Safety Series Vol. 2: Dog First Aid. StayWell Publishing, 2007

Pet First Aid and Disaster Response Guide: Critical Lessons from Veterinarians by G. Elaine Acker and Pets America, Jones and Bartlett Publishers, 2008

DISASTER PREPAREDNESS, EMERGENCY PET PREPAREDNESS

www.aspca.org

PET FIRST-AID INSTRUCTION AND KITS

ASPCA Pet First Aid Kit
www.aspca.org

Animal Use First Aid Kits, Field First Aid Kits
www.outdoorsafety.net

CPR Savers and First Aid Supply
www.cpr-savers.com

Red Cross
www.redcross.org/services/hss/courses/pets.html

ORAL SYRINGES

Drs. Foster and Smith
www.drsfostersmith.com

Quake Kare, Inc.
www.quakekare.com

MICROCHIPPING AND TATTOO COMPANIES

AKC Companion Animal Recovery (microchips and tattoos)
www.akccar.org

Home Again Companion Animal Retrieval Microchip System
www.homeagain.com

National Dog Registry
www.nationaldogregistry.com

PET INSURANCE

ASPCA Pet Insurance
www.aspcapetinsurance.com

Pets Best Insurance
www.petsbest.com

Veterinary Pet Insurance
www.petinsurance.com

PET-SAFE HOME AND GARDEN PRODUCTS

FERTILIZER, WEED KILLERS, AND OTHER GARDEN PRODUCTS

Safe N' Simple Pre-emergence Weed Control
www.blueseal.com/lawncare/safensimple

Safe N' Simple Pet Friendly Fertilizer
www.blueseal.com/lawncare/safensimple

Shop at Riley's
www.rileycare.com

ICE-MELTING PRODUCT

Safe Paw Ice Melter
www.safepaw.com

PET SAFETY COLLARS AND LEASHES

See Spot Glo
seespotglo.com

Visiglo Collars and Leashes
www.visiglo.com

POISON HOTLINES AND INFORMATION

24-HOUR HOTLINES

ASPCA Animal Poison Center Hotline (North America)
888.426.4435 (fees apply)

Vetfone 24-hour Helpline (U.K.)
09065 00 55 00 (fees apply)

Pet Poison Helpline (U.S. and Canada)
800.213.6680 (fees apply)

PESTICIDE INFORMATION

National Pesticide Information Center (U.S.)
800.858.7378
www.npic.orst.edu

Pesticide Action Network
www.pesticideinfo.org

POISON INFORMATION

ASPCA
www.aspca.org

POOL AND BOATING SAFETY PRODUCTS

PupGear Corporation
www.pupgearcorporation.com

Ruffwear
www.pupgearcorporation.com

Poolguard PGRM
www.carefreepools.com

SKIJORNING COMMUNITY WEBSITES

Midwest Skijorers
www.skijor.org.

Sled Dog Central
www.sleddogcentral.com

SUPPLEMENTS AND HOLISTIC INFORMATION

Pet Essences
www.petessences.com

Rescue Remedy
www.rescueremedy.com

Optimum Choices, LLC
www.optimumchoices.com

TRAINING BOOKS

101 Dog Tricks by Kyra Sundance and Chalcy, Quarry Books, 2007

Dog Sense by Kathy Santo, A Borzoi book published by Alfred A. Knopf, 2005

How to Be Your Dog's Best Friend: The Classic Training Manual for Dog Owners, (Revised and Updated Edition), by The Monks of New Skete; Little, Brown and Company, 2002

The Beginner's Guide to Agility by Laurie Leach, TFH Publications, 2006

The Dog Bible, Everything Your Dog Wants to Know by Tracie Hotchner, Gotham Books, 2005

Dog Tricks, Teaching Your Dog to be Useful, Fun and Entertaining by Capt. Arthur J. Haggerty and Carol Lea Benjamin, Howell Book House, 1982

About the Authors

WENDY NAN REES is an author and entrepreneur who has been involved in the pet industry for more than 25 years. Her career began when she founded Lip Smackers, Inc., a company dedicated to providing healthy all-natural treats to consumers concerned about their pets' well-being.

She is an author of *The Natural Pet Food Cookbook: Healthful Recipes for Dogs and Cats* (2007), *No Barking at the Table* (1996), and *No Catnapping in the Kitchen* (1996). She orchestrated the book *The Name Game*, a collection of over 100 celebrity essays and more than 1,000 suggestions for pet names. A percentage of the proceeds from *The Name Game* goes directly to PAWS, a nonprofit organization dedicated to helping people with HIV/AIDS care for their pets.

Her many successes have led to numerous television appearances and newspaper and magazine articles. She was the Pet Lifestyle Advisor on Animal Planet's *Petsburgh, USA* and has also appeared on the Home Shopping Network. She also wrote a monthly column, "In the Kitchen with Wendy," for *Your Pet Magazine*.

Today, Wendy is the host of an Internet radio show called "Wendy's Animal Talk" on www.healthylife.net (see website for broadcast schedule). Wendy also contributes weekly pet tips for www.lovetoknow.com.

Wendy lives in Los Angeles with her dogs Senator, Cappy, and Little Man. **For more information, visit Wendy at www.petlifestyleadvisor.com.**

KRISTEN HAMPSHIRE is an award-winning writer and author of four outdoor design and landscaping books, including *John Deere's Lawn Care & Landscaping; 52 Backyard Projects: Design, Build, and Plant the Yard of Your Dreams One Weekend at a Time; Hobby Farms;* and *Stonescaping Made Simple*. Hampshire has been published in more than thirty periodicals including *Ladies' Home Journal, Fortune Small Business, Vogue Knitting, The Tennessean, Ohio magazine,* and *Consumers Digest.*

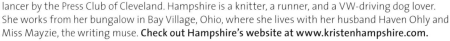

Hampshire launched her business, WriteHand Co., in 2004 after serving as an editor at a green industry journal. She holds a degree from Ohio University's E.W. Scripps School of Journalism, and today she speaks to writers' groups and students about freelance writing. She's a member of the prestigious American Society of Journalists and Authors (ASJA), and was awarded Best in Ohio Free-lancer by the Press Club of Cleveland. Hampshire is a knitter, a runner, and a VW-driving dog lover. She works from her bungalow in Bay Village, Ohio, where she lives with her husband Haven Ohly and Miss Mayzie, the writing muse. **Check out Hampshire's website at www.kristenhampshire.com.**

About the Photographer

DOGUMENTARIAN KENDRA LUCK has created a style and body of work from a past career as an award-winning photojournalist and day-to-day life with her canine muse, Gladys (1992–2008). For Luck, watching a dog is akin to watching children play, waves breaking at the beach, or a bonfire blaze—it's hypnotic. Luck documents the American dog's rising role in the family household.

Luck lives in Albany, California, and travels throughout the United States for private photo commissions as well as editorial and commercial projects. Her work is featured in the book, *Animal Reiki,* the *San Francisco Chronicle, Bay Woof* and several private art collections. Commercial clients include Purina and Aqua Pure Breed. **For more information, visit her website: www.dogumentarian.com.**

Photo: Scott Finsthwait